Christians
in Secular India

Christians in Secular India

Abraham Vazhayil Thomas

Rutherford • Madison • Teaneck
Fairleigh Dickinson University Press

Associated University Presses, Inc.
Cranbury, New Jersey 08512

Library of Congress Cataloging in Publication Data
Thomas, Abraham Vazhayil, 1934–
    Christians in secular India.
    Bibliography: p.
    1. Christians in India. 2. Church and state in
India. I. Title.
BR1155.T46   280′.0954   72-420
ISBN 0-8386-1021-8

*The author wishes to thank the Christian Institute for the Study of
Religion and Society, Bangalore, and the National Christian Council of
India, Nagpur, for permission to quote from copyrighted material.*

Dedicated
to
the Memory of
My Mother
Mrs. Chachykutty Abraham
(1911-1971)

Contents

Preface

This study attempts to understand the meaning and practice of the secular-state ideal and the mutual relationship between the state and the Christian community in India. It will also suggest some guidelines for the future relationship that should exist between the two.

Even though the Christian community is a small minority in India, it has played a constructive role in the evolution of the secular state. But the community needs constantly to reevaluate its role and to make necessary adjustments if it is to make an ever-increasing contribution to the life of India, particularly in maintaining the secular character of the state. While India is called a secular state, it is by no means perfect in its practice of the secular-state ideal. An appreciation of what its basic principles are and incessant examination of its practice of these principles are necessary to assure the maintaining of an atmosphere of religious freedom, mutual respect, and tolerance among the religious groups in India—among themselves and in their relationship to the state as well. It is hoped that this work may make some contribution to the continuing process of dialogue and critical examination.

I am most grateful to Dean Walter G. Muelder, Dr. Paul K. Deats, Jr., Dr. Herbert E. Stotts, and Dr. Amiya Chakravarty (now at the State University of New York, New Paltz, N.Y.) of Boston University for their invaluable help in this study. During my stay in Bangalore, India (1965–1967), I received much help from the distinguished director of the Christian Institute for the Study of Religion and Society, Dr. M. M. Thomas, as well as from Dr. Herbert Jai Singh, Mr. Mark Sunder Rao, and Mr. Richard W. Taylor of the Institute, for which I am indebted to them. I am also thankful to the Edward W. Hazen Foundation for their generous grant which made possible my research in India.

During the course of this research, I had the privilege of interviewing a number of distinguished political and religious leaders in India and outside who gave generously of their time and interest. A number of friends in India and in the United States helped me gather important material. To these and others who have helped me in different ways in connection with this research project, I express my sincere thanks. Thanks are also due to Mrs. Mathilde E. Finch, who did an excellent job in editing the manuscript and to Mrs. Stanley Carlin of Melrose, who typed it most satisfactorily.

To members of my family and my friends who have encouraged me and given their moral support at every stage, I shall ever be indebted. Perhaps the book would never have seen the light of day except for the constant encouragement and support that I received from my wife, Santhamma. For this, I am more than grateful.

This book is dedicated to the memory of my mother, Mrs. Chachykutty Abraham, who passed away on October 31, 1971. She was a gentle soul, full of self-giving love and concern for others, which encompassed not only the immediate family, but an ever-widening circle of neighbors and friends. She personified the best characteristics of traditional Christian piety and Indian motherhood. Along with those of my father, her immeasurable love for and faith in me have been constant sources of inspiration for my life.

Bridgewater, Massachusetts

Christians
in Secular India

Introduction

The Christian Community, Secularism, and the Secular State

When India became independent in 1947, the world watched to see how this potentially powerful country would evolve. Since then, India has proclaimed herself to be a secular state and it has generally traversed the path of religious toleration and freedom. While many a neighboring country has opted for the model of religious state, India has remained a secular one. It has become a model for many newly independent countries in their relation to religious communities within their boundaries. But it is not always clear what is meant by the term *secular state*. Different authors give different definitions of the concept. Some do not even consider India to be a secular state.

The Christian community in India is the second largest minority community in India, and it has an ancient and honorable history. The Syrian Christians of Kerala trace the origin of their church to St. Thomas the Apostle. Then there are also the Christian communities established as a result of the dedicated work of Roman Catholic and Protestant missionaries from the West.[1]

The Christian community as a whole has been active in various degrees during the different periods of Indian history. In spite of the fact that Christians form only 2.4% of the Indian population, the Christian community has played an important part in the social, educational, political, and religious spheres of recent Indian life.

---

1. For history of Christian churches in India see P. Thomas, *Christians and Christianity in India and Pakistan* (London: George Allen and Unwin, Ltd., 1954). Hereinafter referred to as *Christianity in India*; L. W. Brown, *The Indian Christians of St. Thomas: An Account of the Ancient Syrian Church of Malabar* (Cambridge: University Press, 1956); and George Mark Moraes, *A History of Christianity in India: From Early Times to St. Francis Xavier* A.D. *52-1542* (Bombay: Manaktalas, 1964).

With the advent of independence and the establishment of a
secular state, the relationship between the Indian state and the
Christian community entered a new stage. After having been
under British rule and to some extent its patronage for 150
years, the Indian Christian community has been trying to find its
rightful place and proper role in the new India. With independence, the nature of the Indian state and the character of the
Christian community have changed. During the last twenty-five
years of independence, the Indian Christian community has, on
the one hand, followed in traditional lines of service and religious
activities, and on the other, has tried to explore new paths in
both witness and service. It is important that the Christian community define its role in the Indian secular state and explore
what modifications it can make in its present role in India.

If this task is to be done, we must understand the meaning of
the secular state in India. With a history of twenty-five years
behind it, it is possible to ascertain and assess its meaning so
that we can further define the new role that the Christian community should play in the Indian secular state. We must also
understand the present state of affairs, that is, the self-understanding and practice of both the Indian state and the Indian
Christian community.

Definitions

Christian community. This phrase is used here to denote all
those who are known as or call themselves Christians in India.
The vast majority belong to different churches, denominations, or
sects. There may be some who are not related to any organized
group of Christians, but their number is few. In spite of vast
differences in doctrine, church organization, and socioeconomic
levels of Indian Christians, they form a separate religious and
social group insofar as they consider themselves, and are considered by others, as followers of one religion, namely, Christianity.

The Christian community consists on the one hand of individual Christians and on the other of the various churches (or
Christian groups) of which they are members. The Indian Christian community acts through individual Christians, through the
churches, and through national, regional, denominational, and
professional Christian organizations.

While the Christian community cannot be identified with the

Church in India (because many individual churches would claim to be *the true Church*), it nevertheless is a religious community. The main basis of its designation as a group is its common allegiance to the lordship of Jesus Christ. Its role has to be interpreted on the basis of this professed allegiance and loyalty to Christ. As one Indian study points out, "No Christian community either in India or elsewhere can understand itself or be understood in purely sociological or purely theological terms."[1] It is both a sociological and a theological reality.

Secular state. This phrase has been defined in various ways by different authors. Donald Eugene Smith, in his *India as a Secular State,*[2] gives the following definition:

> The secular state is a state which guarantees individual and corporate freedom of religion, deals with the individual as a citizen irrespective of his religion, is not constitutionally connected to a particular religion nor does it seek either to promote or interfere with religion.[3]

Smith describes his concept of the secular state from "the liberal democratic tradition of the West,"[4] and gives a qualified "yes" to the question whether India is a secular state.

W. Cantwell Smith has defined *secular state* as "a form of state so contrived as to win and hold and deserve the loyalty and warm allegiance of any citizen of whatever religion or of none."[5] In one article he emphasizes the moral and theoretical content of the concept, but, although it hints at some broad features of the secular state, especially its democratic, equalitarian, and non-discriminatory character, it is too general to be of use here.

In his treatise *The Concept of the Secular State and India,* Ved Prakash Luthera equates *secular state* with the separation of state and religion. The United States, according to him, is the best example of the secular state.[6] For him, India is not a secular state but a jurisdictionalist state, one which "maintains equal status for the confessions within its domain." The state is not separated from the churches but is intertwined with them.[7]

---

1. "Editorial: The Church of Christ and the Christian Community in India," *Religion and Society* 10, no. 4 (December 1963) :3.
2. Princeton, N.J., 1963.
3. *Ibid.*, p. 4.
4. *Ibid.*, p. 3.
5. "The Problem," *Seminar* 67 (March 1965) :12. Special issue on Secularism.
6. London: Oxford University Press, p. viii.
7. *Ibid.*, p. 22.

Donald Smith agrees that the Indian state does not strictly conform to the concept of the secular one. He finds that while India is essentially secular in spirit, it has compromised its secular nature in many ways. The nature of the Hindu religion and the strong identification of most of Indian society with this religion have made it inevitable that the state regulate many aspects of life traditionally defined as religious. The preferential treatment accorded to low-caste people (on the basis of their caste), and legislative measures passed affecting only one religion (e.g., the Hindu Code Bill), are, according to Smith, further examples of this compromise. By the same logic he recognizes that the U.S. is not a pure example of the secular state, either.

Since the secular state has many interpretations, it has to be studied afresh in each given context. As one reviewer of Luthera's work says, if concepts like secular state and democracy are not studied in their historical contexts, the result will be lopsided conclusions.[8]

In India the concept of the secular state is a means to an end, and the end includes not only religious freedom and harmony but also economic and social progress. A *Religion and Society* editorial describes it as

a technique of building a national *political* community in a situation of religious pluralism and a means of cooperation of all citizens irrespective of their faith, to work for new common goals.[9]

Two recent publications in India containing articles mostly by eminent Indians, as well as publications of the Christian Institute for the Study of Religion and Society,[10] in general emphasize that the secular state should be an instrument of both modernization and social reform.[11] For example, V. P. S. Raghuvanshi writes,

Secularism implying the neutrality of state in religious matters does not however rule out legislation for common national goal

8. Kusum Madgavakar, "The Concept of the Secular State and India: A Review," *Seminar* 67 (March 1965):44. In categorically denying that India is a secular state, Luthera has committed this fallacy.

9. "Editorial: The Idea of a Secular State," *Religion and Society* 9, no. 1 (1962):1.

10. Hereinafter referred to as CISRS.

11. See *Seminar* 67 (March 1965), a special issue entitled "Secularism," and G. S. Sharma, ed., *Secularism: Its Implications for Law and Life in India* (Bombay: N. M. Tripathy Private Ltd., 1966).

or discriminatory social legislation to meet the demands of social justice.[12]

(We will see later that *secularism* and *secular state* are often used interchangeably.) A definition of *secular state* that does not include the possibility of legislating against the custom of barring untouchables from entering certain temples, giving preferential treatment to "Harijans" (the untouchables) and legislating for social reform even when it affects certain religious practices, cannot be adequate for India. As Blackshield says regarding Luthera's thesis,

> The very fact that temple entry authorization is inconsistent with the "separation of powers" model of secularism, ought to suggest that the "separation of powers" model must be wrong.[13]

As far as its attitude to religion is concerned, a state that is indifferent to religion is often called a secular state. But here there can be two types of "indifference." One is that of the secular state of the old French style, which claimed to be "indifferent" to religion but was in fact hostile to it. Religion was relegated to the private sphere; and by denying its social dimension, the government tried to eliminate religion from social life.

The other type of indifference is not hostile to religion. It is a careful respect for positive and negative attitudes of citizens towards religion.[14] Here religion "is neither prohibited, nor eliminated, nor officially promulgated, but is *voluntary,* a matter of choice for each person."[15] From the following statement by Dr. Zakir Hussain, the late President of India, made at the inauguration of the Eucharistic Congress in Bombay in 1965, it will be clear that this is the Indian state's attitude toward religion. He said:

> India is proud to be a secular state, which means that it does not have any special ties with any religion in particular but accords to them all the same reverence and the same rights under law. This disposition enshrined in the Constitution reflects the innate respect of the people of India for all spiritual values wherever they are found.[16]

---

12. "State Policy in India and Secularism," in Sharma, ed., *Secularism: Its Implications* . . . , p. 205.

13. A. R. Blackshield, "Secularism and Social Control," in *ibid.*, p. 59.

14. A. F. Carrillo de Albornoz, *The Basis of Religious Liberty* (London: SCM Press Ltd., 1963), p. 50.

15. *Ibid.*

16. *Christian Focus* (Madras) 6, no. 1 (15 January 1965):3.

The nature of the Indian secular state has to be understood in both the historical and present social context of India. In defining the concept of the secular state, however, the present Indian state can not stand as the ideal type from which a definition may be derived. Nor should we take the U.S. model as an ideal type, either. Any definition of the phrase should be comprehensive enough to include both types.

An operating definition might be suggested here, of the secular state as a state where there is 1) institutional separation between religion and state, 2) religious freedom for individuals and groups, and neutrality of state toward religion, 3) equality of citizens before the law, and, 4) pursuit of social justice and social reform even when this involves control over religious freedom in its secular aspects. While the first three clauses are found in the common Western understanding of the secular state,[17] the last one may be a distinctive contribution from the Indian experience. However, we see that in the United States too, religious freedom is circumscribed by the needs of the state in matters of "public order, morality and health."[18]

Secularism is a word that is used in many senses. Traditionally it refers to a rationalistic philosophy developed in the nineteenth century and associated primarily with the name of A. J. Holyoake. It is a system of ethical principles emphasizing the material improvement of man, concern for this world, and an independent rational morality.[19] Secularism may be defined as a "system of thought which attempts to organize life apart from God."[20] Dean Walter G. Muelder defines secularism to mean "both the practical attitude and the philosophy which finds its highest good in the creative satisfactions of the present age: worldly success, power, wealth, comfort, and pleasure."[21] It was in this sense that the Jerusalem Conference of the International Missionary Council in 1928 understood it and considered it as a challenge to Christianity.[22]

---

17. See definition of D. E. Smith, p. 5.

18. See provisions of the U.S. Constitution regarding secular state in Ch. 2.

19. C. C. West, "Towards An Understanding of Secularism," *Religion and Society* 11, no. 1 (March 1962):47.

20. V. E. Devadutt, "A Christian Apologetic in Relation to Secularism," *National Christian Council Review* 63, no. 3 (March 1943):105.

21. Walter G. Muelder, "Communism, Secularism and Christianity," *Zions Herald* (19 April 1950), p. 370.

22. West, pp. 48–49.

In India *secularism* is often used to mean "the concept of the secular state." G. C. Pande writes:

> Secularism has two distinguishable senses. It may mean the independence of the state from religion or it may mean the advocacy of a worldly outlook which is hostile to religion and seeks to replace it by nonreligious, even irreligious beliefs and institutions. When we speak of the secular state, the former meaning would be obviously appropriate.[23]

I have already referred to Raghuvanshi's statement, in which he equates secularism with the state policy of neutrality in religious matters.[24]

The materialistic philosophy of secularism is not considered the basis for the Indian secular state. Most Indian leaders have repeatedly affirmed that Indian secularism, or the secular state in India, is not opposed to religion. Indian secularism in this sense is sometimes referred to as *open* secularism as opposed to *closed* or *integral* secularism, which is the "delegitimation of all dimensions of ultimate concern or transcendence. . . ."[25] *Open* secularism not only guarantees religious freedom but is "also open to the influence of social ethics inspired by religious beliefs."[26] I shall here use *secularism* to mean (unless otherwise specified) the concept of the secular state and the ideology behind the Indian secular state, namely, *open secularism.*

As with *secular state* and *secularism, secularization* is also used with different meanings. Larry Shiner distinguishes six major categories of meanings for the word and analyzes them. The meaning that comes nearest the usage in this study is the third category, under which *secularization* is understood in terms of "disengagement of society from religion."

> Society separates itself from the religious understanding which has previously informed it in order to constitute itself an autonomous reality and consequently to limit religion to the sphere of private life.[27]

---

23. G. C. Pande, "Secularization and Educational Policy," in Sharma, ed., p. 207.
24. *Ibid.*, p. 205.
25. Albert Terril Rasmussen, "Book Review: *Man in Community,*" ed. Egbert de Vries (New York: Association Press) in *Social Action and Social Progress* (January-February 1966).
26. *Religion and Society* 9, no. 1 (1962):2.
27. Larry Shiner, "The Concept of Secularization in Empirical Research," *Journal for the Scientific Study of Religion* 6, no. 2 (Fall 1967): 212.

The distinction made by many Christian thinkers between *secularization* or *secularity* and *secularism* (according to my terminology, *integral secularism*) is that the former signifies "the rejection of religious or ecclesiastical tutelage of society," while the latter signifies "an all-embracing ideology which seeks to deny religious institutions or viewpoints any formative role in society "[28] West's definition of secularization is in conformity with this. He defines secularization as

> the withdrawal of areas of thought and life from religious— and finally also from metaphysical—control, and the attempt to understand and live in these areas in the terms which they alone offer.[29]

As Shiner points out, *secularization* has also been used to mean "decline of religion," conformity with "this world," "transposition of religious beliefs and institutions," "desacralization of the world," and the "movement from a 'sacred' to a 'secular' society." Some of these meanings complement, while others are opposed to, the meaning given in the last paragraph.[30]

While secularization refers to a worldwide movement that includes "a breakthrough from traditional social structure," in the context of the secular state it means the removal of religious control of society. In a country like India, "where religion pervades all human endeavors, and culture is bound up with religious ideas,"[31] law (especially personal law), education, and social customs have to be emancipated from the control of religious institutions and traditions. Thus secularization involves the secularization of law, education, and so on. This process is not opposed to religion, and many Christians see it as developing from the impact of the Gospel on the world.[32] However, secularization may degenerate into a complete negation of the religious or transcendental dimension of life and involve acceptance of the negative philosophy of secularism. Generally speaking, however, secularization is seen as a desirable process.

---

28. *Ibid.*
29. West, p. 50.
30. *Ibid.*, pp. 209-17.
31. "Editorial: The Secular Ideal," *Deccan Herald* (Bangalore) (6 February 1966), p. 4.
32. See Leslie Newbigin, *Honest Religion for Secular Man* (Philadelphia: Westminster Press, 1966), pp. 10ff.

1

The Historical and Cultural Roots of the Secular State in the Indian Tradition

Scholars are divided in their opinion as to how far each period in Indian history has contributed to the idea of the secular state. There is a strong tendency in modern Indian nationalism to affirm in very vehement terms the continuity of modern Indian renaissance with that of its hoary past. Every modern trend in India that is supposed to be good is traced back to some precept or practice in ancient India. Thus democracy, tolerance, equality, social justice—all these are traced to Vedic and puranic periods.

In contrast to this, some modern scholars, among whom K. M. Panikkar could be considered one of the foremost, denies any connection between modern Indian government and ancient Indian polity. He says categorically, "In its political and constitutional aspects, New India does not clearly owe anything to the ancient Indian political ideas." The main reason he gives for this is that Indian political thought ceased to grow after the thirteenth century (i.e., with the establishment of Muslim rule in North India), for it did not have new political experience to guide it.[1] However, in his study of the Hindu polity he shows that it was essentially secular in its outlook and practice. While there may have been a discontinuity in the growth of Indian political thought, the early historical background of India cannot but have great influence, both in the evolution and in the practice of the secular-state ideal in modern India. It would be safe to assume that the truth about the influence of ancient Indian polity on the

1. K. M. Panikkar, *The Ideas of Sovereignty and State in Indian Political Thought* (Bombay: Bharatiya Vidya Bhavan, 1963), pp. 101-2. Hereinafter referred to as *Sovereignty and State*.

21

present-day Indian state lies between the two extremes—that while it is not wholly based in ancient Hindu polity, it has not been completely immune to its pervasive influences.

Regarding the influences of the Muslim period and particularly of the British period, there can be less doubt about their influence in shaping the form of modern Indian government. Along with these we shall examine the influence of Western culture and political thought and the Indian freedom movement in shaping the secular-state ideology.

Hindu Polity and Culture

Ancient India did not develop any formal political philosophy, but the science of statecraft was highly developed. The earliest and most important textbook specifically dealing with statecraft is Kautilya's *Arthasastra*, attributed to the famous minister of Chandra Gupta, the Mauryan Emperor (322–298 B.C.).[2] It gives very detailed instructions in the control of the state, the ordering of state economy, and the waging of war. The *Santi Parvam*, the twelfth book of the great epic *Mahabharata*, is a collection of many passages dealing, among other things, with statecraft. It is dated around the first century of the Christian era. The other great epic, *Ramayana*, also contains sections on statecraft. The legal literature, called *Smrti*, particularly the seventh section attributed to the sage Manu (second and third centuries A.D.), are of great importance. These were "manuals explaining scriptures."[3] Many medieval jurists wrote lengthy commentaries on the *Smrti* literature. *Mitaksara* of Vijnanesvara (who wrote at the court of the Chalukya Emperor, Vikramaditya VI, c. 1075–1127) "a commentary on the law book of Yajnavalkya, played a very important part in the forming of civil law in India." So has Jimuthevahana's (twelfth century) treatise on inheritance, *Dayabhega*, influenced the law of modern India.[4] From those and ancient Indian literature, from *Rig Vida* onwards in general, we get much valuable information about kingship and polity in pre-Muslim India.

There are two theories regarding the origin of kingship in

---

2. A. L. Basham, *The Wonder That Was India* (New York: Grove Press, Inc., 1956, 1959), pp. 79ff.

3. *Ibid.*, p. 112.

4. *Ibid.*, p. 113.

India—one is divine origin and the other primeval election.[5] Hindus considered government as a misfortune, but as necessary when men became evil and the strong persecuted the weak. The gods themselves had to appoint a king (Indra) to win their battle against the demons. He was appointed by the High God, as in the case with the human king. By means of Royal consecration (Raja-suya) and sacrifices (asvamedha, the horse sacrifice) the king's divine appointment was confirmed and strengthened.[6] "Nearly all Hindu legends on the origin of kingship depict men in a state of anarchy as praying to the Gods to save them."[7]

But, for Buddhists, kingship was dependent on consent, based on social contract. Due to the gradual process of cosmic decay, man became earthbound, attached to property and with that began theft, murder, and other crimes. So the people came together and decided to appoint one man among them to maintain peace and order and rewarded him with a portion of their produce for his services. He was called "The Great Chosen One" (Mahasam-mata). The contractual theory and the mystical theory were coalesced in the different traditions.[8] "On the lowest estimate the Hindu king is a charismatic figure, divinely appointed, at the most he is a great divinity himself."[9]

Kautilya's *Arthasastra* emphasizes the contractual theory, even though he advises that the divine theory may be used to keep the ordinary people loyal to the king. The king is pictured as an autocrat and his main duty is the protection of the people from internal disorder, as well as from external aggression. "The idea that kingship has been instituted for protection is one of the cardinal tenets of Hindu political philosophy."[10] The protection included the order of society, "the right way of life for all classes and ages" (Varnasrama dharma), as prescribed by the sacred texts. So the primary powers of the king were limited by dharma. If he infringed sacred customs too openly, he may incur the displeasure of the brahmins as well as the people in general and there was sanction in the *Mahabharata* for revolt against an oppressive king who does not protect.[11]

---

5. V. P. Sarma, *Studies in Hindu Political Thought* (Delhi: Motilal Banarsidas, 1st ed., 1954; 2d ed., 1959), p. 171.

6. Basham, pp. 81-82.

7. C. H. Philips, ed., *Politics and Society in India* (London: George Allen and Unwin, Ltd., 1963), p. 15.

8. Basham, pp. 82-83.

9. Philips, p. 15.

10. Varma, p. 188.

11. Basham, p. 87.

But the king was also the maker of the age ("kalasya kara-nam"). "Again the king is the cause of setting in motion the customs, usages and movements and is the cause and maker of the time."[12] He could not change the sacred law, but the secular law of Hindus, as Panikkar points out, is based not only on the *Smritis* derived from Vedas, but also on acharas or usages.[13] As such, the king had great power to modify, amend, or even abrogate certain customs and usages which he considered to be against the spirit of the age. This gave a dynamic quality to law in spite of the unchangeableness of *dharma*. The king is thus both the conserver as well as the transformer of social tradition. He was considered responsible for the events of the age, and the merits of the people accrued to him also.[14] So the right of the individual was not given much recognition.[15]

The relationship of the king, who belonged to the *kshatriya* caste, and the brahmins is of great importance and interest. The councillors of the king were often brahmins. With an orthodox king, the *purohita* or the court chaplain was very influential.[16] As the Hindu laws laid down different degrees of punishment for the same crime according to the caste of the person, the brahmins were in a privileged position. But in some other cases, since a higher standard of morality was expected of those belonging to the higher castes, a more severe punishment was prescribed for the same crime in *manu smriti*.[17]

In the later vedic period some brahmins claimed to be above the law altogether. Some even claimed that their only king was Soma (God).[18] They claimed many special privileges but they were never beyond punishment, though exempt from execution, torture, and corporal punishment in most cases. The brahmins who followed regular occupations did not command so much respect as those who practiced a religious occupation.

According to Buddhist tradition, since Buddha was born a *kshatriya*, kshatriyas were the highest caste. But even the Buddhist texts gave respect to the brahmins. They served as mutual checks. "A strong king was always a check on brahmanic preten-

---

12. Panikkar, *Sovereignty and State*, p. 39.
13. *Ibid.*, pp. 39–40.
14. *Ibid.*
15. Varma, p. 188.
16. *Ibid.*, p. 100.
17. *Ibid.*, pp. 120–21.
18. *Ibid.*, p. 120.

sions, just as the brahmins were a check on the pretensions of the king."[19]

Panikkar points out that because there was no organized church in Hinduism, the separation of the religious life from civil government was natural and easy. The Dharma was above the king and the state and he could not change it. But in the field of *artha* or "worldly affairs" the state was supreme.[20] Just as there was separation between dharma and artha, there was separation between brahma and kshatra.

The brahmins served as a check on the king, to keep him from becoming an absolute monarch, but they could not convert themselves into a theocracy.[21] There is no instance of a priest-king in India, unlike Babylonia and Egypt.[22]

Thus we find that monarchy was the normal system of government in ancient India.[23] Monarchy was essentially a secular office in spite of occasional attributes of divine origin given to the office. Monarchy, which was originally contractual in character and later hereditary and more powerful, was not subservient to the priesthood. Its primary obligation was to afford protection to the people, and the king was limited only by the demands of Dharma, which he was to uphold. The essential secular character of Indian monarchy set an ancient precedent for the modern Indian state.

There are certain other aspects of Hindu polity that may be pointed out as forerunners of the present secular state of India.

One is the fact that republics and democracies existed in ancient India up to the fourth and fifth centuries A.D.[24] According to *Mahabharata* five republican peoples—the Andhakas, the Vrishnis, the Yadavas, the Kukuras, and the Bhojas—formed themselves into a confederation and Krishna was made its president. According to Panikkar, "the republican tradition was a persistent factor in Indian history."[25] The very fact that modern Indian historians have given this so much importance shows that it is looked upon as a source of inspiration for the modern Indian government.[26] This is not to claim any direct lineage for the present-day Indian state from the ancient Indian republics.

19. *Ibid.*, p. 141.
20. Panikkar, *Sovereignty and State*, p. 52.
21. *Ibid.*, p. 66.
22. Varma, p. 45.
23. Philips, p. 14.
24. *Ibid.*
25. Panikkar, *Sovereignty and State*, p. 7.
26. Philips, p. 14.

That in the social structure of the ancient Hindus, brahmins, the people of learning and renunciation, were given a higher status than the kshatriyas, the warriors and the rulers, indicates that the ancient Hindus gave primacy to spiritual values over political goals and aspirations. In identifying the individual soul with the Supreme Being the position of the individual is exalted. "In his inmost essence, man is a divine spark."[27] This spirituality of Hindu political thought was particularly emphasized in the writings of modern Hindu sages and political thinkers like Dayananda, Vivekananda Tilak, Aurobindo, and Mahatma Gandhi. According to Varma, "this emphasis on spirituality and morality in Hindu political thought is a great contribution to world political thought."[28] The protection given to the dignity and rights of the individual under the Indian constitution may be thought to owe some debt to this tradition in its formation.

Tolerance is one of the professed cardinal principles of modern Indian state. One of the classic examples of tolerance in world history is given by the rule of Asoka[29] and his example has undoubtedly influenced the founding fathers of modern India, especially Nehru. The special emblem of India is the replica of the top of an Asoka pillar showing four lions and the wheel. In one of his rock edicts (XII) Asoka wrote that "there should not be honour of one's own sect and condemnation of others without any grounds."[30] Asoka, himself a Buddhist, allowed freedom for all religions to flourish.

The modern civil service of India, an essential element of a secular state, is usually thought of as a legacy of the British rule in India. While this is true, it has also to be noted that the Kautilyan state had an elaborate bureaucracy that collected revenues, maintained law and order, and supervised every aspect of life. According to Panikkar,

> the traditional Indian administrative system was inherited by the Muslims from their predecessors and was taken over with changes of nomenclature by the East India Company.[31]

Panikkar sees a dual origin, Indian and European, for the vast

---

27. Varma, p. 256.

28. *Ibid.*

29. Asoka ruled the Mauryan Empire between 269 and 232 B.C. See Basham, pp. 53, 56.

30. *Ibid.*, p. 132.

31. Panikkar, *Sovereignty and State*, p. 105.

economic activity of the government of India. Modern experiments with decentralized government and *Panchayati Raj* (village level rule) also hark back to ancient times when administration, even under the largest empires, was based on villages and groups of villages.[32]

It is debatable how far and to what extent the models and ideas of ancient Hindu thought have influenced and are still influential in the formation and development of the Indian secular state. Indian political thinkers and reformers like Ram Mohan Roy, Gokhale, and Gandhi knew about the ancient heritage, but

> in most cases their efforts were directed rather at finding prototypes of modern Western ideas in ancient India than at interpreting basic ancient Indian concepts in terms suitable to contemporary conditions.[33]

In the discussions during the writing of the constitution and present-day legislative debates, one often hears references to Hindu Dharma and the sacred texts, but it is difficult to say how far these are determinative in the formulation of the constitution and new laws. One may, however, agree with Basham that many principles found in Hindu polity are valid for a secular state. Some of these principles are: 1) that the government should be subject to the needs of the social order, 2) that the king's duty is not only to protect but to please the people, and 3) that the government should not be considered an end in itself. It should help each individual to attain peace.[34]

Muslim Influence

The Muslim period extended from the beginning of the thirteenth century to the middle of the eighteenth century, the time of the Delhi Sultanate (1211–1504) and the Moghul Empire (1526–1757). By the time Muslim influence was established in India, the classical Islamic polity of the Caliphate had come to an end. In Mohammed, the religious and secular powers were combined, and the same was the case with the early Caliphs. But by the ninth century the *ulama* (doctors of Islamic law) claimed for themselves exclusive right to define orthodox dogma.

---

32. *Ibid.*, p. 106.
33. Philips, p. 23.
34. Basham, p. 23.

In India, the Muslim ruler was considered the *de facto* Caliph for its own dominions and he was guided by the counsels of the *ulama*.[35] The *sadr-us-sadur* was the chief theologian of the state and the one to guide the ruler in implementation of religious principles. But the influence of the ulama waxed and waned with the rule of different monarchs.

One result of Muslim invasion was that the Hindu rulers who had to defend their countries came to consider themselves as defendants of the Hindu religion. According to Panikkar "Religious faith became an active factor of policy with Hindu kings as a result of Islam."[36]

The Muslim rule in India embraced the two extremes of suppression and intolerance of Hinduism, and complete tolerance practiced by Akbar. During the period of the Delhi sultanate, heretical Shia sects were severely persecuted by the orthodox Sunni government. Public worship of Hindu idols was generally forbidden and Hindus were not allowed to build new temples or repair old ones. Sometimes temples were desecrated and destroyed. In 1669 Aurangazeb issued a general order for the destruction of all Hindu temples and schools.[37] He reenforced the *jizya* tax on Hindus. Deviating from the earlier part of his rule, Aurangazeb came to regard himself as the head of a Muslim state rather than as president of all India.

In marked contrast was the policy of his forebear Akbar. One of his wives was a Rajput princess and he appointed several Hindu leaders to high offices of the state. He also abolished the pilgrim tax and the poll tax on Hindus. "Akbar's aim was a national monarchy which his Hindu subjects did not consider as a burden on them."[38]

The most remarkable aspect of his rule was his policy of religious toleration. From 1578, exponents of other religions were admitted for discourses on various aspects of religion. Akbar received in his court religious leaders and priests belonging to Christian, Parsi, Jain, and Hindu religions, and had earnest discussions with them.[39] He forbade forcible conversions to Islam

35. Theodore de Bary, *Sources of Indian Tradition* (New York: Columbia University Press, 1958), p. 465.
36. K. M. Panikkar, *A Survey of Indian History* (Bombay: The National Information & Publication, Ltd., 1947), p. 134.
37. Percival Spear, *India, A Modern History* (Ann Arbor: University of Michigan, 1961), p. 143.
38. Panikkar, *A Survey of Indian History*, p. 156.
39. *Ibid.*, p. 158.

and permitted followers of other religions and sects also to make converts. He removed all bans on the building of temples. Hindu and Jain saints were held in high honor and Hiravijaya Suri was granted the high title of Jagad Guru.[40]

Akbar curbed the power of the ulamas by the so-called infallibility decree of 1579, by which he claimed the power to judge doctrinal disputes and to issue religious orders in accord with the Koran. He was to be, in effect, the Khalifa as well as emperor. In 1580 Akbar inaugurated a new cult, the *Din Illahi* or Divine Faith, which contained elements of different religions. Its influence was mainly confined to the court and the aristocratic circle around the emperor.

Akbar's tolerance of all religions and his leanings toward a syncretistic religion provide one of the historical prototypes for the modern secular state of India. While the Muslim period on the whole was marked by suppression of the Hindus and religious intolerance, Akbar's rule was an exception.[41]

British Administration

The British, who came as traders and remained as rulers for over one hundred and fifty years, left the most profound impression of their rule on Indian life. It was British rule that again unified India and gave her an efficient civil service and judicial administration. It also paved the way for English education and the tremendous influence of Western and Christian thought on Indian political, social, and religious thinking. According to Natarajan, "the three main channels through which modern ideas have found their way to India are British rule, English education and Christian missionaries."[42] I shall briefly discuss some of the policies of British administration in India that contributed toward the formation of the secular state in India.

Having commercial motives and gains primarily in mind, the British tried to follow a policy of complete religious neutrality in India, and this met with some success. However, in the implementation of this policy there were many variations. In addition to its commercial-imperial objectives, the British government tried

40. *Ibid.*
41. D. E. Smith, p. 65.
42. Natarajan, *A Century of Social Reform in India* (Bombay: Asia Publishing House, 1962), p. 5.

to fulfill its role as an Indian ruler and as a "Christian government."[43]

The British East India Company, which began its commercial enterprise in India in the early part of the seventeenth century, differed from the Portuguese who came a century earlier in that it was not particularly interested in undertaking any proselyting mission. This was true of the French and Dutch traders also, who, after a brief stay in India, were ousted by the British. The East India Company did not want missionaries to come to India and there was a clause in their charter that prohibited sending missionaries there.[44] The charter granted to the company by the Parliament in 1698 contained the directive that the company's chaplains should learn the local language of the country to instruct Indian servants or agents of the company in the Protestant faith.[45] But this was practically ignored. The order given in Bombay in 1662 said "There shall be no compulsory conversion, no interference with native habits, and no cow killing in Hindu quarters," and this remained the guiding policy of the company.[46] The company was very sensitive about disturbing the religious feelings of the Hindus and Muslims lest it hinder their commercial enterprise. The early representatives of the company were in no way the kind of people who would be able or willing to spread Christian religion in India.

Until 1813 the East India Company actively discouraged the spreading of Christianity in India.[47] No missionary was allowed to land in India without a license from one of the directors, and this was not easy to obtain. William Carey, one of the early missionaries, was refused a license and had to start work in the Danish colony of Serampore near Calcutta. A few chaplains were sent out by the company to look after the religious needs of the European employees, but even this was not a consistent practice. Only one was added between 1760 and 1800.[48]

In 1793 William Wilberforce made an attempt to include in the charter, which was being discussed for renewal in the Parliament, a clause making it obligatory on the part of the company

43. D. E. Smith, p. 66.
44. Thomas, *Christianity in India*, p. 151.
45. D. E. Smith, p. 66.
46. *Ibid.*, p. 66.
47. Arthur J. Mayhew, *Christianity and Government of India* (London: Faber and Gwyer Ltd., 1929), pp. 26-38.
48. *Ibid.*, p. 47.

to send missionaries to India. This was opposed by the company and was not accepted.[49] In 1813, when the charter was again reviewed, the right of missionaries to come to India was recognized by the Parliament. Also, a Bishop was appointed with jurisdiction over all the dominions of the East India Company and having headquarters in Calcutta.[50] The Church of England was established in India by this step.

With this, several missionaries started work in India, and they studied critically the relationship of the company with the Hindu religion. The company, as the ruling power, had taken over some of the functions of the previous rulers, which included protection of Hindu temples and control of pilgrims to great Hindu shrines. According to the missionaries, the company "took upon itself the office of dry nurse to Vishnu."[51] In 1837 a memorial was presented by the missionaries to the government of Bombay pointing out some of the anti-Christian practices, such as official attendance of government servants at Hindu festivals and the employment of Brahmins for the purpose of making invocations for rain and good weather.[52]

As a result of petitions from different quarters in India and England, the Court of Directors gave orders to completely sever any government connections with religious practices of the people. The salute provided by the army at Hindu festivals was stopped, as was collection of pilgrim tax. The governance of temples and temple property was handed over to Hindu trustees.

> Thus a good deal of neutrality was obtained. All told, the East India Company and the missionaries conceived a wholesome check on each other which helped the smooth progress of both Christianity and British rule in India.[53]

In its attempt to prove that the government was not favoring Christians, rules were sometimes passed that discriminated against Indian Christians. They were by law debarred from appointment to several military and judicial posts. As a result of several representations made, the directors ordered the governor-general in 1831 to remove these injustices, saying that

> neutrality which we think is our duty to observe does not re-

49. D. E. Smith, p. 68.
50. Thomas, *Christianity in India*, p. 180.
51. *Ibid.*, p. 181.
52. *Ibid.*, p. 182.
53. *Ibid.*, p. 183.

quire that converts to Christianity should be placed by law in a less advantageous situation than other persons.[54]

The severance of the company's connection with Hinduism seems

to have been followed by an active campaign by the servants of the company to Christianize India, and an interference with Hinduism was reported.[55]

In a dispatch of the Court of Directors we find that strict instructions were issued to the Governor General to impress upon the servants of the company the need for neutrality and noninterference. The extent of this interference is not known, but it may have been short-lived.[56]

Britain established the principle of equality before the law. Criminal law was administered uniformly without regard to caste or religious distinctions. In civil law, Hindu and Muslim law were enforced by the courts; this raised certain problems, particularly regarding inheritance. Under both Hindu and Muslim laws apostasy entailed loss of inheritance. For the Hindus, performance of funeral obligations was considered a precondition to inheritance. In 1832 the Bengal government removed the legal disability of loss of inheritance on conversion to Christianity, and in 1850, at the instance of Christian spokesmen, it enacted the Caste Disabilities Removal Act and made it law for all of British India. The Act also protected the converts' right of guardianship of children.[57] "The Act of 1850 was offensive to both Hindus and Muslims who regarded it as an incentive to apostasy."[58] There was general apprehension during this period that British government was attempting mass conversion of Indians to Christianity by its laws. The Widow Remarriage Act, passed in 1856, was also received this way. But in spite of the general fear,

it is true that the fear was absolutely unfounded and the British

---

54. Frank Penny, *The Church in Madras* (1912), p. 348. Quoted in D. E. Smith, p. 69.

55. Thomas, *Christianity in India*, p. 185.

56. *Ibid.*

57. D. E. Smith, pp. 70-71.

58. R. C. Majumdar, ed., *The History and Culture of the Indian People*, vol. 9, *British Paramountcy and Indian Renaissance*, pt. 1 (Bombay: Bharatiya Vidya Bhavan, 1965), p. 422.

government had no intention of encouraging, far less making, conversions to Christianity.[59]

In 1854 a system of grants-in-aid to educational institutions managed by private agencies was instituted. The main beneficiaries of this aid were Christian schools, being the most numerous, but the grants were given on the merit of secular subjects being taught in the schools.[60]

It was generally believed that the Vellore Mutiny of 1806 and the Great Rebellion ("Sepoy Mutiny") of 1857 were largely caused by the suspicion of Hindus and Muslims that the British rulers in India unduly favored Christians and Christian missionary work and were deliberately undermining India's religions by social reforms, preparing the stage for complete Christianization of India. The British government was very sensitive about this and whenever there was any sign of discontent, it tried to prove that it was not supporting missionaries. "There was everywhere the uneasiness of men who resented the intrusion of firebrands into a powder magazine."[61] The Vellore Mutiny led to the expulsion from Madras of London Mission agents who had been admitted only a few years ago. The Bengal Campaign against the Serampore Mission could also be attributed to British nervousness during this period.[62]

But in spite of the official policy of neutrality and sometimes opposition to mission work in India, the very presence of the British and the protection and peace guaranteed by the rule gave prestige and help to the work of the missionaries. It was also inevitable that several officials of high and low rank were favorably inclined toward missionary work and actively supported such activities. The missionaries also benefited by the teaching of the English language and the help received from the government for conducting educational institutions. As a result, mission work flourished during the nineteenth century.

While the present-day Hindu historians concede that the British government had no proselyting designs, those who lived in the period had grave misgivings. The very ambivalence in the policy of the government created suspicion among Hindus. On the one hand the authorities disavowed any support for the work of the

59. *Ibid.*, p. 423.
60. D. E. Smith, p. 71.
61. Mayhew, p. 81.
62. *Ibid.*

missionaries, but on the other hand, there was often indirect support. The support that the government gave to schools seemed particularly calculated to undermine the foundations of caste.[63]

According to Mayhew this situation arose because of the inherent ambiguity of the British policy. He says that even as Asoka actively tried to propagate Buddhism, at the same time being tolerant of other religions, the British also should openly have professed their religion and officially promoted it. The patronage of a state religion, along with toleration of other religions, was part of the Hindu idea of kingship, and if Britain had openly followed this policy, it would have been acceptable to the Hindus.[64]

In 1858 (after the Great Rebellion of 1857) the British crown assumed governance of India. In her proclamation, Queen Victoria again affirmed the principle of religious neutrality. She declared that all religions will "enjoy the equal and impartial protection of law" and that no special favor would be shown to any one religion.[65]

The above brief description of British administration's dealings with religions in India shows that, in spite of certain ambiguities, the British administration in India tried to be neutral in religious affairs. This is an important historical root for modern India's secular state.

The Influence of Western Education, Culture, and Political Thought

The impact of the British rule and, through it, the influence of Western education, thought, and culture was most profound in India. This affected the social, religious, and political thought as well as the institutions of the people. As Panikkar says,

The organization of the democratic state, its secular character, the structure of its institutions and the political principles underlying them are also essentially European in their inspiration.[66]

To begin with, the East India Company was interested only in

---

63. *Ibid.*, p. 87.
64. *Ibid.*
65. Quoted in D. E. Smith, pp. 71–72.
66. K. M. Panikkar, *The Foundations of New India* (London: George Allen and Unwin, Ltd., 1963), p. 16.

commerce and it left India undisturbed in other areas. In the seventeenth century Indian civilization was considered alien but not inferior. But by the eighteenth century the general British outlook was that "Indian institutions were . . . effete, many customs odious, and Indian peoples barbarous."[67] The Renaissance produced a new confidence and a crusading spirit in Europe. Europe had found a new secret, namely the principle of reason, and this resulted in great scientific progress and the introduction of the principle of social justice.[68] It was the people who were imbued with this spirit who influenced the course of events in India in the nineteenth century.

At the beginning of the nineteenth century two streams of thought were prominent in England, namely, the Utilitarian and the Evangelical, both of which influenced India. The Utilitarians, under Jeremy Bentham, believed in reason, utility, and the possibility of social reform. They were against custom and vested interest and privilege. To them India provided a field where these new ideas could be put into practice. Bentham found very little to be admired in India and much that needed change. James Mill, Bentham's leading disciple, and his son John Stuart Mill were key officials in India House. Indian administrators, like Elphinstone, Holt, Mackenzie, Metcalfe, and Bentick, were imbued with their ideas and were instrumental in introducing the new policy of attacking the obvious abuses and practices found in Indian society. Bentick's suppression of *Sati*, in spite of opposition on religious grounds from orthodox Hindu leaders, is a good example of this new policy. But there was no attack on caste. And even though there was more opposition, the right to change religion without losing inheritance was granted on the basis of natural justice.

The Evangelicals, though opposed to the naturalistic philosophy of the Utilitarians, were in accord with them on the need for reform in India. They were motivated by the humanism of the Gospels and missionary zeal to convert souls. They were against idolatry and many superstitious practices. Evangelical leaders like William Wilberforce and Charles Grant were also influential in the government. It was under Wilberforce's instigation that the 1813 Charter Act allowed Christian missions to operate within the Company's territories even though without government sup-

---

67. Spear, pp. 254-55.
68. *Ibid.*, p. 255.

port. The Company's commercial monopoly was abolished and thirty thousand dollars was set aside for annual promotion of learning among Indian people.[69] The social reforms that the radicals and the Evangelicals were instrumental in introducing into India were appealing to Indian humanitarians like Rammohan Roy.

The introduction of Western law into India and its institutionalization there had tremendous effect. It shaped the modern Indian legal system and undermined traditional Indian institutions.[70] Under Bentick, Thomas Babington Macaulay, who had been called "India's New Manu," laid the foundation for modern legal systems of India.[71] He had to fight for the principle of equality of all before the law and the right of the accused to be considered innocent until proven guilty. According to Hindu practice, a Brahmin could not be punished on the evidence of a Sudra (of lower caste), and the degree of punishment varied according to caste. Under Muslim law, an unbeliever's testimony against a Muslim was not acceptable; but now all were made equal before the law.

Sir William Jones, who arrived in India in 1783, had discovered the wealth of Sanskrit literature and translated much of it to English. He and his colleagues in the Royal Asiatic Society gave a great boost to India's morale by showing to the world some glories of its ancient past.

English Education in India

Of all the influences of the British period, the introduction of English education had perhaps the most transforming effect in the life of India. India, which was essentially parochial and divided and sunk in the morass of old fossilized traditions and stagnant superstitions, was awakened from its sleep of lethargy and inaction and put in contact with the newly vibrant Western civilization. Out of this contact emerged a new India, which, by the end of the nineteenth century, was unified with the spirit of nationalism and infused with Western ideas of democracy and secularism. This influence, while mainly touching only the elite, who alone benefited from English education, was enough to give

---

69. *Ibid.*, p. 258.
70. *Ibid.*, p. 260.
71. Panikkar, *A Survey of Indian History*, p. 210.

a dynamic quality to Indian society. R. C. Majumdar points to English education as the greatest transforming influence in India in the nineteenth century.[72]

Consistent with the policy of religious neutrality, the British were first reluctant to sponsor any alien system of education in India lest it might offend the religious sensibilities of the people. There was also genuine appreciation in many quarters for classical Indian learning. In 1781 Warren Hastings established the Calcutta Madrasa (or Muhammaden College) to teach Arabic and Persian languages and Muslim law. Jonathan Duncan, Resident in Benaras, founded the Sanskrit College at Benaras in 1791. But the demand for English education came from the elite of the major cities like Calcutta, Bombay, and Madras where, through contact with the English, they had come to appreciate the value of English as a medium of culture and expressed the desire to imbibe the new spirit of the West through the study of the English language. The Hindu College was founded in Calcutta in 1817 as a result of the initiative taken by Hindu and European leaders of Calcutta. The Christian missionaries also founded schools in Serampore (1818) and elsewhere.[73]

An annual grant of 1 lakh of rupees ($30,000) was to be spent for the advancement of learning in India according to the new charter of the company passed in 1813 by the Parliament. The company, however, did not develop any policy and none of it was spent until 17 July 1823, when the General Committee of Public Instruction was formed in Calcutta and put in charge of the existing government institutions and the grant. Under the influence of the Utilitarians and James Mill, the Directors now suggested that the learning imparted should be useful and this meant not "the useless fables of Hindu mythology or the tenets of the Quran."[74] William Bentick, the Governor-General of India, himself a Benthamite, believed in general education as the panacea for the regeneration of India.[75] The famous "Minute on Education" by Macaulay unequivocally affirmed that the learning of the East was nothing compared to the new learning of the West and that the latter alone could free the Indian mind from superstition and ignorance. His object was to "form a class of persons, Indian in blood and in colour, but English in tastes, in opinions, and in

---

72. Majumdar, 10:31.
73. Ibid., pp. 30–34.
74. Ibid., p. 44.
75. Ibid., p. 45.

morals and in intellect."[76] This sentiment was earlier echoed in a letter written by Raja Rammohan Roy in December 1823 to Lord Amherst, the then-Governor-General, protesting against the government proposal to establish a Sanskrit school under Hindu pandits. He wrote that the Sanskrit system of education would only keep the country in darkness. What was needed was a liberal and enlightened system under which mathematics, natural philosophy, chemistry, and other useful sciences would be taught.[77] As a result of pressure from England and support in India, Bentick issued his Resolution of 7 March 1835, which supported this position and allocated all the funds for education exclusively to English education.[78] English also supplanted Persian as the official language of government business, diplomacy, and courts of law. As a result, thousands of people who would have learned Persian to get a job learned English.[79]

In spite of some protests from the Orientalists, the cause of English education prospered. The government of India Educational Dispatch No. 49 of 19 July 1854, drafted by Sir Charles Wood, provided a firm basis for the further development of education in India. In 1857 universities were started in Calcutta, Bombay, and Madras. The Hunter Commission of 1882, and the Universities Commission of 1902 (under Lord Curzon), made further recommendations, all of which contributed toward higher education in India.

The popularization of English education opened the floodgates of Western ideas into the Indian religious, social, and political scene. The introduction of English education broke the intellectual isolation of India from the Western world.

The most important effect of Western culture on India was that it replaced blind faith with the spirit of nationalism and free enquiry.[80] In Bengal, one of the early effects of English education was the revolt of many young Hindu students against their traditional religion and practices. While this new spirit may have had the effect of demoralizing and denationalizing Indian youth of the period, its most positive effect was that it "instilled in the minds of Indians a spirit of rational inquiry into the basis of their religion and society."[81] This spirit is typified by the personality of

---

76. *Ibid.*, p. 46.
77. *Ibid.*, pp. 34–35.
78. *Ibid.*, p. 47.
79. Spear, p. 261.
80. Majumdar, 10:89.
81. *Ibid.*, p. 92.

Rammohan Roy and the founding of the Brahma Samaj. In opposition to traditional Hindu religion, Rammohan Roy proclaimed a monotheistic religion, which he based on the Upanishads. Devandra Nath Tagore and Keshub Chander Sen succeeded him in giving leadership to the movement.

Until English education was introduced, the source of all knowledge was supposed to reside exclusively in the Sanskrit classics by the Hindus. By learning the English language and Western thought, one challenged this orthodox assumption. The new ideas learned in the English schools and the old ideas from one's birth were kept in watertight compartments by many. Even so, in the long run mutual influence cannot be avoided. The textbooks used in English education contained many radical ideas that were strange to Indian thought and that were closely in line with the philosophy of secularism and the secular state ideal. For example, prose writers like Burke, Macaulay, and John Stuart Mill were full of ideas that were basically "Christian and Classical" as well as essentially secular in outlook. The writings of English poets, the Bible, and other works, portions of which were used as textbooks, contained ideas of the worth of the individual, primacy of conscience and reason, and the equality of all men before God— ideas that often militated against orthodox Hindu concepts. Political ideas like nationalism, self-government, personal liberty, rule of law, and the like were also implicit in English literature as well as in the political works. Many European writers and political philosophers were read and enjoyed in English translation. Modern scientific studies were introduced and this again involved the acceptance of reason over tradition and superstition. Thousands of people who were educated in this new system and exposed to Western ways of thinking and reasoning became not only tame civil servants, but also fiery leaders of an awakening India, the awakening of which finally led to the formation of the secular state. Most of the great leaders of modern India who left a deep mark on Indian life were men who were influenced by Western thought and ideals. Raja Rammohan Roy, Tagore, Ghose, Gandhi, and Nehru are some of the outstanding examples. Not all accepted Western ideals, however, and some even became leaders in reacting against them. Nevertheless, the impact of Western influence on them cannot be doubted.[82]

The work of foreign missionaries in India cannot be ignored

82. Spear, pp. 360-62.

in this connection, and this will be examined in greater detail later. Missionary attempts at converting high castes were not very successful. Yet they were able to influence and win over many distinguished men belonging to the high castes, especially in Bengal. The missionaries were more successful with the lower castes. While many Hindus bitterly resented their proselyting activities, they learned a lesson from the missionary concern for the untouchables and the "depressed classes." Their hospitals, orphanages, and other humanitarian work also deeply impressed Hindu India. While the large number of schools and colleges started by Christian missions did not account for many conversions to Christianity, it was notably instrumental in spreading Western and Christian ideas among the Indian intelligentsia. In evaluating the influence of Christian missions during the British period, Natarajan says,

> Christian missions have played a large part in introducing India to the humanistic side of Western civilization. . . . Christian missions have incidentally and indirectly done much good to the country. The fear of Christianity has been the beginning of much social wisdom in India. The first impulse to start orphanages, for instance, came from the desire to prevent famine orphans from being swept into the missionary fold through mission orphanages.
>
> Social service as distinguished from social reform is a new feature of Indian life, which we owe chiefly to the example of Christian missions.[83]

These influences also form part of the background and historical roots out of which the Indian secular state evolved. Missionaries, sometimes in spite of themselves, were allies in the process of westernization.

Secularism in Hindu Thought

We have noted the Hindu polity and political ideas in their relation to the secular state. Equally important is the philosophy of the people as a whole. The secular state, as we have seen, presupposes not only a form of administration but also a general attitude of the people toward life. By implication, the secular state ideal should have a world-affirming, rather than world-negating, attitude. A healthy "this-worldliness" and an attitude

83. Natarajan, pp. 7–8.

that considers the affairs of this world, including social welfare, as sufficiently important to warrant the attention and efforts of people should be present. So also, a general attitude of tolerance toward different religions and ideologies is necessary to have a secular state as opposed to a theocratic one. A secular state that is intensely concerned with the welfare of the people and that works for social change also presupposes a citizenry willing to change and think in rational terms, not guided merely by super-stition and outmoded tradition. In all these respects, we find that certain aspects of Hindu religion and thought and some social movements within Hinduism have made significant contributions.

The Hindu religion is usually supposed to be otherworldly, and to teach renunciation of the world. While this is true about ortho-dox Hinduism, it is not true about popular Hinduism. Moreover, Hinduism is a composite of many traditions and it contains cer-tain ones that express a trend toward secularism or interest in this world. As Devanandan points out, present-day Hinduism is very much concerned with discovering and bringing into the open some of the secular strands within Hinduism:

> The essential quest in contemporary Hindu renaissance, there-fore, is to discover a religious basis for this new secularism which could lend support to this earthly preoccupation calling for active involvement in purposive plans for the development of long neglected natural resources, the re-ordering of time-honoured social institutions and for determined effort to con-centrate attention more on present welfare of all men rather than on the realization of the ultimate destiny of the individual.[84]

In the classical work the *Sarva Darsana Sangraha* (Compen-dium of Philosophies) compiled in the fourteenth century, one of the nine Darsanas or philosophies of Hinduism discussed in it is the Charvaka system, or materialism. Even though it was not one of the "orthodox" or "Brahmanical" systems, as a philosophical system "it has had an ancient and continuous history in India since Vedic times."[85] Even though the writings of neither its supposed founder, Brihaspati, nor his followers are extant, the system of thought "has been important enough to evoke the vigor-ous criticism of the other schools against it."[86]

---

84. P. D. Devanandan, "Contemporary Hindu Secularism," *Religion and Society* 9 (March 1962):21-22.

85. P. Narasimhayya, "The Rational Quest for Philosophy and Discipline: The Materialism of Charvaka," *Bhavan's Journal* 13, no. 6 (1966):71.

86. *Ibid.*, p. 73.

Charvaka means "the sweet" because of its ideal of pleasure (kama). It is also known as *Lokayata,* the worldly.

The Charvaka system is atheistic and completely materialistic. It considers the pursuit of individual pleasure as the only valid aim of man and accepts only perception as the means of knowledge. The sense experiences of touch, hearing, sight, smell, taste, and heat or cold are the only means of verification of truth. There is no independent mind and the spirit dies with the body. This repudiates the doctrine of *karma.* Charvaka accepted only *artha* (wealth) and *kama* (pleasure) and not *dharma* (duty) and *moksha* (salvation). According to Charvaka,

> since reality consists of physical sensations and human life consists only of the consequent mental feelings, the natural and proper goal of life is pleasure, as steady, as permanent or continuous, and as intense, as man's efforts and calculations can make it. . . . Pleasure is the highest dharma, duty, standard and goal.[87]

The Charvaka social and political ideal is one of equality and liberty for all to pursue their own welfare and pleasure without interfering with others. "So peace, order and a strong state organization and a practical policy are essential."[88] The state is not a moral organization but is nonmoral or amoral.

As we can see, in spite of its many weaknesses the Charvaka system makes certain contributions that strengthen the forces of secularism. It emphasizes rationalism and the principle of knowledge through experience as opposed to adherence to and emphasis on metaphysical reasoning and categories of thought.

> It does a great service, however, in emphasizing physical realities, sense experiences and pleasures, and a strong egalitarian society and state. By demanding universal and sense-perceptual proof, it challenges all claims to transcendentalism, and revelations closed to reason. It is also a good corrective to extreme and tortuous asceticism which crushes out all pleasures and feeling from life.[89]

Some scholars doubt the extent of the influence that Lokayata philosophy exerted at any time in Indian history, but references to it in other literature show that it was well enough known to merit refutation. In any case, it is necessary to recognize the

87. *Ibid.,* p. 76.
88. *Ibid.*
89. *Ibid.,* p. 77.

existence of this unorthodox system in the history of Indian philosophic thought.

The *artha* tradition gained emphasis in succeeding works like the *Panchatantra*, the *Hitopadesha*, and *Kathasaritsagara*, compiled between 700–1000 A.D. Dharma was considered the moral basis for the pursuit of worldly goods. But the growth of *Dharmasastras*, which gave a lower place to castes following agricultural and trade vocations, again emphasized withdrawal and renunciation as the ideal of Hindu culture.[90]

During the Muslim period, Hinduism kept to its orthodox traditions, which became rigidified. The emphasis was in renunciation and withdrawal from the world. But we find a Hindu renaissance in the nineteenth century as a result of contacts with the West. It posed challenges that orthodox Hinduism could not escape by mere withdrawal. The Western spirit challenged the traditional religious attitudes and moved Indian thought toward nationalism and secularism.[91]

Rammohan Roy typified the new spirit in Hinduism, which took a "spirit of rational inquiry into the basis of their religion and society."[92] Rammohan did not merely borrow a few principles or ideas from the West at random, but brought traditional Hindu religious principles and practices under the burning fire of reason. He challenged Hindu orthodoxy as not consonant with the principles of its own scriptures. He opposed multiplicity of gods and idol-worship, which formed the essence of current popular Hinduism, on the ground that they were against the teaching of the Vedas.[93] The Brahma Samaj, which he founded, tried to present what he considered to be the pure form of Hinduism based on the Upanishads, devoid of abuses and corruptions and incorporating what was best in the Western tradition. The Brahma Samaj was perhaps too intellectual and exclusive to ever become popular.[94]

In 1875 Swami Dayananda Saraswati founded the Arya Samaj. He too was opposed to many of the traditional doctrines of orthodox Hinduism. The Arya Samaj considered only the Vedas as authoritative. Dayananda rejected caste and the superiority of the Brahmins. Intercaste marriages were encouraged and child marriage was discouraged. The Arya Samaj also initiated the

90. Devanandan, "Contemporary Hindu Secularism," p. 24.
91. Spear, p. 295.
92. Majumdar, 10:92.
93. *Ibid.*, p. 92.
94. Spear, p. 293.

Suddhi movement, by which Hindus who were converted to other religions might be received back into Hinduism. Even though Muslims particularly resented this, the Samaj looked upon it as a means for achieving the religious and political unity of India, which was the cherished ideal of the Samaj. The Samaj instilled the spirit of nationalism in the Punjab, even though combined with anti-Muslim feeling.[95] Social services like famine relief and the spread of English education were two distinctive features of the Samaj. In these and in the revolt against traditional religion, it showed certain secular elements.

The contemplative aspect of Ramakrishna Paramahamsa's teachings was given a social and dynamic content by his chief disciple, Swami Vivekananda. He taught that out of contemplation, social service should ensue. In 1897 the Ramakrishna Mission was established, and in many ways it resembled a Western missionary association. Vivekananda emphasized "Karma yoga, purposeful action in the world as the thing needful for the regeneration of the political, social and religious life of the Hindus."[96] Much philanthropic work is carried out by the Mission even now in many parts of India. Vivekananda wrote once to a disciple, "The poor, the ignorant, the illiterate, the afflicted—let these be your God: know that service to these is the highest religion."[97] By his travels in America and the West, and his defense of Hinduism, Swami Vivekananda increased national self-respect. His work also greatly enhanced the national spirit and he was in line with Rammohan Roy's work in rejuvenating the Indian life. According to some, Vivekananda paved the way for the regeneration of India.[98] The Ramakrishna Math and Mission has been called the "greatest spiritual force in modern India."[99] By rejuvenating India, stimulating nationalism, and engaging in social service, Vivekananda and the Ramakrishna Mission have contributed to the formation of the secular state.

The Indian National Movement and the Establishment of the Secular State

A study of the emergence of Indian nationalism and the Indian

---

95. *Ibid.*
96. Devanandan, "Contemporary Hindu Secularism," p. 26.
97. Quoted in Majumdar, 10:129.
98. *Ibid.*, p. 130.
99. *Ibid.*

freedom movement, which culminated in Indian independence and the establishment of the new state, is necessary to further understand the nature of the secular state in India. Some of the ideas that dominated the national movement are the very same ones that formed the basis of the new government and the constitution. At the same time we may also notice some ideas that were against the concept of the secular state (and that may yet again emerge to the forefront) that were dominant in certain periods of the national movement. The course of the development of communal politics in India and the formal division of India into India and Pakistan is also relevant for our understanding of the nature of the Indian secular state.

Indian nationalism arose during the second half of the nineteenth century as a result of many forces. Reaction against foreign rule, revelation of India's past as a result of the studies of oriental scholars and the consequent pride that Indians felt in their past, the influence of European nationalism and liberal political ideas, and the propagation of the new ideas through the medium of the printed word—these are some of the reasons for the emergence of the feeling that India was one nation and that it had a destiny and goal that should be developed. The newly emergent spirit of nationalism was defined mainly in two ways—one based on the Hindu religion (and in the case of Muslims, on Islam), the other a pluralist society based on economic and political interests. Both elements were equally wedded to the idea of national independence.

In tracing the communal element of Indian nationalism, one has to go back to the founding of the Brahma Samaj by Raja Rammohan Roy and the attempt to assert the ability of a reformed Hinduism to withstand the cultural and religious onslaught of the British rule in India. The activities of Keshub Chunder Sen, including his controversies with the missionaries, made him popular with the educated classes in Bengal and throughout the country.[100] But Brahma Samaj remained essentially a religious organization and did not continue to wield much influence in the political field.

The Arya Samaj founded by Dayananda gave great impetus to nationalism in the Punjab. It imbued the people with a spirit of self-confidence. The Arya Samaj was a militant sect and its patriotism was based on the rejuvenation and protection of Hindu

---

100. *Ibid.*, pp. 468–69.

religion. It was particularly hostile to Islam and was not friendly toward Christianity.[101] However, it worked for political independence.

The role of the Theosophical Society in the national movement should also be mentioned. Mrs. Annie Besant, the most gifted representative of the society in India, extolled the glory of the ancient Indian past and advocated the reconstruction of Hindu society on the model of the old.[102] Even though theosophy recognized the spiritual unity of all religions, it was closely linked with the Hindu religion. She wrote, "If there is to be an Indian nation, patriotism and religion must join hands in India."[103]

During the First World War, or shortly thereafter, Pundit Madan Mohan Malaviya and Lala Lajpat Rai organized the Hindu Mahasabha with a view to spreading doctrines of Hinduism and showing its contemporary relevance. The Mahasabha has since then been a strong force in pleading for a nation based on Hinduism. The Hindu Mahasabha acted as the voice of Hindu orthodoxy, particularly in opposition to the Muslim League.

We have so far surveyed the considerable part played by Hindu nationalism in the Indian national movement. Its concept of nationalism was firmly based in 1) revival of Hinduism, and 2) close identification of the Hindu religion with the concept of the Indian nationhood. India was to be free from foreign yoke, but the new India was to be built on the cultural and religious heritage of Hinduism. India was to be indeed free from foreign yoke— not only politically, but also culturally and religiously.

The other element of communal influence in the national movement was the activities of the Muslim League, which was formed in 1906. During the period when the Hindu community benefited from its Western education, which resulted in Hindu renaissance and reform movements, the Muslim community was by and large left behind. It was still nursing the pain of having lost the empire and unwilling to have any contacts with the "idolatrous" Hindus and the British "infidels." It was Sayyid Ahmad Khan who first paved the way for Muslim resurgence by founding the Anglo-Arabic College (renamed Aligarh Muslim University in 1920) in 1875.[104] When the Indian National Congress was formed he advised the Muslims to stand aloof from it. He preferred British rule

---

101. *Ibid.*, p. 475.
102. Majumdar, 9:492.
103. *Hindustan Review* 15:545. Quoted by Heimsath, p. 315.
104. Spear, p. 297.

to what he thought would be Hindu hegemony.[105] According to him, India was inhabited by different nationalities like the Muslims, the Marathas, the Brahmins, the Sudras, and the Madrasis. The Congress, according to him, could not "rationally prove its claim to represent the opinions, ideals and aspirations of the Muslims."[106] The Muslim League was formed partly because of the reaction against the activities of the Arya Samaj and the agitation against partition of Bengal, as a result of which in East Bengal the Muslims had a majority. A Muslim deputation secured from Lord Minto, the Governor-General, a promise to grant separate electorates for the Muslims. To Iqbal, the great Muslim poet, Muslim unity was provided by Islam. He demanded the creation of a "Muslim India within India."[107] Muhamad Ali was the next great leader of the Muslims. It was under his leadership that Hindus and Muslims worked against the British for the preservation of the Caliphate in Turkey. But the unity of Hindus and Muslims was short-lived. Differences of opinion arose between the Congress and the Muslim leaders and the first breach came in 1930. The leader who finally engineered the creation of a separate state for Muslims in the formation of Pakistan was Muhamad Ali Jinnah. He started off as a Congressman, but finally became the spokesman for an independent Muslim state.

Thus we find that communal nationalism of both Hindus and Muslims which finally led to the division of India and the setting up of Pakistan as an independent state. When we examine the activities of the Indian National Congress we shall find that the vast majority of Hindus and a considerable number of Muslims were in favor of the establishment of a noncommunal state, as advocated by the Congress. Even within the Congress there were both secular and communal tendencies, but the former was by far the predominant philosophy of the Congress. The role of the Christian community in the national movement will be discussed in a later chapter.

The Indian National Congress, the most important organization to carry on the freedom movement was founded on 28 December 1885 in Bombay. The idea was originated by a retired English Civil Service official, A. O. Hume, and several Englishmen served as its presidents during the beginning years. Even though the Congress was not the first nationalist organization to be started,

---

105. De Bary, p. 742.
106. *Ibid.*, p. 747.
107. *Ibid.*, p. 767.

from its inception it became the main vehicle for nationalist expression. In the beginning the Congress represented leaders of the new, liberal, educated class of India. They were great admirers of the British.[108] At its third meeting, in Allahabad, Pandit Madan Mohan Malaviya, founder of the Hindu College at Banaras with Annie Besant and a great champion of orthodox Hinduism, was present and was one of the early leaders of the Congress. But most of the early leaders did not represent orthodox Hindu ideas.[109]

However, a change in spirit came with the next generation. Indian nationalism took on a spirit of fervor and dedication. The defeat of Russia by Japan stirred hopes of Asian greatness in the minds of people. As noted earlier, Tilak, the "father of Indian unrest," infused nationalism with Hindu religious fervor, which was highly appealing. Upon his arrest and incarceration he became a national hero. The partition of Bengal further accelerated the national movement, which took on a religious hue and fervor. The latter may be noted in the oath that Bengalee youth took when they decided to boycott foreign goods:

> Invoking God Almighty to be our witness, and standing in the presence of after generations, we take this solemn oath that so far as practicable, we shall use home-made articles and abstain from the use of foreign articles. So help us God.[110]

Tilak, Lala Lajpat Rai, and Aurobindo Ghose were among the leaders of the radical section of the Congress. They split with the Congress in the Surat Session held on 21 December 1907.[111] As Panikkar says, the Congress's nationalism at this stage was basically Hindu and revivalist.[112]

As noted earlier, the attitude of Muslims like Sir Saiyed Ahmad Khan was not favorable to the Congress. As a counterblast to this, the "Patriotic Association" was started at Aligarh in 1888. However, the entire Muslim community was not opposed to the Congress. Some were associated with it from the beginning. Justice Badruddin Tayabji, Rahamatulla, and Muhammed Say-

---

108. Panikkar, *A Survey of Indian History*, p. 225.
109. *Ibid.*
110. Surendrarath Banerjee, *A Nation in Making*, p. 229. Quoted by K. K. Datta, *Renaissance, Nationalism and Social Changes in Modern India* (Calcutta: Bookland Private Ltd., 1965), p. 29.
111. *Ibid.*, p. 33.
112. Panikkar, *A Survey of Indian History*, p. 225. See also Heimsath, p. 312.

yani were some of the early prominent Muslim leaders in the Congress.

Many Indian historians believe that the British government followed the policy of *Divide et Impere*. The government was alarmed at the rapid growth of nationalism under the Congress and it is held that they deliberately encouraged the Muslim community to ask for special and favored treatment.

There were attempts at Hindu-Muslim unity, which resulted in the "Lucknow Pact" of 1916 between the Congress and the Muslim League, according to which the Congress agreed to separate electorates. Both agreed on a scheme of reforms and on the objective of self-government for India.[113] At the close of the First World War, Muslims were very much agitated about the dismemberment of Turkey, for which Britain was greatly responsible. The Khilafat Movement, started by Maulana Abul Kalam Azad and the two Ali brothers (Shaukat and Muhamad), was wholeheartedly supported by the Congress. This achieved a high watermark in Hindu-Muslim unity.[114] But with the proclamation of Turkey as a Republic, the abolition of the institution of the Caliphate, and the declaration of Turkey as a secular state in March 1924, the main plank for joint action was lost and along with it Hindu-Muslim unity. The Muslims again became active in politics and communal riots took place in 1923. The unity conferences in 1927 with Pandit Motilal Nehru and Muhamad Ali as leaders were of no avail in bringing the communities together.

While the Muslim League under the leadership of Jinnah continued to press for the creation of a separate state for Moslems, the Congress Party developed more and more into a nationalistic organization. From 1920 onwards, Gandhi became the undisputed leader of the Congress. Under Gandhi's leadership, the Congress became a "truly nationalistic instrument, a political microcosm of the national life. As a result of his tactics and attitudes at various times, it became identified with most of the progressive movements in the country."[115] The Congress was able to win the loyalty of almost all the communities of India except the Muslims, although even among these the Congress had a sizable following.

Gandhi's appeal was not based on orthodox Hinduism, even though he was a pious Hindu. He was influenced by what was

---

113. Datta, p. 39.
114. *Ibid.*, p. 51.
115. Spear, p. 363.

best in both the West and the East. In contrast to the appeal of the nationalist and revivalist leaders of the earlier period, his appeal was emotional as well as universal. His concept of the destiny of India, though expressed in terms of *Rama Rajya* (Rama's rule or kingdom), was not sectarian. Even though he was often misunderstood by missionaries and others on this score, it was because his idea of Hinduism was so catholic and universal that he expressed his vision in Hindu terms.

While some may identify Gandhi with at least some aspects of Hindu revivalism, none could so regard the other towering leader of the Congress, Jawaharlal Nehru. He was wholly liberal, nonsectarian, and secular in his outlook, and he stamped the Congress with his philosophy. The Congress accepted the goals of a secular, democratic, and socialistic pattern of society under his leadership.

While the Congress was wholly dominated by these two figures from 1920 up to the time of independence, there were those who followed the two leaders completely and also those who did not and were communal in their outlook. The Congress inevitably contained people of different ideological shades. But the molding influences were those of Gandhi and Nehru and those who stood in their line of thought.

The partition of India and independence were followed by massacres and mass migration, which occurred on the eastern and western borders of India and Pakistan. The disturbances were worst in the Punjab. It is estimated that more than ten million people became refugees and that about a million people were killed.

It is against this background that the Constituent Assembly of India (appointed before independence and now reorganized) completed its task of drawing up the Constitution for independent India, and India became a secular democratic republic on 26 January 1950.

In this chapter we have briefly examined the historical and cultural roots of the secular state in India.

Historically speaking, the origin and nature of Hindu kingship gives some precedent for the concept of the secular state. The kingship was not primarily considered as divine in origin, and its relationships with people, at least theoretically speaking, was contractual. Also, the kingship was seldom dominated by the Brahminical priesthood. Asoka exemplified in his rule (even though as a Buddhist monarch) the ideal spirit of tolerance for all religions. We have also noted the existence of republics that were secular in nature.

During the Muslim period, the emperor was supreme because in some ways he represented the Caliph in a local sense. While many Muslim rulers persecuted Hindus and forced conversion, rulers like Akbar followed a policy of tolerance, impartiality, and having Hindus in high positions of government. Akbar is the shining example of the secular spirit during the Muslim period.

The British administration, by and large, followed a policy of religious neutrality, which was certainly a good preparation for the Indian secular state. The independent civil and judicial systems left by the British provided a good frame for the secular government. The national freedom movement also developed, mainly favoring the establishment of a noncommunal state, and the disturbances immediately preceding and following independence only reinforced the will of the founding fathers of the nation to keep India secular in government and outlook.

In the cultural and religious realm we found that the spirit of tolerance in Hinduism is an important element of the historical roots of the secular state. The existence of the Lokayata or *nastika* (atheist) tradition and the emphasis on *artha* (pursuit of wealth), which are to be found as part of Hindu thought, also form part of the secular tradition in India. Perhaps the greatest contribution to the evolution of the modern secular state in India has been made by the nineteenth-century liberal thought of the West, which transformed the outlook of the leaders of the nationalist movement—the Indian middle class, and also permeated the social and political thought of the country. The westernizing influences of English education and the work of Christian missions also cannot be discounted in this respect. All these historical, cultural, and religious heritages of India provided a firm foundation for the evolution of the modern secular state in India.

Of course there were strong forces that were against the spirit of the secular state. The close relation between religion and state in the Hindu tradition, the idea of the theocratic state and communal tension during much of Islamic rule, the divisive policies of the British government and the communal aspects of the Congress party—all these militated against the evolution of the secular state. But the impact of the overwhelming forces of history and culture described earlier has resulted in the formation of the secular state. The next chapter will consider the meaning that the secular-state concept has acquired in India since independence.

2
The Meaning of the
Secular State in India

Having considered the historical and cultural roots of the idea of the secular state in India, we may now examine what meaning the idea has acquired in present-day India. One way to do this is to determine the meaning that the Indian National Congress, the major political party of India, ascribed to the secular state, both by its pronouncements and its practice. The secular-state ideal was incorporated into the Constitution of India after lengthy debates and discussion in the Constituent Assembly of India. Studying the relevant portions of the debates will throw much light on what the founding fathers of the nation meant by the secular state (even though the term itself is not used in the Constitution). We shall further examine the relevant clauses in the Indian Constitution. Jawaharlal Nehru was the foremost exponent of the secular-state ideal during the national movement, as well as in independent India, until his death in 1964, and it will be rewarding to look at some of his ideas regarding the secular state. We shall also survey attitudes that major political organizations, as well as representative political leaders, have expressed with regard to the secular state. Here the writer will incorporate the results of the interviews that he was privileged to have had with some of the outstanding political and social leaders of India.

The Indian National Congress and the
Idea of the Secular State

The Congress's espousal of the secular-state ideal is primarily based on two concerns: 1) the desire to foster communal unity

52

and harmony in India, and 2) to affirm and promote the fundamental rights of the individual—of every individual, irrespective of caste, color, creed, language, place of birth, and so on, as basic to the practice of democracy.

What was the Congress's attitude toward communalism and communal representation in elections? It was wholly opposed to communalism in politics based on one's loyalty to one's caste or religion. The Congress, in claiming to be a "national" party, had, by and large, eschewed communal politics.

Even though the Congress was at times dominated by Hindu extremists (especially during the first decade of this century when Tilak, Ghose, and others dominated the scene), during most of its history it tried, with a great measure of success, to represent all the peoples of India. Even when the Muslim League became very strong and most of the Muslims supported it, distinguished Muslim leaders like Maulana Abul Kalam Azad and large numbers of Indian Muslims still maintained their loyalty to the Congress and were well represented in the organization.

Nevertheless, the Congress has been accused of practicing communalism.[1] It is pointed out that Congress membership was predominantly Hindu and that the psychological and philosophical background of Congress ideology was Hindu. But in reply to this it should be noted that the Congress was predominantly Hindu in membership because the population of the country mainly consisted of Hindus. The Congress was open to all people and in the Lucknow Pact and in later resolutions, the Congress has shown high solicitude for protecting the fundamental rights of the minorities.[2] Gandhi claimed at the second session of the Round Table Conference in London in 1931 that the Congress was the only all-India-wide national organization and that it represented all minorities.[3]

The desire of the Congress to promote communal unity and to accommodate the views of the minorities, especially the Muslim community, is seen in the Lucknow Pact of 1916, the Khilafat Movement, and the pronouncements of Congress leaders like Gandhi and Nehru. In deference to the wishes of the Muslims, the

1. See R. Coupland, *The Indian Problem: Report on the Constitutional Problem in India* (London: Oxford University Press, 1944), pp. 86, 102.

2. P. D. Kaushik, *The Congress Ideology and Programme 1920–47: Ideological Foundations of Indian Nationalism during the Gandhian Era* (Bombay: Allied Publishers Private Ltd., 1964), p. 61.

3. A. C. Bannerjee, *Indian Constitutional Documents: Vol. III, 1917–1939* (Calcutta: A. Mukherjee & Co., 1949), p. 190.

principle of separate electorates was accepted by the Congress. It also wholeheartedly supported the Khilafat Movement, through which the Indian Muslims demanded the restoration of the Caliphate in Turkey. In 1927 and in 1931 the Congress accepted the principle of joint electorate with reservation of seats for minorities. It was accepted as "a compromise between the proposals based on undiluted communalism and undiluted nationalism."[4] The Congress was adamant until the very end on only one question, i.e., preserving the unity of India. But in the face of civil war and the prospects of indefinite postponement of freedom, the Congress agreed to the partition of India.

Another aspect of the secular policy of the Congress may be seen in its concern to ensure fundamental rights for all citizens, especially the minorities. It would not be wrong to assume that, even apart from the communal question, the Congress would have been concerned with the question of the rights of man *per se* because of the influence of Western political thought on its ideology. But the problem of minorities made it imperative that the Congress define its stand early.

As early as 1919 at the Amritsar Congress Session, the party passed a resolution on Fundamental Rights, guaranteeing freedom of speech, freedom of the press, and equality before the law.[5] The resolution on Fundamental Rights that the AICC passed in August (6–8) 1931 in Bombay also dealt with freedom of conscience and nondiscrimination on the basis of religion, caste, creed, and sex.[6] The Congress did not waver from these decisions and when the new Constitution of India was written, its leaders redeemed their pledge by incorporating almost identical clauses in the Constitution.

These principles of secularism and religious tolerance were reiterated again and again until the advent of independence. Since independence (in 1947), the Congress has been the ruling party in the central government and its policies are reflected in the actions of the government.

The Secular State in Nehru's Thought

Prime Minister Jawaharlal Nehru's views on the secular state

---

4. *Resolution of the Congress Working Committee*, July, 1931, in Bannerjee, *ibid.*, pp. 206, 209.

5. B. Pattabhi Sitaramayya, *The History of the Congress* (Allahabad: Congress Working Committee, 1935), p. 46. Also see pp. 180 and 310.

6. *Ibid.*, pp. 779-80.

have to be understood in terms of his views on religion, his strong reaction to communalism, and his views on religious freedom and fundamental rights. For Nehru, a secular state meant more than an arrangement by which different religious communities and the government could coexist peacefully; it reflected a view of society and life in general.

Nehru grew up in a family that was Hindu, but not traditionally Orthodox. The interest in Theosophy that he gained from his tutor was but a passing phenomenon.[7] In his *The Discovery of India* he has described his early philosophy as a scientific humanism.[8] As he says later, he was "essentially . . . interested in this world, in this life, not in some other world or a future life."[9] He was not so much interested in the questions regarding the existence of God as in the service of man. His approach was essentially a human approach. According to Nehru, "The moment we forget the human approach, somehow the foundation of our thinking is removed."[10]

In spite of his apparent agnosticism, as Nehru looked around the world, he felt, in his words, "a sense of mysteries, of unknown depths" and an urge "to understand it, to be in tune with it and to experience it in its fulness."[11] He also believed in an ethical approach to life and recognized that some religious values "were still the foundation of morality and ethics."[12] In 1960, in an interview with the Indian journalist R. K. Karanjia, he said:

> The old Hindu idea that there is a divine essence in the world and every individual possesses something of it and can develop it, appeals to me in terms of a life force. I do not happen to be a religious man, but I do believe in something—call it religion or anything you like, which raises man above his normal level and gives the human personality a new dimension of spiritual quality and moral depth. Now, whatever helps to raise man above himself, be it some god or even a stone image, is good, obviously it is a good thing and must not be discouraged.

---

7. S. Abid Hussain, *The Way of Gandhi and Nehru* (London: Asia Publishing House, 1961), p. 88.

8. Jawaharlal Nehru, *The Discovery of India* (New York: The John Day Company, 1946), p. 10.

9. *Ibid.*, p. 12.

10. Jawaharlal Nehru, *Speeches* 111, 86 (14 April 1956). Quoted by M. N. Das, *The Political Philosophy of Jawaharlal Nehru* (New York: The John Day Company, 1961), p. 35.

11. Nehru, *The Discovery of India*, p. 13.

12. *Ibid.*, pp. 11-14, 110.

Speaking for myself, my religion is tolerance of all religions, creeds and philosophies.[13]

While Nehru found it difficult to accept the divinity of any religious founder or the divine authority of any scripture, his main quarrel was with organized religion. In his autobiography he wrote:

The spectacle of what is called religion, or at any rate, organized religion, in India and elsewhere has filled me with horror, and I have frequently condemned it, and wished to make a clean sweep of it. Almost always it seems to stand for blind belief and reaction, dogma and bigotry, superstition and exploitation and the preservation of vested interests.[14]

In India and elsewhere he found organized religion causing and promoting hatred and violence between peoples and being a reactionary force in society. Nehru's antipathy toward organized religion was based on his belief that it promoted superstition and, above all, communalism.

Nehru would make absolutely no compromise with communalism. He firmly believed that communalism was fostered by the vested interests to gain their own ends. Religion was used to support this.[15] The communalism that led to the partition of India is based on a medieval theory, that religious groups constitute a political community.[16] Nehru also pointed out that the real solution to the communal problem will come when economic questions arise that transcend communal lines.[17] In his early years he gave communalism a Marxian interpretation—that it was a middle-class problem of search for office and employment. In 1928 he said:

It has nothing to do with the masses, but the masses are deluded and misled and made to forget their real troubles. If you direct their attention to economic facts which matter, you will automatically turn away from communalism and pseudo-religious mentality.[18]

13. R. K. Karanjia, *The Mind of Mr. Nehru* (London: George Allan and Unwin, 1960), p. 33. Quoted by M. M. Thomas, "Nehru's Secularism–An Interpretation" in *Religion and Society* 9, no. 1 (March 1962):13.

14. Jawaharlal Nehru, *Toward Freedom: The Autobiography of Jawaharlal Nehru* (New York: The John Day Company, 1941), p. 240.

15. *Ibid.*, p. 382.

16. *Ibid.*, p. 383.

17. *Ibid.*, p. 407.

18. *Presidential Address at U.P. Provincial Conference*, Jhansi, 27 October 1928. Quoted by Kaushik, p. 299.

But communalism was more than merely an economic problem —it was emotional and often irrational. Nehru and other Congress leaders finally recognized the strength of Muslim communalism in consenting to the partition of India at the time of independence. But India was still left with a large Muslim population and there were other religious minorities like the Sikhs, Christians, and others. The forces of Hindu communalism that wanted a Hindu state were also strong. Nehru fought an incessant war against the divisive forces of communalism. Soon after independence he became, in effect, the greatest champion of the rights of Muslims in India.[19] He was against both Hindu and Muslim communalism. In a speech in the Constituent Assembly (Legislative) on 3 April 1948, he said: "But the combination of politics and religion in the narrowest sense of the word, resulting in communal politics is—there can be no doubt—a most dangerous combination and must be put an end to."[20]

His idea of the secular state in India was that India should be a "common home to all those who live here, to whatever religion they may belong. . . . Ours is a composite nation, as all great nations must necessarily be."[21] If different religions are to co-exist peacefully, there must be a spirit of toleration on the part of the religions as well as of the government. To Nehru the basis for the unity of India was not one religion but the common cultural heritage of all Indians, irrespective of their religion.[22] Another element of unity should be the common aspirations for India's future.

Nehru's outlook on tolerance was very similar to the Hindu idea. He has described it in terms of "secularized paganism."

There are two things about paganism which do attract me. One is the essential tolerance in a pagan. The other is harmony with nature such as the old Greeks and the old Indians had.[23]

This paganism, according to Nehru, is opposed to the semitic attitude of having the whole truth. "The whole truth is too big

19. Michael Brecher, *Nehru: A Political Biography* (London: Oxford University Press, 1959), pp. 428, 625-26.
20. Jawaharlal Nehru, *Jawaharlal Nehru's Speeches, Vol. I, Sept., 1946– May, 1949* (New Delhi: The Publications Division, Government of India, 1958), p. 74.
21. *Ibid.*, p. 55.
22. *Ibid.*, pp. 337-38.
23. *Link*, 15 August 1961. Quoted by M. M. Thomas, "Nehru's Secularism," p. 14.

for any people to grasp completely."[24] This outlook of tolerance and coexistence he finds in Indian thought and philosophy. According to M. M. Thomas, we may consider Nehru's secularized paganism as influenced by Hindu metaphysics, but not identical to it.[25] Related to this was Nehru's dislike for slogans and his opposition to dogmatism of any type. Answering a question regarding strengthening the United Nations, Nehru said:

> Some of the slogans are not bad, but I dislike most slogans. They prevent the person from thinking. All slogans, I think, are rather confusing, although they may contain an element of truth in them. So let us face this problem, certainly in a moral way, in a spiritual way, and, if I may say so, in a reverent way and, if I may also say so, with always the idea at the back of my mind that I may not be wholly right. There may be something else that might help me. There may be something else that has escaped me.[26]

As is evident from this quotation, Nehru like to approach every question with an open mind and he liked others to have the same approach to life. It was on this basis that different religious groups should coexist with each other.

In reviewing Nehru's views on the secular state we see that while he was not a follower of any religion he did not hold any anti-religious or militantly atheistic type of secularist ideology either. He believed passionately in the usefulness of science and technology for modern life and in a scientific outlook on life. He was also a humanist. At the same time he was aware of other dimensions of thought.

> Nehru's secularism is not a total philosophy of life, but an approach which is conscious of its own limitations. It is an "open secularism" which "while it puts questions to religion, as any secularism should, it listens to religious questions both from within and without."[27]

As a scientific humanist, he judged organized religion by its usefulness for the integration and welfare of man. His secularism also demanded that people of all religions and secular creeds should be tolerated and accommodated. There was to be a "com-

---

24. *Ibid.*, p. 16.
25. *Ibid.*
26. Jawaharlal Nehru, *Talks with Nehru: A Discussion between Jawaharlal Nehru and Norman Cousins* (London: Victor Gollancz Ltd., 1951), p. 61.
27. M. M. Thomas, "Nehru's Secularism," p. 20.

posite nation" where all religions and creeds found freedom to exist. At the same time he was vehemently opposed to the forces of communalism, which tried to impose the views and interests of one religion on the nation at the expense of others.

The Debates of the Constituent Assembly

The Cabinet Mission of the British Government, which came to India to arrange for the transfer of power to Indian hands, declared through its statement of 16 May 1946 its decision to assemble a constituent assembly that would draw up the new constitution of India. The Assembly, which was elected by the provincial legislatures, met for the first time on 9 December 1946.[28] The Muslim League did not take part. On 24 January 1947, in pursuance of Paragraph 20 of the Cabinet Mission's Statement of 16 May 1946, the Assembly elected an Advisory Committee on Minorities and Fundamental Rights.[29] Sardar Patel was the Chairman of the Committee. It was this committee that made important recommendations to guarantee the rights of minorities in independent India. When the Constituent Assembly first met it was still hoped that India could remain united, and many of the early discussions, particularly of the Advisory Committee on Minorities, took place in the context of the demands of the Muslim League and the necessity to reassure the minorities, especially the Muslims, of their honorable and secure future in independent India. But the inexorable movement of events led to the partition of India and the emergence of India and Pakistan as two separate nations. Still the work of the Constituent Assembly continued, and the new constitution of India was promulgated on 26 January 1950. In the Advisory Committee on Minorities, the minorities were well represented and Sardar Patel and other leaders were very eager to redeem the pledges that the Congress had made regarding minority rights. Thus, in spite of the fact that partition had taken place, the rights of minorities and the fundamental rights of all persons were well taken care of by the Committee and the Assembly. Dr. H. C. Mukherjee, a Christian, was the vice-president of the Constituent Assembly. This was one sign of the solicitude shown for the minority communities.

---

28. A. C. Bannerjee, *The Constituent Assembly of India* (Calcutta: A. Mukherjee and Co., 1947), pp. 38, 74.
    29. *Ibid.*, p. 310.

The clauses regarding fundamental rights and religious freedoms were discussed at great length in the Assembly, and these discussions show what idea the founding fathers of the country had in mind regarding the secular character of the Indian state. In spite of the fact that the term "secular state" was used very often during the discussions, the term did not become part of the new constitution. Professor K. T. Shah tried twice to have the term incorporated into the constitution, but without success.[30] Suggestions that the name of "God" should be inserted in the constitution were also not acceptable to the Constituent Assembly.[31]

The areas that elicited detailed discussion and particularly throw light on the meaning of the secular state are 1) the question of separate electorates and reservation of seats for minorities; 2) the right to propagate religion; 3) religious education; and 4) a uniform civil code. A new clause was added regarding cow protection and discussion regarding this is also of special interest in this context.

The leadership of the Assembly was particularly concerned about creating confidence among the minority communities of India. When partition took place, some Hindu members complained that the generous guarantees incorporated in the Draft Constitution were put there on the basis that there would be no partition. The Fundamental Rights Committee was appointed before partition and the rights were also written before partition. Professor Saksena, the conservative Hindu member, said that Sardar Patel had told him and some others: "Kindly do not interfere with these rights, religious and cultural, because they form part of an agreement arrived at before partition." Saksena added that it would be ungrateful for anyone to say that these rights were not enough.[32] The same attitude of making a concession, rather grudgingly, may be seen in the statement of Sri Purushottamdas Tandon regarding Christians and the right of conversion.

> We Congressmen deem it very improper to convert from one to another religion or to take part in such activities and are not in favour of this. . . . But it is only at the request of some persons, whom we want to keep with us in our national en-

---

30. *Constituent Assembly Debates* (India), 7:400, 815–16. Hereafter referred to as CAD.
31. *Ibid.*, pp. 341, 1049.
32. *Ibid.*, p. 944.

deavour, that we accepted this . . . we want to carry our Christian friends with us.[33]

These statements show that there were powerful groups who represented Hindu revivalism and who would have liked to have Hinduism shown special favor as the religion of the majority. M. Thirumala Rao cited the example of Great Britain, where the church is "associated with their universities, with their Parliament, with their courts of law and so on." Without going to that extent in imposing religion, he wanted national traditions and culture to be protected.[34] In understanding the meaning of the secular state, it is important to recognize this element of the background in which the clauses were passed. We may note here a continuation of the tradition of Hindu nationalism, the history of which was traced in previous sections. It was only because of the new fervor of freedom and nationalism that these voices did not become stronger or were not allowed to dominate the discussions.

If the Hindu majority was anxious "to carry [the minorities] with them," at least some sections of the minorities themselves were highly cooperative and farsighted for their part. They insisted on rights that they considered fundamental, but they were also willing to trust the majority. This may be seen especially in the Christian members' attitude to clauses regarding propagation of religion (see below) and the question of reservation of seats for minorities for elections.

The Congress had always been opposed to the principle of separate electorates, which the Muslim League had demanded and the British Government had practiced. But the Congress had, as a compromise, accepted the principle of having reservation of seats for minority communities (these would be elected by joint electorates) in general elections. The Committee on Fundamental Rights and Minorities had recommended that there be reservation of seats for minorities.[35]

The question of separate electorates and reservation of seats was opposed by several members on the ground that they were against the spirit of the secular state.

Many speakers belonging to the majority as well the minority

33. *Ibid.*, pp. 492-93.
34. *Ibid.*, p. 348.
35. Articles 292 and 294, *Constituent Assembly of India: Draft Constitution of India* (New Delhi: Government of India Press, 1948), pp. 139-40.

communities pointed out that the safety of the minorities could best be assured by trusting the majority. Even when rights are enshrined in the Constitution, it is the majority that has to give effect to them in practice. Pandit Govind Ballabh Pant pointed out that separate electorates would isolate the minority communities from the majority and this was not good. It could lead to the oppression of the minorities.[36] In other words, the safety of the minorities depends on the development of mutual relations and trust between majority and minority communities.

The recommendations of the Advisory Committee on Fundamental Rights, presented in 1947, had provided for reservation of seats for minorities, including Christians.[37] At the insistence of some leaders of the minority communities themselves, especially Christians, the Advisory Committee on Fundamental Rights recommended in May 1949 that this provision be removed except for reservation of seats for scheduled castes and tribes (mainly the low-castes who had been for long socially, economically and politically backward). This was accepted by the Committee and the Assembly. Jerome D'Souza (a Roman Catholic priest), supporting the change, said that the passing of Fundamental Rights that were justiciable had reassured the minorities. Muslim, Parsi, and Sikh members also supported the move. Some Muslim members, however, were not convinced of the wisdom of support.

While the vast majority agreed to reservation of seats for Scheduled Castes, some were opposed. Mahavir Tyagi said that there was no justification for reservation, even for ten years. Reservation, if necessary, should be on the basis of class—the illiterates, the poor, and so on—and not on caste. H. C. Mukherjee also made the same point.

The second area that produced much discussion was that part of Article 19(1) in the Draft Constitution which equally entitled all persons not only to freedom of conscience and the right freely to profess and practice religion, but also to propagate the same. As already mentioned,[38] the right to propagate religion was inserted particularly at the insistence of the Christian community. While the freedom of conscience and the right to profess and practice religion clauses were readily seen as essential for a modern state, the right to propagate religion and convert others was

36. CAD, 5:8, 223.
37. The "Interim Report on Fundamental Rights" was presented to the Constituent Assembly in April 1947.
38. Statement by Tandon, referred to earlier in this section.

seen by some as against the spirit of India and something that would promote communalism. It was pointed out by some members that there was no need for this particular sub-clause, because it was already implied in the clause guaranteeing freedom of speech. S. V. Krishnamurthy Rao said:

> One thing I would like to see omitted is the provision for freedom to propagate religion. This right which has been claimed by some has been the bane of our political life. In a secular state, such a provision, especially with the guarantee for the free exercise of religion and freedom of thought, is out of place in our Constitution.[39]

Another member[40] saw Article 19 as a "charter for Hindu enslavement," "the most disgraceful article, the blackest part of the draft Constitution." Rightly or wrongly, India had been declared a secular state. If any religion was to receive favored treatment, it should be Hinduism.

> But this unjust generosity of tabooing religion and yet making propagation of religion a fundamental right is somewhat uncanny and dangerous. Justice demands that the ancient faith and culture of the land should be given a fair deal, if not restored to its legitimate place after a thousand years of suppression.[41]

K. Santhanam said that Article 19 was not so much about religious freedom as religious toleration. Propagation comes under freedom of speech, but there should be no rights for mass conversion. Another member said that "propagation" was all right as long as there was no "mud-slinging" on other religions, especially by Christian missionaries.[42]

One Muslim member moved that the words "practice and propagate religion" should be replaced by "and practice religion privately." Since the practice of religion was a private matter, it should not be referred to in the Constitution.[43]

Another member moved that there should be no conversion in hospitals, schools, and asylums maintained partly or wholly by state funds. Other propaganda might be allowed. M. Ananthasayanam Ayyangar moved that "conversions from one religion

---

39. CAD, 7:382.
40. Lokanath Misra.
41. CAD, 8:823.
42. *Ibid.*, 7:835–36.
43. *Ibid.*, pp. 817–18.

to another brought about by coercion or undue influence shall not be recognized by law." Supporting this, he said that the minorities were communal minorities and mass conversions might be used for political purposes. "All people have come to the same opinion that there should be a secular state here; so we should not allow conversion from one community to another." If somebody does want to convert, he should swear before a judge that he wishes to be converted.[44] None of these motions was passed.

The right to propagate religion was not incorporated in the resolutions of the Congress Party before independence. The Karachi Congress Resolution of 1931 did not mention it. The first draft of the article on religious freedom drawn up by the Advisory Committee on Minorities and Fundamental Rights, followed the Karachi Statement closely and did not mention propagation of religion.[45]

Largely because of the endeavors of H. C. Mukherjee and other Christian members of the Constituent Assembly and the magnanimity of Sardar Patel, the draft article on freedom of religion contained the important word "propagate." But the Report also contained Clause 1, which stated: "Conversion from one religion to another brought about by coercion or undue influence shall not be recognized by law."[46] K. M. Munshi moved an amendment to add that conversion of a minor under 18 years of age also should not be recognized. This was opposed by Christian members. F. R. Anthony said that "children should be allowed to be brought up in the faith of the parents even after conversion, unless grown-up children object." J. J. M. Nichols-Roy pointed out that a person under 18 also has a conscience and can decide in matters of religion. Jerome D'Souza looked at this from the point of view of the authority that a man should have over his family, and this should be a fundamental right.[47]

B. R. Ambedkar, the law minister, strongly opposed the Munshi amendment and the clause was referred back to the Advisory Committee. Christians objected to the whole clause on the basis that the clause was inappropriate and unnecessary, for no one claimed a right to convert somebody by coercion or fraud or undue influence. The Christian members of the Constituent Assembly, under the leadership of H. C. Mukherjee, presented a memo-

44. *Ibid.*, 5:11, 364.
45. See D. E. Smith, pp. 181-84.
46. CAD, 3:427-28.
47. *Ibid.*, pp. 491-92, 498.

randum to Sardar Patel explaining their objections to Clause 17.
At the suggestion of Patel himself, the whole clause was dropped
by the Advisory Committee and the suggestion was accepted by
the Constituent Assembly.[48]

While there were many voices opposed to the clause regarding
propagation and conversion, voices in favor of the same and in
support of the Christian demand were not lacking. In supporting
the clause several Hindu members took the occasion to praise the
Christian community and missionary work.

Lakshmi Kanta Maitra, referring to previous remarks about
Christians, said, "The Indian Christian community happens to be
the most inoffensive community in the whole of India." He continued:

> Sir, I feel that every single community in India should be given
> this right to propagate its own religion. Even in a secular state,
> I believe there is necessity for religion. . . . If we are to re-
> store our sense of values which we hold dear, it is of the utmost
> importance that we should be able to propagate what we hon-
> estly feel and believe in. . . . If different religionists would
> expound their faith it will help towards mutual understanding.[49]

L. Krishnaswami Bharathi said that it was generally understood that the word "propagate" was intended only for the Christian community. But it was necessary for all communities. It
was necessary to educate people in their religious tenets and
doctrines. Christians "have not transgressed their limits of legitimate propagation of religious view. . . ." The Minorities Committee

> came to the conclusion that this great Christian community
> which is willing and ready to assimilate itself with the general
> community, which does not want reservation or other privi-
> leges, should be allowed to propagate its religion along with
> other religious communities in India.[50]

T. T. Krishnamachari pointed out that *propagate* is open to all.
It will allow Arya Samajists to carry on the Suddhi movement
(reconverting to Hinduism those who became Muslims and Christians). The Christian educational institutions where he studied
for fourteen years had not attempted to convert him.

---

48. D. E. Smith, pp. 183-84.
49. CAD, 7:831-33.
50. *Ibid.*, p. 834.

I am very well aware of the influences that Christianity has brought to bear upon our own ideas and our own outlook, and I am not prepared to say here that they should be prevented from propagating their religion.

Moreover, he said, in the past conversions mainly took place among the lower castes. When their social and economic conditions are improved, there won't be large-scale conversions.[51]

K. M. Munshi, in supporting the clause, said that Christian missionaries might have lost their particular influence with the Collectors (administrative heads of districts) since 1933, when the Congress ministries came into power. *Propagate* is an essential part of freedom of speech. It is also part of a compromise with the minorities. Christians insisted on it as fundamental to their faith and this arrangement should not be disturbed.[52]

The main import of the clause on religious instruction was that no religious instruction should be provided by the state in any educational institution wholly maintained through state funds. In educational institutions recognized by and/or receiving aid from government, no one should be compelled to attend religious classes or worship. In general it was felt that religious instruction was useful but that because of the diversity of India's religions it was physically impossible for the state to make provisions for the teaching of all religions.

S. Radhakrishnan pointed out the rightness of the state's eschewing religious instruction in schools wholly supported by it while allowing aided schools to give religious instruction. But a person of another faith would not be compelled to join classes in religion. So far as the state schools were concerned, "we cannot allow any religious instruction of a denominational character."[53]

One important clause of the Directive Principles of State Policy states that "the state shall endeavour to secure for the citizens a uniform civil code throughout the territory of India" (Art. 35 in Draft Constitution; Art. 44 in the present Constitution). Even though this is not part of the Fundamental Rights, it forms part of the important policy guidelines for the nation that the Assembly had suggested. The development of a uniform civil code, which would apply equally to all people of the country, was considered essential for the nature of the secular state that India had opted for itself. At the same time there was the opposition from Mus-

51. *Ibid.*, pp. 836-37.
52. *Ibid.*, pp. 837-38.
53. *Ibid.*, 5:358.

lims that their personal law was part of their religion and hence the state should not legislate on those matters. This brought out several important attempts at definition of the secular state.

Many Muslim members argued that Muslim personal law was part of the religion of the community and hence any legislation regarding the same would be considered as interference with religion. According to Maulana Hasat Mohani,

> There are three fundamentals in their personal law, namely, religion, language, and culture which have not been ordained by any human agency. Their personal law regarding divorce, marriage, and inheritance has been derived from the Quoran and its interpretation is recorded therein.[54]

Other Muslim members conceded the necessity for a uniform civil code and the necessity for change in their personal law. But the change had to be gradual and should be implemented only with the consent of the community, consent previously ascertained by the Union Legislature by law. Nazirmuddin Ahmed said, "I have no doubt that a state would come when the civil law became uniform. But then, that time has not yet come."[55]

B. R. Ambedkar, the law minister, rejecting the view that personal law is religious law and hence should not be changed, said:

> The religious conceptions in this country are so vast that they cover every aspect of life, from birth to death. There is nothing which is not religion and if personal law is to be saved, I am sure about it that in social matters we will come to a standstill. . . . There is nothing extraordinary in saying that we ought to strive hereafter to limit the definition of religion in such a manner that we shall not extend beyond beliefs and such rituals as may be connected with ceremonials which are essentially religious.

He said that there was no need that laws relating to tenancy or succession, for example, should be governed by religion.

> I personally do not understand why religion should be given this vast, expansive jurisdiction so as to cover the whole of life and to prevent the legislature from encroaching upon that field.

The government must have freedom to legislate for social reform, he added. However, he conceded that the state could not enact laws that would totally estrange a community.[56]

---

54. *Ibid.*, 7:759.
55. *Ibid.*, p. 542.
56. *Ibid.*, p. 782.

Discussion on cow protection illustrates certain views and trends regarding secularism in the Indian Constituent Assembly. In spite of Hindu propaganda and agitation in favor of including a cow protection clause, there was no such clause in the Draft Constitution. One committee had already rejected the idea of including a clause to ban cow slaughter in the Fundamental Rights on the grounds that Fundamental Rights are for human beings![57]

However, during the debate on the Draft Constitution, Thakur Das Bhargava, a member of the Congress, proposed that such a clause be included in the Directive Principles of State Policy. Bhargava said that he was not making the appeal in the name of religion but in the light of economic requirements of the country.

In spite of the economic arguments propounded by the sponsors of the new clause, it was obvious that the dominant motive was religious.[58] Some Muslim members were quick to point this out. Syed Muhammed Sa'adulla of the Muslim League said that he would not object to the clause if his "Hindu brothers" wanted it to be included in the Coonstitution from the religious point of view. But this was bringing it in under cover of economic reasons. Actually there were many economic arguments against it.[59]

Ambedkar, probably taking into consideration the strong Hindu sentiment behind it, accepted the amendment and the Constituent Assembly passed it. Thus the ban-on-cow-slaughter clause became Article 48 of the Constitution.

Having reviewed the discussion regarding some important aspects pertaining to the secular-state idea, we may find it useful to review some of the more direct attempts at defining the meaning of the secular state in the Assembly. This would further help us to understand more clearly the meaning that the secular state had for the framers of the Indian Constitution. We shall look at them in the context in which they were spoken.

Moving that a new article be added to ensure neutrality of the Indian state toward all religions, K. T. Shah said that the state

---

57. D. E. Smith, p. 484.
58. See footnotes in D. E. Smith, pp. 484 and 485 for references to the economic aspect of cow protection, also page 486. It is obvious that total ban on cow slaughter is not a sound economic policy for India, with its large unproductive cow population.
59. *Ibid.*, p. 578.

should not concern itself with the actual profession of faith or belief.[60]

The form of oath for various offices given in the Draft Constitution did not mention God.[61] Advocating that oath of office should be taken in the name of God, H. V. Kamath said that the nation had

> a heritage which is of the Spirit—a spirit that is, ever was, and ever shall be, a heritage that is eternal.

The Assembly, he continued, should not "squander this invaluable heritage."[62]

In discussing the secular state, K. M. Munshi said that the religious-mindedness of the people should be taken into consideration. The essence of Indian culture is belief in God and in the dignity of man because man can be an instrument of God. "We need not fear that a secular state is inconsistent with a religious mind among the people."[63] Jerome D'Souza also pointed out that while the secular state does not make any choice among different religions, "it does look with sympathy upon the convictions, the feelings, the desires, the hopes and aspirations of the entire people."[64]

Ambedkar answered the criticisms by saying that the secular character of the state was not compromised by using the name of God for oath of office. In the final version, two alternate forms were given, namely, "I, A.B., do swear in the name of God/ solemnly affirm that . . ." (Third Schedule).

It is very interesting to note that even though it was declared time and again during the debates that India was a secular state, the Assembly did not approve Professor Shah's repeated attempts to declare it formally by incorporating the term into the Constitution itself. By the very same token the Assembly did not accept the suggestion to incorporate the name of God into the Consti-

---

60. CAD, 7:816. Shah moved "that the following new article be inserted under the heading 'Rights relating to Religion' occurring after Article 18.

" '18-A. The state in India being secular shall have no concern with any religion, creed or profession of faith: and shall observe an attitude of absolute neutrality in all matters relating to the religion of any class of its citizens or other persons in the Union.' " The motion was not accepted.

61. I, A. B., do solemnly affirm (or swear) that I will . . . etc.

62. CAD, 7:1049.

63. *Ibid.*, p. 1057.

64. *Ibid.*, p. 1059.

tution (except in the form for taking oaths).[65] While neither the official drafting committee nor Ambedkar made clear why they did not include the term, it may be surmised that the term *secular state* seemed to give too negative an idea of the state's attitude and relation to religion, which might hurt the religious sensibilities of the vast majority of the people. It is also possible that the leaders did not want to commit India to any stereotyped pattern of secular state, whether American, Russian, Turkish, or any other country's, but wanted to develop India's own unique way of dealing with the question of religious freedom and the state's relationship to religious bodies in accordance with the unique situation of India.

In reviewing the debates of the Constituent Assembly on some important issues, we find new light thrown on its understanding of the meaning of the secular state. From these discussions certain points emerge that define some of the essential elements of the secular-state idea in India. They are:

1) The secular-state idea has to deal with an arrangement by which people belonging to different religious and cultural communities may live together in mutual trust and harmony. This has to be understood in the context of the communal struggle in the pre-independent and the immediate post-independent period and the strong desire to unify and solidify the country. The secular-state idea did not contain any judgment on the idea of religion as such, but only an attitude of neutrality toward religious communities as well as toward religions.

2) But this neutrality, this nondiscriminatory or noncommunal approach, does not mean anti-religious policies. This was asserted over and over again by many speakers. In recognizing the right of religious freedom at all, the state made a positive recognition of religion.

3) The secular-state idea meant that the Assembly recognized the need for social reform. In a country like India, where the sphere of religious influence is so vast, the state may have to interfere in certain areas that have traditionally been considered religious spheres. But there won't be any infringement of religious freedom as far as freedom of conscience and essentials of religious beliefs and practices are concerned.

4) In the secular state the sentiments of the people should not be ignored. While, for the sake of unity and harmony, religious

---

65. *Ibid.*, p. 341.

instruction was excluded from public schools, it was hoped that some kind of moral education could be given in all schools so as to foster the cultural and spiritual heritage of the country.

5) The secular-state idea also contained many compromises. To many conservative members of the Assembly, guaranteeing the right to propagate religion was a compromise, the price paid to get the cooperation of minorities and particularly Christians. The passing of the ban on killing cows as a Directive Principle of State Policy, even though under the guise of an economic measure, represented a compromise on the part of the leadership of the Assembly and some of the minorities, with the conservative element of Hindu membership, so that there would be no open hostility or attack on the fundamental principles of the secular state.

6) Finally, as Nehru and some other members mentioned, the secular-state idea represents a mechanism for different religious communities not only to live together in harmony but also to think beyond membership in religious or social communities alone to membership in economic, political, and other types of communities too. In a secular state people have to learn to belong to mixed groups and look at things from different perspectives. This involves a new outlook and a new habit of thinking, as far as traditional communal societies are concerned.

Provisions in the Indian Constitution
Regarding the Church-State Relationship

From a review of the debates of the Constituent Assembly, we have been able to see the interplay of different currents that finally resulted in the making of the Constitution of India. We shall now examine the more important clauses of the Indian Constitution that have a bearing on the nature of the secular state in India.

Religious Nondiscrimination

Article 15(1) says "The state shall not discriminate against any citizen on grounds only of religion, race, caste, sex, place of birth or any of them." Article 15(2) prohibits any discrimination on the above grounds with regard to access to public places like shops, hotels, entertainment houses, wells, roads, etc. Article

16(2) similarly guarantees nondiscrimination in respect of employment or office under the state. Article 23 prohibits traffic in human beings and different forms of forced labor. Section 2 of the same clause prescribes that this will not prevent the state from imposing compulsory service for public purposes but that "the state shall not make any discrimination on grounds only of religion, race, caste, or class or any of them." Article 29(2) deals with admission to educational institutions and it states:

> No citizen shall be denied admission into any educational institution maintained by the state or receiving aid out of state funds on grounds only of religion, race, caste, language or any of them.

The fundamental rights conferred by Articles 15 and 16 are conferred on a citizen as an individual. It is a personal right and hence the fact that others of his caste or religion are being discriminated against cannot be used as an excuse to deny his rights. The two clauses of Article 15 and Article 16(2) ensure that "religion shall not be the ground for any disqualification or discrimination in any public matter." *Discrimination* can mean beneficial discrimination also. Under these clauses nobody can claim any special privileges on grounds of religion only.[66]

Article 16, clauses (1) and (2) guarantee equality of opportunity to all citizens as far as state employment or holding of a state office is concerned. Religion shall not be used to discriminate. Article 23(2) gives the state power to require compulsory service for public purposes. This would include compulsory military service or conscription, even though the Indian state now has no system of compulsory military service. Conscription for national defense cannot be avoided by anybody on the ground simply of religion. Article 29(2) gives the citizen guarantee against discrimination in getting admission to state or state-aided educational institutions only on the ground of religion, race, etc. or of any one of them.

By the Constitution (First Amendment) Act of 1951, Clause 4 was added to Article 15. Provisions had already been made (16(4), 46, and 340) to show special consideration for "backward classes of citizens," scheduled castes and tribes. This amendment brings Articles 15 and 29 in line with the Articles mentioned

---

66. Durga Das Basu, *Commentary on the Constitution of India*, 1 (Articles 1-151), 3d ed. (Calcutta: S. C. Sarkar and Sons Ltd., 1955):137. Hereinafter referred to as *Commentary*.

above and makes it constitutional for the state to reserve seats for the above-mentioned classes of people in public educational institutions as well as to make other special arrangements for their advancement.[67]

Another area of the principle of nondiscrimination is voting and representation in the legislatures. Article 325 states that no person shall be ineligible for inclusion in the general electoral roll on grounds of religion, race, caste, or sex. There shall be no special electoral roll based on these categories. Elections are to be conducted on the basis of adult suffrage (Article 326).

In accordance with this, the system of separate communal electorate (first introduced in 1909) was abolished. However, the Constitution provides for the reservation of seats for Scheduled Castes and Tribes (Articles 330 and 332). This special privilege will cease after 20 years from the commencement of the Constitution (Article 334). (Originally it was for only 10 years.) Special provisions are also made for the President of India and Governors of States to nominate Anglo-Indian members to the Parliament and State Legislatures when necessary (Articles 331 and 333).

One of the important qualifications of the nondiscriminating clauses is represented by the word "only" in Articles 15(1), 16(2), 23(2), and 29(2). Even though there is a difference of opinion about the same, it is generally held by the courts that the word *only* in Articles 15 and 16 has great significance. Religion, race, caste, sex, place of birth, or any of them cannot be made the *sole* basis for discrimination.[68] However, the state may make any of those grounds a basis for legal discrimination if it can show that there is another ground of discrimination accompanying it. Hence religious discrimination is possible, provided religious grounds are accompanied by other grounds.

Personal and Corporate Religious Freedom

The main clauses that deal with individual and corporate religious freedom are Articles 25 and 26.[69] These clauses are very vast in their scope and have various ramifications, some of which have already been dealt with.

Article 25 guarantees to *all* persons (irrespective of national-

---

67. *Ibid.*, p. 136.
68. Luthera, p. 68.
69. See discussion on The Constituent Assembly debates.

ity) freedom of conscience and the right freely to profess, practice, and propagate religion. However, these rights are restricted by the following grounds:

i) Public order, morality and health
ii) Other provisions of Part III of the Constitution
iii) Regulation of non-religious activity associated with religious practice
iv) Social welfare and social reform
v) Throwing open of Hindu religious institutions of a public character to all classes and sections of Hindus.

Explaining the phrase "freedom of conscience," the eminent commentator on the Indian Constitution, Durga Das Basu, says:

A Secular State therefore means a State which has no religion of its own and which refrains from discrimination on grounds of religion.[70]

As Basu points out, it is true that no religion could be singled out for favor or disfavor by the state. But the word "equally" in "all persons are equally entitled" may mean that the state is free to aid all religions equally or restrict all religions in the same way. There is no clause in the Indian Constitution that imparts a rigid "wall of separation" doctrine, as is evident from the several clauses that give the state powers to interfere with several aspects of religious affairs.[71] It has to be emphasized that the Indian Constitution, unlike many others, does not recognize specially any one religion.

"To profess, practice and propogate." Article 25 gives the right not only to profess one's religion but also to practice and propagate the same. In the words of the Supreme Court,

Every person has a fundamental right not merely to entertain such religious belief as may be approved of by his judgement or conscience but to *exhibit* his belief and ideas in such overt acts as are enjoined or sanctioned by his religion and further to *propagate* his religious views for the edification of others.[72]

Professing one's religion, i.e., stating one's creed in public, would least interfere with secular interests or the rights of others. But

---

70. Basu, *Commentary*, p. 317.
71. P. K. Tripathi, "Secularism: Constitutional Provision and Judicial Review," in Sharma, ed., p. 172.
72. Ratilal v. State of Bombay (1954), S.C.A. 538 (546) in Basu, *Commentary*, p. 318.

the "practice" of religion, which is "the external and applied part of religious belief and philosophy," as well as "propagation" of religion may come more under the concern of the state.[73] However, in the name of "public order, health and morality," the state cannot deprive the individual of the substance of his religious freedom.[74]

The two other major restrictions put on the right to freedom of religion are, 1) secular activities associated with religious practice, and 2) social welfare and reform. The state may regulate any "economic, financial, political or other secular activity" associated with religious practice. Entry 5 of the Concurrent List of Schedule VII of the Constitution gives the legislative power in this respect to the Parliament and state legislatures. The list includes such subjects as marriage and divorce, succession, and personal law.[75] Freedom to practice religion would apply to those rites and observances which are of the *essence* of religion. Matters of personal law (relating to marriage, adoption, etc.) are secular activities. Article 44, which is part of the Directive Principles of State Policy, specifically directs the state to endeavor to secure for the citizens a uniform civil code throughout India. Even though only tentative steps have been taken in this direction, they represent the attempt of the state to disentangle religious and secular activities.[76] Article 25 (2)(b) gives the state broad powers to enact for social welfare and reform when religious practices run counter to the interests of social welfare. Prohibition of bigamy and prohibition of excommunication have been justified under this clause. Regarding a case involving excommunication, the Bombay High Court said,

> a sharp distinction must be drawn between religious faith and belief and religious practices. What the state protects is religious faith and belief. If religious practices run counter to public order, morality, health or a policy of social welfare upon which the state has embarked, then the religious practices must give way.[77]

73. Sharma, ed., p. 173.
74. Basu, *Commentary*, p. 320.
75. See Article 246 regarding subject-matter of laws made by Parliament and by the Legislatures of States.
76. D. E. Smith, pp. 108-9.
77. Saifuddin v. Moosaji, 40 A.I.R. 183 (187) in William O. Douglas, *We the Judges: Studies in American and Indian Constitutional Law from Marshall to Mukherjea* (Garden City, N.Y.: Doubleday Company Inc., 1956), p. 343.

As Ambedkar pointed out during the Constituent Assembly debates,[78] the conception of religion in India may cover every aspect of life from birth to death. But this definition of religion will not be allowed, as far as freedom of religion is concerned. Article 25 (2) (a) and (b) opened up the way for regulating the financial administration of many Hindu religious institutions when needed and also for social reform.[79]

However, it is not always easy to determine what constitutes the essence of a particular religion. No set rule can be followed, because religions vary. The Supreme Court has set the guideline that "what constitutes the essential part of a religion is primarily to be ascertained with reference to the doctrines of that religion itself."[80]

Article 26 deals with corporate or collective freedom of religion. It recognizes the right of a religious denomination or sect to maintain religious and charitable institutions of its own, to have autonomy in conducting its domestic affairs in matters of religion, to own property and administer it according to law.

In interpreting this clause, questions as to what constitute "matters of religion" and the limitations to the freedom "to administer such property in accordance with law" have been the ones raised most frequently. Matters of religion involve a fundamental right, whereas administration of property of a religious organization is subject to law.

In a case involving excommunication, the Bombay High Court held that a religious denomination did not have the right to expel a member, thus depriving him of his legal rights and privileges. The Court did not consider this a "matter of religion."[81]

In the Commr., H.R.E. v. Lakshmindra case,[82] and Ratilal Panchand v. State of Bombay,[83] the Supreme Court had occasion to rule on several matters concerning Article 26. The Court ruled that the state has the right to supervise and regulate the economic affairs of a religious institution as long as the administration is not taken away from the hands of the religious authorities. The proper government officials also had the right to fix the scale of

---

78. 7:781.
79. D. E. Smith, p. 109.
80. "Commr., H. R. E. v. Lakshmindra" (1954) S.C.A. 415 (432) in Basu, Commentary, p. 321.
81. Saifuddin v. Moosaji, A.I.R. (1953) (Bombay), p. 183 in D. E. Smith, pp. 110ff.
82. (1954) S.C.A. 415 in Basu, Commentary, pp. 323-24.
83. (1954) S.C.A. 538 in ibid.

expenditure in order to avoid waste in conducting ceremonies and rites. But no unreasonable restrictions should be put on the trustee. Regarding entry into religious institutions by proper government officials for inspection, this may be done provided it is done with due notice and having respect for the religious rules and sentiments connected with the institution (for example, temple).

The Bombay Public Trusts Act of 1950 was held valid in its main points. Thus, trustees of religious trusts were required to register and pay Rs. 25 for registration. The trustees were also required to keep accounts in a prescribed manner. The establishment of the Public Trusts Administration Fund and obligatory contributions to this fund by every public trust were ruled valid, for this fund was to be specifically used for Public Trusts Administration. The contribution levied was a fee, not a tax. But here again the court struck down a clause that would empower it to appoint the Charity Commissioner as trustee of the religious fund. This was against the right of a religious institution to manage its own religious affairs.[84]

Religious Bodies and Taxation

The Indian Constitution[85] guarantees freedom from payment of taxes for the promotion of any particular religion. Public funds raised by taxes shall not be appropriated for the benefit of any particular religion or religious body. This does not mean that the state cannot help religious institutions along with other secular institutions of its kind without discrimination. Denominational schools and charitable institutions aided by the state would come under this category. The clause also does not prevent levying fees or contributions from religious trusts or endowments for the specific purpose of the proper administration of the same. Presumably nondiscriminatory taxes for the benefit of all religions or religious institutions would also be legal.[86] Article 290A provides for annual payment of a fixed amount of money to the Devaswom funds in Kerala and Madras for the maintenance of Hindu temples that were formerly in Travancore and Cochin, which are ruled by Maharajahs. This is in accordance with the

---

84. Luthera, pp. 115f. Also, Douglas, pp. 344-47.
85. Article 27.
86. D. E. Smith, p. 129.

agreements entered into with the former rulers of these states before they became part of the Indian union.

Religious Instruction and the Rights of Minorities to Conduct Educational Institutions

Articles 28, 29(2), and 30 deal with the right of religious minorities to conduct schools, and the problem of imparting religious instruction in educational institutions.

According to Article 28 no educational institution wholly maintained by state funds is to provide religious instruction, but those institutions only partly subsidized by the state may. But in the latter case, religious instruction has to be given on a completely optional basis. Nobody should be compelled to attend such classes against his (or in the case of a minor, of his guardian's) will. It should be noted that the state may impart "moral instruction which is an essential part of training in citizenship, maintenance of law and order in the state, and growth of social cohesion." But the task of differentiating morality from religion will not be an easy task.[87]

Article 29(2) has been amended by the Constitution (First Amendment) Act, 1951, by inserting Clause (4) in Article 15. This amendment validates reservation for members of the backward classes, and Scheduled Castes and Tribes. It does not condone communal reservation as a whole. Article 30 gives religious minorities the right to run schools. These schools shall not be discriminated against in granting aid on the basis that they are under the management of a religious minority. In its advisory opinion on the Kerala Education Bill of 1957, the Supreme Court held that even though private educational institutions had no constitutional right to receive any grant from the state (except Anglo-Indian institutions), nevertheless, since they would not be able to function without government help this help should be given. It declared void certain clauses of the Bill that gave the state government power to take over the entire management of aided private institutions.[88]

Uniform Civil Code, Cow Protection, and Social Reform

The Indian Constitution includes a section called "Directive

---

87. Basu, *Commentary*, p. 328.
88. D. E. Smith, p. 114.

Principles of State Policy." These provisions, though not enforceable by any court, do give important direction to the state regarding governance and legislation.

Article 44 of this section directs that "the state shall endeavour to secure for the citizens a uniform civil code throughout the territory of India." As we have seen, this clause caused a lot of controversy and discussion in the Constituent Assembly. The purpose of this directive is to achieve national consolidation through the introduction of uniform personal law. The article assumes that there is no necessary connection between religion and personal law in a secular state. The purpose of this article is not to restrict religious liberty. Adequate powers for regulating the same for the sake of social reform and legislating in matters of economic, political, and other secular activities that may be associated with religion, are given by Article 25 (2).

Our interest in Article 48, one of the Directive Principles of State Policy, is in its directive to prohibit the slaughter of "cows and calves and other milch and draught cattle." Even though, according to the article, this is to be done for the sake of "organising agriculture and animal husbandry on modern and scientific lines," it is evident from the debates on the clause in the Constituent Assembly that the main reason was the strong Hindu sentiment against the killing of cows.

Interpretations Given to the Secular State by Representative Political Organizations and Leaders

We have examined the meaning of the secular state as understood by the founding fathers of the nation, as envisaged in the Constitution and interpreted by the courts, and also as it has evolved in the ideology of the Congress party and in the thought of the prime individual architect of the present Indian secular state, namely, Jawaharlal Nehru. The Constitution of India was promulgated on 26 January 1950. How has the concept been understood and interpreted by the major political parties and representative political and national leaders since then? It is necessary to explore whether there is general unanimity in understanding the meaning of the secular state and whether this corresponds to the meaning given by the Constitution and the courts. We shall therefore examine the attitudes of the major political parties and groups, and some of the national leaders who also represent different parties and ideologies, many of whom the writer has had the privilege of interviewing.

The leaders interviewed represented some of the major political parties of India, namely, the Communist Party, the Samyukta Socialist Party, the Swatantra Party, the Jana Sangh, and the Revolutionary Socialist Party. The writer also interviewed some eminent nationalist Muslim leaders, as well as Christian leaders. It may be noted that the Congress Party is omitted from this review because we have already considered that party's concept of the secular state in India.

Definition, Roots, and Meaning of the Secular State in India

There is general agreement regarding the desirability of the secular state as far as protection to minorities and nonpreference of any particular religion are concerned. Some of the phrases commonly used by different political leaders to describe and qualify the concept of the secular state in India were, "not anti-religious or irreligious," "noncommunal," "having no state religion," and "pluralistic." There seemed to be a general eagerness to dispel any notion that the word *secular* in *secular state* has any anti-religious connotation. However, A. K. Gopalan emphasized the point that the secular state is one that does not encourage religion.[89]

Two qualifications need to be added to this general picture. Ram Manohar Lohia, the articulate leader of the Samyukta Socialist Party (Dr. Lohia died recently), said that the phrases "nondenominational" and "nonsectarian" or the "idea of nonpreference among various faiths" describe only certain aspects of the secular state. They do not represent the whole idea. It should be understood in the broader context that "Indians should engross themselves in the fascinating problems and urges of this world rather than of the next"—of "aiheek" (this world) rather than of "para loheek" (other world). "This present living world should be our main present concern and subject of study." Lohia said that to this extent India has not understood the full meaning of the secular state. A secular state presupposes secularism, taking the world as it is, enjoying it and revealing it. But this does not mean being anti-religious or denying the importance of spiritual urges.[90]

89. Interview with A. K. Gopalan, Member of Parliament and leader of the Communist Party of India, New Delhi, December 1966.
90. Interview with Ram Manohar Lohia, late Member of Parliament and leader of the Samyukta Socialist Party, New Delhi, 1966.

According to the Bharatiya Jana Sangh, the basis of the secular state should be *Bharatiya Sanskriti and Maryada* (Indian culture and tradition). Professor Madhok, the president of the Party, said in an address:

> We stand for "Bharatiya Sanskriti" whose roots go back to the Rigved. Rigved says: "God is one. Wisemen call Him by many names." You may call Him Indra or Varuna. You may call Him Ram or Rahim. You may call Him Allah or anything else. It does not matter so long as you think that the goal is one. That is the basis of Indian tolerance. So long as Indian culture, which is essentially vedic Hindu culture, survives in India, there is nothing to fear for Muslims, Christians and others. They will live with us as equal citizens. . . . Therefore roots of secularism, roots of tolerance, in India are not in Gandhi or Nehru or Congress or this or that party. The roots lie in Indian culture and the philosophy as set out in the Vedas.[91]

The Jana Sangh believes that there is only one culture in India. Even when people follow different religions, the culture is the same. Indian culture is indivisible. So it is both meaningless and dangerous to talk about a composite culture.[93]

While the All-India Muslim League is a comparatively small party, it is influential in certain regions of the country. There are also other Muslim organizations that are not political, and these have also expressed themselves on the secular state. Since the partition of India, the Indian Muslims, many of whom had supported the idea of an Islamic state, had to adjust themselves to the concept of a secular state in which non-Muslims formed the vast majority. In the early years, the Muslim population understood the word *secular* (following the then-current Urdu translation) to mean "irreligious" or "atheistic," and it was easy for the common man to conclude that the Indian state was against religion. With the use of more accurate translation of the English word *secular* in Urdu publications, this misunderstanding has been somewhat cleared.[94]

The following statement of the Jama'at-i-Islami organization (1960) may be taken to represent the attitude of a large number of Indian Muslims to the secular state.

---

91. Balraj Madhok, *What Jan Sangh Stands For* (Ahmedabad: Ahmedabad Junior Chamber, 1966), pp. 7-8.

93. Quoted in J. R. Chandran and M. M. Thomas, ed., *Political Outlook in India Today: A Pre-election Study* (Bangalore: Committee for Literature on Social Concerns, 1956), pp. 102-3.

94. Ziya-ul Hasan Faruqi, "Indian Muslims and the Ideology of the Secular State," in Donald Eugene Smith, ed., *South Asian Politics and Religion* (Princeton, N.J.: Princeton University Press, 1966), p. 140.

In propagating a religious ideal in a country which is avow-edly secular, the Jama'at is not contravening any accepted article of the Indian Constitution. Secularism is a state policy which implies that there should be no discrimination or par-tiality on the basis of religious minority. But if beyond this *utilitarian expediency* some people have the deeper philosophi-cal connotations in mind, we beg to differ. These philosophical connotations are essentially Western in origin, and carry a spirit and a history which are totally foreign to our temper and needs.[95]

Many nationalist Muslim leaders interpret the formation of the secular state as the result of a covenant between the Muslims and the non-Muslims of India. Then this would be in the tradition of the mutual contract (mu'ahadah) that the Prophet Muhamad initiated between the Muslims and the Jews of Medina.[96]

Humayun Kabir, the eminent Muslim political leader and author, pointed out that the secular state was necessary not only for Muslims and other minorities but also for the Hindus, other-wise the different factions of the Hindus might fight against each other.[97] Another eminent Muslim leader, who wished to remain anonymous, said that India has a positive attitude toward religion since India gives the greatest freedom for religion. He would also like the government to give grants to all religions, to build tem-ples, churches, and mosques, as in Malaysia. S. S. Nigam, Pro-fessor of Law at Banaras Hindu University, also thinks that the

Constitution has not adopted merely a negative or passive atti-tude towards religion, but has assumed a positive role to protect it, and encourage a reasonably free interplay of religious ideol-ogies.

He also thinks that the state can give aid to different religious institutions without showing discrimination.[98]

The roots of the secular state are traced by most of the leaders to the Western tradition, the example of the British impartiality and noninterference in religious affairs of India, and the Pakistan movement that led to the partition of India, along with the spirit

95. Quoted in *Ibid.*, p. 140.
96. *Ibid.*
97. Interview with Humayun Kabir, Member of Parliament and Muslim Nationalist leader, New Delhi, December 1966.
In Pakistan, several sects of the Muslim religion consider each other as heretic and this causes friction in political life. See Badr-ud-Din Tyabji, "A Means to an End," in *Seminar* 67 (March 1965):33-34.
98. "Uniform Civil Code and Secularism," in Sharma, p. 158.

of Hindu tolerance. But the Jana Sangh, as we have already seen, finds the Vedic idea that God is one and that all religions are different pathways, to God, to be the exclusive basis of the secular-state idea.

Religious Freedom—Particularly the Freedom to Propagate Religion

All the leaders interviewed, including the Communist member of Parliament, A. K. Gopalan, wholeheartedly supported the principle of religious freedom as embodied in the Constitution. However, there were differences of opinion regarding certain aspects, especially about the right to propagate religion. Sreekantan Nair (leader of the Revolutionary Socialist Party) said that this clause compromised the idea of the secular state. The right to propagate should be only an individual right, not a corporate one.[99] Dr. Lohia did not like the idea of converting people from one faith to another. At the same time, he would not take away the right of any faith to convert people to its own fold. If foreign Christian missionaries are allowed to preach religion and convert, the same privilege should be given to missionaries from Russia to preach the idea of "no-God." But native missionaries may do the work of converting if they see fit to do so.[100] Madhok (Jan Sangh) said that there should be freedom to convert, but not with the aid of foreign missionaries. Indian Christians should have every freedom to convert.[101]

Uniform Civil Code

Most of the political leaders interviewed and parties agree on the desirability of having a uniform civil code as directed by Article 44 of the Directive Principles of State Policy in the Constitution. Frank Anthony, Member of Parliament and leader of the Anglo-Indians, pointed out that "every civilized country had a uniform civil code." The Indian government, according to the opinion of Frank Anthony, need not wait to get the permission of each community to change its personal laws and introduce a common civil code applicable to all people. He was critical of the

---

99. Interview by the author, December 1966.
100. Interview by the author.
101. Interview by the author with Balraj Madhok, Member of Parliament and President of the Bharatiya Jan Sangh, New Delhi, December 1966.

fact that Christian bishops were opposed to the Christian Matrimonial Bill introduced by the government, on the grounds of allowing divorce.[102]

Both Ranga (president of the Swatantra Party) and Lohia were for having a uniform civil code for India. Ranga, however, cautioned that in the case of Muslims, the government should exercise restraint, otherwise they might think that what they practice was being done away with. Hindus were in favor of modernizing their laws and so there was no difficulty.[103]

The Jana Sangh is wholeheartedly for a uniform civil code. But its members opposed the Hindu Code Bill in the Parliament on the ground that it did not apply to all citizens of the country. The Sangh accused the Congress party of being communal in this respect. Madhok said:

> So, we are opposed to it. Civil code must be common to all irrespective of caste or creed and so long as Government does not do it, we will be justified in calling the Congress a communal party and not a nationalist party.[104]

Muslim opinion is divided regarding the constitutional directive concerning a uniform civil code. Kabir suggested that the state might indicate certain directions in which the personal laws of different religious communities could be modified and then opinion among the communities should be mobilized. A committee of Muslim legislators should be appointed for this purpose. He also said that religious bodies themselves might initiate reform.[105]

According to Faruqi, all sections of the Muslim intelligentsia (with the exception of the Barelwi school, which is reactionary) are in favor of a thorough review of the Muslim personal law as it exists today. But there is sharp difference of opinion "regarding the competent authority to make such a review and suggest reforms and the extent of reforms."[106] A representative meeting of Muslim leaders of different shades of opinion, convened by Zakir Hussain, the president of India (then vice-president), in July

---

102. Interview by the author with Frank Anthony, Member of Parliament and leader of the Anglo-Indian Community, New Delhi, December 1966.
103. Interview by the author with Professor N. G. Ranga, Member of Parliament and president of the Swatantra (Freedom) Party, New Delhi, December 1966.
104. Madhok, p. 46.
105. Interview by the author.
106. Faruqi in D. E. Smith, ed., *South Asian Politics and Religion*, p. 147.

1963, unanimously advised the government of India to give up the idea of appointing a committee to study the possibility of reforming Muslim personal law and leave the matter entirely to the Muslims themselves. As a result the law minister (Asoke K. Sen) made a statement in the Parliament that the initiative for reforming their personal laws should come from the minorities themselves. It was not the policy of the government to take any lead in this matter.[107] Because of strong protest from sections of the Hindu community, the government of India had to go slow with the passing of the Hindu Code Bill.[108]

Cow Protection

In November 1966 there were huge demonstrations in New Delhi, supported by leaders of the Jan Sangh and Hindu communal organizations, demanding that the Parliament should enact laws banning the slaughter of cows throughout India. A. K. Gopalan said that the government, in acceding to some of the demands, forfeited India's claim to be a secular state.[109]

Though economic reasons are given for the Directive Principle concerning the protection of cows (Article 48), it is generally agreed that the article represents a concession to Hindu reverence for the cow. The Jana Sangh bases its demand for the law to ban the killing of cows on economics as well as on the sentiment of the vast majority of the people. If the government is to be considered democratic, it should pay attention to the sentiments and emotions of the large majority.[110]

Lohia said that although the anti-cow slaughter agitation might be sponsored by revivalists and obscurantists, this should not blind one to the unique situation in India. All over the world, 99% of the people are nonvegetarians; in India more than half of its 500 million people do not eat meat or fish. Reverence for all life has been a peculiar feature of India, and cow protection is an extension of reverence for life. The rational way would be to protect the cows and also pass laws to punish those who treat the cow cruelly. Lohia pointed out that the latter clause is necessary because, along with nonkilling, there also exists great cruelty in the treatment of animals.[111]

107. *Ibid.*, p. 146.
108. D. E. Smith, *India as a Secular State*, pp. 279-81.
109. Interview by the author.
110. Madhok, p. 53.
111. Interview by the author.

Frank Anthony thought the anti-cow killing agitation was a bad thing and it showed the strength of the obscurantist position. However, he and the Muslim leaders were of the opinion that the minority communities should not take issue, because it would only exacerbate relations with the majority community. In the opinion of Kabir, the majority community themselves will demand cow slaughter within ten years, for many groups of Hindus (e.g., villagers in Bihar and Assam) already do eat meat.[112] The other Muslim leaders also advocated a policy of "give and take."

Communal Tensions, Pakistan, and the Secular State

An appraisal of the current understanding of the secular state will not be complete without reference to the communal tensions in India, especially between Muslims and Hindus, and such a state's ties to Indo-Pak relations. The historical events that have led to the partition of the country and the birth of Pakistan have already been dealt with. The Kashmir issue, which led to a full-scale war in 1965, has kept alive the bitterness in the relationship between the two countries.

One of the main planks of the Jan Sangh program is reunifying India—achieving Akhand-Bharat (undivided India). Speaking of Pakistan, Madhok said, that India cannot run away from the fact that Pakistan was its born enemy and that it was going to remain so as long as Pakistan existed. Madhok claimed that the Indian Muslims still look up to Pakistan.[113] M. S. Golwalkar, head of the Rashtriya Swayam Sevak Sangh (R.S.S.), closely allied to the Jan Sangh, said regarding Muslims and Christians in India:

> Together with the change in their faith, gone are the spirit of love and devotion for the nation. Nor does it end there. They have also developed a feeling of identification with the enemies of this land.[114]

The above statements show that some Hindu leaders directly and indirectly question the loyalty of the large Muslim population (and sometimes of the Christians) to India. But generally high praise is given to them by nationalist leaders and the press and

---

112. Interview by the author.
113. Interview by the author.
114. M. S. Golwalkar, *A Bunch of Thoughts* (Bangalore: Vikrama Pra-kashan, 1966), pp. 127-28, in Herbert Jai Singh and Mark Sunder Rao, eds., *Indian Politics After Nehru* (Bangalore: The Christian Institute for the Study of Religion and Society, 1967), p. 144.

this was especially evident during the August–September, 1965 Indo-Pakistan conflict. Muslims took an active part in the fight against Pakistan.[115]

The Government of India has always treated the Kashmir issue in the context of the secular nature of the Indian state. Nehru was particularly firm on the Kashmir issue because, to him, to surrender Kashmir to Pakistan on the mere basis that Kashmir had a Muslim majority, was to compromise dangerously the secular nature of the Indian state. He also linked the future of India's Muslim minority with that of the Kashmir crisis, and said that a firm rejection of the nonsecular arguments by Pakistan was necessary to ensure the cementing of the secular-state ideal in India and thus assure the security of the Muslim minority.[116]

Thus the friction in relations with Pakistan, especially regarding the Kashmir issue, gives the Hindu communal parties opportunity to whip up distrust and antipathy for the Muslim community. Naturally the Muslim community also feels rejected and insecure, to the same extent. This chain of action and reaction is very injurious to the character of the secular state but is part of the current picture of the understanding of and interpretation given to the secular-state concept.

The interpretations given to this concept by different political leaders and parties seem to move in a continuum. On the one hand they represent a negative attitude toward the role of religion, especially organized religion, in civil life, and the realization of the need to separate religion as well as restrict it from interfering in affairs of state. This may involve a repudiation of the usefulness of religion as such (as with Communists), or just the repudiation of the extensive involvement of religion and religious traditions in civil life. The Congress, the Socialist Party, and the Swatantra Party may be considered to hold this latter view, generally.

The communal parties and religiously minded leaders would understand the Indian secular state as one in which religion had a positive though restricted role to play. Here there may be difference of opinion as to the relative role that the religion of

---

115. P. N. Masaldan, "Political Programmes and the Concretization of Secularism," in Sharma, ed., p. 228. This was also true in the more recent conflict with Pakistan which finally resulted in the creation of Bangladesh as a nation independent of what had been East Pakistan.

116. Ronald Segal, *The Anguish of India* (New York: Stein and Day, 1965), pp. 259-60.

the majority (Hinduism) and others (Islam, Christianity, etc.) should play. But the life of the people as a whole should be guided by religious values and principles. While leaders say that religion has a positive role to play, they do not generally spell out the way in which this role can be performed. But they are certain that the state should not unduly restrict religion for exercising its beneficial influence on the people.

3
Indian Christians, Nationalism, and the Secular State

The objective of this study is to investigate the actual and potential role of the Christian community in a secular state, with particular reference to India. To this end we have examined the meaning of the Indian secular state in Indian history, and in contemporary understanding and practice, and have come to the conclusion that India is essentially a secular state in both principle and practice in that it follows a policy of religious neutrality, grants religious freedom, and guarantees the fundamental rights of the individual. Indigenous as well as foreign influences have been equally important in providing the foundation of the Indian secular state. The concrete historical situation of India, during the freedom movement and at the time of independence, was also important in determining its secular character. It is obvious that the Indian secular state did not originate in a vacuum and does not exist in one. The different communities and peoples of India have contributed positively and negatively toward the evolution of the secular state in India. We shall now examine the part that the Christian community has played in the evolution of the Indian secular state. For this we shall survey the history of the relationship that the Christian churches have had with the political authorities in India. We shall also examine the role that Christians played during India's freedom struggle, and their attitude toward communal representation. It has been acknowledged that some of the most creative thinking about the nature of the secular state in India is being done by some Christian bodies.[1] We shall in

---

1. D. E. Smith, *Secular State*, p. 438.

addition examine the views of the major Christian bodies in India regarding the secular state.

Historical Note on Church-State Relationship in India

For studying the relationship between the Christian community in India and political authorities during its long history, we may divide the Christian community into three groups, namely, Syrian Christians, Christians of Goa and other Portuguese colonies, and Christians of the former British India. This excludes Christians in the princely states of India (except those of Travancore and Cochin—now part of the state of Kerala—who are the Syrian Christians), but these represent only a very small portion of the total Christian community and in some respects we may infer the pattern of relationship of these from what we learn of the history of Syrian Christians in the former princely states of Travancore and Cochin.

Syrian Christians

The Syrian Christian community traces its origin to the church founded by St. Thomas the Apostle in A.D. 52.[2] Not many details are known about its history until the sixteenth century, when the Portuguese came to India. However, there are certain well-documented incidents that are of interest to us in the present context. In the fourth century there was a Syrian immigration of 400 Christians from Baghdad and Jerusalem under the leadership of Thomas of Cana, the merchant prince, to the Malabar coast. It is believed that Cheraman Perumal, the ruler of Cranganur, received them and conferred privileges on Thomas and the Syrian and local Christians.[3] Syrian Christians were merchants and seem to have occupied a highly honorable position in the state and to have continued to enjoy the patronage of the rulers for a long time. Some of the copper plates on which were inscribed charters giving special privileges to Christians are still extant. There was also a tradition that the Syrian Christians had their own kings around the tenth century.[4]

---

2. P. Thomas, *Christians and Christianity in India and Pakistan*, pp. 12f.
3. S. G. Pothen, *The Syrian Christians of Kerala* (New York: Asia Publishing House, 1963), pp. 22-23.
4. *Ibid.*, p. 32. See Fr. I. Daniel, *The Malabar Church and Other Orthodox Churches* (Haripad, Travancore: Suvarna Bharathi Press, 1950), pp. 29-34.

We have almost no knowledge of the community in the Middle Ages. But we again pick up the trail with the arrival of Vasco da Gama, the Portuguese navigator in Calicut (on the Malabar coast) in 1498. When he came to Cochin in 1502, a deputation of Syrian Christians sought Portuguese protection against Muslims and others. The Portuguese were only too glad to have local allies, and entering into treaties with local rulers, they saw to it that the local Christians were protected and privileges granted to them.[5] But the friendship with the Portuguese was short lived, because they tried to bring the Syrian Church under the rule of the Roman See. In trying to force the Syrian Church to be subject to Rome, the Portuguese authorities even enlisted the support of the Rajah of Cochin.[6]

But traditionally the local rajas had for centuries recognized the honorable position of the Syrian Christians and their special privileges. They numbered about 200,000 and they were a martial people. In many local matters they were autonomous and they showed their loyalty to the bishop not only in spiritual matters but also in civil matters. The state's power intervened only in criminal matters.

Most of the Christians had lived under the realm of the Maharajah of Cochin. But with the decline of that House, many moved to different parts of the kingdom of Travancore. The authorities here were at first not very favorable to Christians, because many of them had fought on the side of the Rajah of Cochin against the Rajahs of Travancore. However, there are no records of active persecution. We do find that during the British rule, Christians were suffering from some discriminatory practices imposed on them.[7]

On the other hand, there are also signs of friendship and favor shown to Christians. One good sign is the fact that many old Syrian churches are situated close to some ancient temples. Only because of royal favor and local friendship with high-caste Hindus would Christians have been able to build churches close to Hindu temples. It is surmised that often Hindu rulers wanted the Christian "god" to be near their own gods and made grants of land for the building of churches near temples.

During the British period the princely or native states under the rule of rajahs did not come under the direct administration

---

5. Brown, p. 13.
6. *Ibid.*, p. 30.
7. P. Thomas, p. 227.

of the British crown. However, all of them accepted the suzerainty of England. British "Residents" were appointed to the states as representatives of the Crown. They wielded great influence and power with the local administration. In Travancore and Cochin, the local Maharajahs sometimes appointed Britishers as "Diwans" or prime ministers.

The first two British residents in Travancore and Cochin, Cols. Macaulay and Munro, took an active interest in the affairs of the Syrian Christian community. At the insistence of Col. Macaulay, one Syrian bishop was deported by the Company from Cochin. He also got the Travancore government to pay a considerable amount of money to the Syrian Christians as compensation for certain injustices (the nature of which is not clear) they had suffered in the past.[8]

The second Resident, Col. Munro, also took an active interest in the affairs of the Syrian community. He was instrumental in securing further financial help for Christians from the rulers. This infuriated certain sections of the Hindu community, especially in Travancore. He also interested himself in the internal affairs of the church. It was at his insistence that the Church Missionary Society sent four missionaries to work in the Syrian church. He considered the missionaries as his agents.[9]

The later Residents were not actively interested in the Syrians, but their very presence gave Christians some prestige (especially Protestants) and support. As Thomas says,

> the removal of their disabilities and the wary eye the British kept on any attempts at discrimination against Christians had a salutary effect on the progress of the community.[10]

Another interesting fact to note is that by 1817 it had become the practice of the Travancore government (Sirkar) to formally recognize a new bishop when he was consecrated. Opposing factions within the church sometimes appealed to the government for recognition, and several cases involving the validity of orders and similar matters were tried in the law courts of Travancore and Cochin.[11]

Two points emerge from the foregoing. The first is that the Syrian Christian community occupied a place of honor and privi-

---

8. Brown, p. 127.
9. *Ibid.*, pp. 132-34.
10. P. Thomas, p. 233.
11. Brown, p. 134.

lege in the kingdoms in which they lived. During most of their history their existence was not merely tolerated but they were welcomed because of their trade enterprises and martial capabilities. They were also considered high caste. However, they also suffered political reverses along with the adverse fate of the rulers whom they served. They were united under their *metran* or bishop, who wielded not only spiritual authority but also some civil authority. They were part and parcel of the high-caste society of Kerala.

Second, during the British period, the Syrian community derived certain benefits, some direct, but mostly indirect, because of the British political presence. As we have noted, the first two British Residents helped the community directly. Indirectly, through British missionary work, the Syrians were able greatly to improve their educational standard. They also received sympathetic treatment from British officials. However, the Syrians on the whole refused to accept the church affiliation of the missionaries and did not accept the outward signs of Western culture. Their direct contact with Westerners was confined to a few people at the top, and the rank and file continued to be Eastern and Indian in their outlook and habits. The Syrian community was never accused of being an appendage of British imperialism.

Christians of Goa and Other Former Portuguese Colonies

The Portuguese came to India in search of "pepper and souls." They conquered all the key positions on the West Coast of India during the first ten years of the sixteenth century. The Pope had charged the King of Portugal with the responsibility of establishing the church "in all lands discovered and still to be discovered" in the Far East. In the name of the Crown and with its financial support, missionaries were sent to convert the native people. In 1533, Goa was made the bishop's see. The Portuguese drove away or massacred the Muslims, who were considered their mortal enemies. Hindus were converted. Those who resisted long were treated as second-class citizens.[12] In this, the Portuguese were following the dogma then prevalent in Europe, that *Cuius Regio, eius religio*. In reward for the zeal that the Portuguese showed

---

12. F. A. Plattner, *Christian India* (New York: The Vanguard Press, 1957), p. 54. For the Portuguese period, see also F. A. Plattner, S.J., *The Catholic Church in India—Yesterday and Today* (Allahabad, U.P.: St. Paul Publications, 1964), pp. 13–23.

in proselytism, the Pope conferred on Portugal the privilege of *Padroado* or patronage. According to this, the king had the authority to name candidates for bishops in the new areas and Portugal undertook the responsibility to protect Christians in these areas. In their treaties with local princes, Portugal did insist on the privilege of looking after the interests of Christians and protecting their interests. This clause was incorporated in Portugal's treaty with the Zamorin, ruler of the northern part of Kerala, where some Syrian Christians lived.[13]

The Inquisition was established in Goa in 1560. Thus the church was very much connected with the Portuguese administration. I have already referred to Portuguese attempts to bring the Syrian church under Rome. In this, Alexis de Menezes, the Archbishop of Goa, was supported by the secular power of the Portuguese administration and its ally, the Rajah of Cochin.

Wherever the Portuguese established their trading posts in India, these became Catholic centers. The converts were highly Westernized in manners, dress, and food; they accepted the Portuguese way of life and even Portuguese names.[14] With the decline of the Portuguese rule in the seventeenth century, they lost most of their territory to other powers. Goa, the last Portuguese foothold in India, was merged with the country in 1961. But the short Portuguese rule in India provided an example where the Indian Christian community was most closely identified with the rulers and enjoyed special privileges due to foreign rule. It also furthered the image of the Christian community in India as foreign and set apart from their Indian compatriots.

The Church in the British Period

While the Syrian Christian community existed in India from the first century, and the Roman Catholics started large-scale missionary enterprise from the sixteenth century onwards, the first Protestant missionary arrived in India only in 1706. He did not come under the aegis of the British, but under the patronage of the Danish king to the Danish territory of Tranquebar in South India.[15]

13. Moraes, p. 123.

14. Thomas Pothacamury, *The Church in Independent India* (Maryknoll, N.Y.: Maryknoll Publications, 1958), p. 13.

15. C. E. Abraham, "The Rise and Growth of Christianity in India," in Haridas Bhattacharya, ed., *The Cultural Heritage of India*, 2d ed. (Calcutta: The Ramakrishna Mission Institute of Culture, 1956), 4:553.

William Carey, the first British missionary, arrived in Calcutta in 1793. The East India Company was not on the whole friendly toward mission work in India. This was based on the fear that missionary work would antagonize Hindus and Muslims and thus jeopardize the trade operations of the company. The Vellore Mutiny of 1808 quickened their fears and the Directors of the Company preferred to follow a policy of religious impartiality which, according to Ingham, "served as a useful cloak for their greater interest in dividends."[16]

In 1813, due to the agitation of evangelicals, the Parliament included in the Charter Renewal Act a clause admitting the principle of missionary activity in India, but missionaries were required to obtain a license from the Company to enter India. In 1833 the free unlicensed entry of missionaries was allowed by the Parliament under the new Charter Renewal Act.[17]

While the official attitude of the company was rather negative toward mission work, individual officers of the company, from the Governor General on, often helped missionaries in their personal as well as official capacities. Missionaries were sometimes pressed into the service of the government. C. F. Schwartz in the South negotiated with Haider Ali and Tipu in behalf of the company's government.[18] But others were indifferent or hostile to missionary work. Speaking of the period from 1793 to 1833, Ingham says:

From the British Governments in India, the missionaries might look in general for approval extending at times to active support, but an incautious step might produce immediate recriminations. Individual officers, from the most junior collector to the Governor-General might give their assistance; yet a Company's Resident might equally effectively undermine the whole structure of missionary work in his district.[19]

The ambivalent attitude shown by the British toward missionary work was evident in their treatment of converts also. Most of the early converts were from the lower castes, with some notable exceptions in Bengal. The government did not want to appear to be showing any favoritism to native Christians. In Bengal,

---

16. Kenneth Ingham, *Reformers in India 1793-1833: An Account of the Work of Christian Missionaries on Behalf of Social Reform* (Cambridge: The University Press, 1956), p. 10.

17. *Ibid.*, pp. 11, 1.

18. *Ibid.*, p. 13.

19. *Ibid.*, p. 19.

Christians were excluded from military service. A sepoy who converted to Christianity had to leave the ranks. Writing in 1859, M. A. Sherring, a missionary in India, complains regarding the treatment meted out to converts: "They were branded by their fellow-countrymen and by the ruling power as a contemptible and incapable race."[20] He says that at the time of the Mutiny the Christian converts were most loyal to the British. He sees this as a reason why the government should encourage missions.

> And the thought, too, presents itself with striking force, that for the natives to become evangelised is for them to be made loyal subjects of the British Crown. . . . Let the Government of India, therefore, as a matter of administrative policy, throw all the weight of its influence into the scale of missions, for by so doing it will add immensely to its own stability and it may be, prevent the possibility of a second rebellion.[21]

Sherring acknowledges that government officials in their private capacity often helped missions and Indian converts.[22]

Until 1831 Indian Christians were by law debarred from appointment to several government posts. The clause was removed after several representations. Another disablement was that, following the traditional laws of Hindus and Muslims penalizing apostasy by disinheritance, Christian converts suffered loss of property on conversion. This disablement was removed by Governor-General Dalhousie in 1850 by the Caste Disabilities Removal Act, passed in spite of some opposition from Hindus. The act also protected the right of guardianship of children of converted parents.[23] In 1854 the government started a system of giving grants-in-aid to educational institutions managed by voluntary organizations. This helped the Christian missions most of all since the majority of such schools were run by them.[24] In 1858 the Crown assumed the rule of India. This followed the Mutiny of 1857, one cause of which was supposed to be the overt support extended by the government to missions. The government officials practiced a greater degree of religious neutrality from that time.[25]

---

20. M. A. Sherring, *The Indian Church During the Great Rebellion. An Authentic Narrative of the Disasters That Befell It, Its Sufferings; And Faithfulness unto Death of Many of Its European and Native Members,* 2d ed. (London: James Nisbet & Co., 1859), p. 336.

21. *Ibid.,* p. 339.

22. *Ibid.,* p. 337.

23. Mayhew, pp. 133-37.

24. D. E. Smith, *Secular State,* pp. 69-71.

25. *Ibid.,* p. 197.

From the beginning, the East India Company had employed chaplains in India to minister to the spiritual needs of its employees. In 1813, along with the clauses permitting entry of missionaries, Parliament also provided for the appointment of a bishop in Calcutta, who was to supervise ecclesiastical matters throughout India (as well as Ceylon and Australia!). The expenses were to be met out of revenues from India. In 1833, the British Parliament created two more bishoprics, in Bombay and Madras. Even though the bishops were not to interest themselves in mission work, Bishop Heber, the second bishop of Calcutta, and those who followed, worked closely with the Church Missionary Society and other missionary societies. The state-appointed bishops were thus also engaged in missionary work. This church-state connection was criticized not only by non-Christians, but also by Christians. As a result, the Church of England in India was disestablished by the Indian Church Measure passed by the Parliament in 1927. Bishops in India were no longer appointed by the Crown and the church came to be known as "Church of India, Burma and Ceylon." However, the government paid a sum to the bishops for superintending the work of the chaplains. Churches that were built with full or partial help from the government continued to receive subsidies for their repair and maintenance.

Presbyterian and Roman Catholic chaplains were also employed by the government and received the same treatment as those of the Church of England, after 1927. When India gained independence and the British troops were moved out of the country, the system of government chaplaincy ended. Government-maintained churches were handed over to local ecclesiastical authorities. The Indian Ecclesiastical Establishment was abolished on 31 March 1948.[26]

In spite of the official policy of the Government of India (during British rule) of religious neutrality, as already pointed out, the individual government officials of high and low ranks often showed sympathy and favor to the missionaries in particular and to Indian Christians in general. Governor-General Wellsley extended official patronage to the work of Bible translation by Carey. William Bentick stood firmly for the rights of Indian Christians. Mayhew says that Lord Dalhousie believed

with an irresistible love of fair play, and a sound conviction that it was not only our Christian duty but our wisest policy

26. *Ibid.*, pp. 78-83.

to show that we were neither ashamed of being Christians nor afraid to protect them.[27]

There were many British governors and officers who were devout, and James Thompson, governor of a state, looked forward to the Christianization of India. We also read about a governor of Bombay who conducted Sunday School classes, and the attendance by officials at the public baptism of converts and at public discourse between missionaries and Hindu religious teachers was not uncommon.[28]

The Madras Government sent its senior chaplain, Dr. Kerr, to Travancore to investigate the condition of the Syrian church there. We have already seen the keen interest that the first Residents, Col. Munro and Col. Macaulay, evinced in helping the Syrian Christian community.

All this shows that Indian Christians were greatly helped, directly and indirectly, by the British rule. The very fact that Christianity was the religion of the rulers gave it many advantages. Many Indian leaders complain about the fact that in many cities and towns choice land was appropriated by mission organizations.[29] I have already referred to the payment that the churches received from the government for maintenance of churches and supervision of chaplains. In 1926, the government spent 30 million rupees for this purpose.[30] It was estimated (in 1946) that with complete disestablishment, the Diocese of Calcutta alone would lose Rs. (rupees) 60,000 a year in salary grants.[31] P. Thomas sums up one aspect of the effect of British rule on Christianity in India when he says:

> Political suzerainty has obvious powers to enhance the spread of the religion of the rulers, and the gains to Christianity during the British period were the most remarkable.[32]

However, there is another side to the picture. We know that not all officials were always sympathetic to the Christian cause. Christians also suffered from British anxiety to show that they were religiously neutral, which at times took the form of discriminating against Christians—what Mayhew called a "nervous disavowal

---

27. Mayhew, p. 115.
28. *Ibid.*, p. 123.
29. Ram Manohar Lohia in personal interview by the author.
30. *Guardian* (Madras), 3 June 1926, pp. 254-55.
31. *Ibid.*, 5 September 1946.
32. P. Thomas, p. 185.

of them [Christian missions] and all their work."[33] K. T. Paul, an eminent Indian Christian giving the presidential address to the All India Christian Conference, said:

> In more recent years, if the profession of Christianity has been again and again a disqualification preventing an Indian access to opportunities he deserved by reason of his undoubted qualifications and tested merit, it was because the British bureaucracy was naturally nervous on the score of religious neutrality. At the same time there was no difficulty for the Maharajah of Mysore to appoint an Indian Christian as his Executive Councillor, or for the Maharajas of Travancore and Cochin to appoint them to some of the highest offices including in one case the Dewanship itself.[34]

One basis for the complaint was that the government chose the European and Anglo-Indian Christians for special favor and looked down upon "native" in Indian Christians. This was particularly true of recently converted communities that were very backward and poor. The *Guardian*, the Protestant Christian newspaper, complained editorially in 1924: "Indeed the community has not yet found its place as a force to be reckoned with by government."[35]

Not all Christians supported the British administration or looked for special favors from it. Many Christians were opposed to the British rule and its policies, as we shall see later. Thus we see that on the part of the British administration in India there were two aspects to its policy toward the Christian enterprise in India: 1) official neutrality and occasional disfavor; and 2) positive encouragement and acceptance, both overt and covert.

In reviewing the history of church-state relationships in India, we find that the Syrian Christian community enjoyed an honorable position in the state (except during the short period of Christian monarchy, if this tradition is true) without being officially connected with the state. It was the beneficiary of the generally tolerant attitude of Hindu monarchs in South India to foreigners and foreign religions, and also of mutual respect and need for one another. During the British period, Syrian Christians, though not directly involved with British administration, generally benefited from their presence.

The Goan and related Christian community was closely allied

---

33. Mayhew, p. 87.
34. *Guardian*, 3 January 1924, p. 7.
35. *Ibid.*, p. 375.

with the Portuguese administration and received advantages. But in the long term it suffered from losing its Indian identity and being part of Western imperialism.

Because of the British policy of religious neutrality, Christians in "British India" were not so identified with the British administration as were those in Portuguese territories. However, to some degree in actual fact, and much more so in popular imagination among non-Christians, Christianity came to be closely identified with the British. It is true that the Church of England was "established" in India for a short period, but on the whole the church did not get much direct help from the government. But the church did receive much indirect help during the period and it utilized it to fulfill its mission. The peace and security that British rule offered, along with factors already mentioned, were conducive to the growth of missions. According to one author, "on the whole we can speak of a favourable situation for missions but not of any actual favouritism."[36] The church, however, suffered grievously from over-Westernization and the stigma, right or wrong, of being an accessory to British imperialism.

Indian Christian Participation in the Freedom Movement

The Indian Christian community as a whole did not take an active part in the national liberation movement. This is freely admitted by responsible Christian leaders. Bishop A. J. Appasamy says:

> But apart from a man here and there, the vast majority of our Christian people stood aloof from the national struggle. It is quite necessary to face facts and to recognize that in the fight for the independence of India, Christians as a whole had little or no share.[37]

Eddy Asirvatham also expresses the same idea when he says:

> During the days of the national struggle, the political record of Indian Christians showed marked moral weakness. Few Indian Christians put their vaunted ideals of service and self-sacrifice into operation when the testing came between 1921 and 1945.[38]

---

36. Plattner, *The Catholic Church* . . . , p. 25.
37. *The Christian Task in Independent India* (London: S.P.C.K., 1951), p. 2.
38. *Christianity in the Indian Crucible*, 2d rev. ed. (Calcutta: Y.M.C.A. Publishing House, 1957), p. 26.

There were many reasons for this. First of all, a large section of the Indian Christian community was closely associated with foreign missionaries and churches. These churches were very dependent financially and spiritually on "mother churches" overseas, and they followed the advice of the missionaries. The English missionaries were by and large identified with the British rulers and in many cases forbade their followers to take part in the political struggle. In any case they did not give encouragement to such participation. Non-British missionaries could enter the country only after pledging that they would not engage in any political activities. Hence they were not allowed to express any opinions on political matters.[39]

There was also the widespread feeling, especially among the uneducated, ordinary members of the community, that the future of Christians would be bleak under a government in which the Hindus would be in the majority. They looked to the British government as the protector of their religious freedom. The missionary churches, whose membership consisted mostly of converts from the low-caste groups, were cut away from the ancient heritage of Indian culture and the members tried to imitate Western customs and manners. Thus they were isolated and held in contempt by the rest of the Indian society. They were economically poor and many depended on government jobs for their livelihood. The "loaves and fishes of office" was one reason for supporting British rule.[40]

The isolation of the Christian community was also caused by the ostracism of Christian converts by the Hindu community. Since the starting of the Arya Samaj movement in 1895, their propaganda caused a hostile feeling to develop against Christians and Christianity. The village Christian peasants were oppressed by their landlords. Hence it can also be said that

> The exclusiveness which the convert developed is not of his own choice, but was thrust upon him by the intolerance of the Hindu community.[41]

Educated Christians on the whole supported the national movement. There was also a cleavage between the officialdom of the

---

39. Appasamy, p. 3.
40. *Guardian*, 3 July 1924, p. 319.
41. E. C. Bhatty, "The Indian Christian Community and the Nationalist Movement," *National Christian Council Review* 62, no. 11 (November 1942) :449.

churches and the members, especially the youth. In Kerala, the Youths' Christian Council of Action protested against the unfavorable stand the bishops and church leaders took against the movement for responsible government in Travancore.[42]

J. C. Kumarappa, a Christian follower of Gandhi and a freedom fighter, wrote to D. F. Westcott, Bishop of Calcutta and Metropolitan of India, urging him to register the protest of the church against the repressive acts of the government and to persuade it to follow the nonviolent path shown by Gandhi. Westcott sent a formal reply quoting Romans 13 and saying that authorities should be obeyed. He could not agree with the Gandhian practice of civil disobedience. In a long reply, Kumarappa repudiated his arguments and said that missionaries seemed to be "Britishers first and Christians afterwards if convenient."[43]

Another example from Travancore may be given of the conservative attitude of the church hierarchy. The freedom movement in British India had its parallel movements in the princely states like Travancore. In the early forties such movements were being put down with an iron hand by the autocratic Dewan (prime minister) of Travancore, C. P. Ramaswamy Aiyer. But while many Christian people and leaders were being sent to jail by the Dewan for taking part in such agitation, the Roman Catholic Archbishop of Trivandrum gave a magnificent reception to the Dewan and presented a citation extolling his services. This was viewed with great dismay by those Christians taking part in the freedom movement.

Of course, there were a number of exceptions. C. F. Andrews, an Anglican missionary, was a close friend of Gandhi and Tagore. Verrier Elwin was another missionary who actively supported the freedom movement. Stanley Jones also was a friend of Gandhi and sympathized with his movement. In 1930, more than 200 British missionaries signed a manifesto appealing to Britain to be sympathetic to Indian demands.[44] Indian church leaders like Bishop Azariah of Dornakal were also openly sympathetic to the freedom movement.[45]

But in spite of the fact that missionaries and the church hierarchy were on the whole opposed to the freedom movement and

---

42. "The Present Situation in Travancore–Statement by the Youths' Christian Council of Action," *Guardian*, 29 September 1938), p. 614.
43. *Guardian*, 19 June 1930, p. 298.
44. *Ibid.*, 13 November 1930, p. 538.
45. *Ibid.*, 17 September 1942, pp. 436-37.

most Christians kept aloof from it, there were a number of Christians who took an active part in the movement at both the national and local levels. Nor were Christians late-comers to the freedom struggle.

Some of the founders of the Indian National Congress in 1885 were Christians. Krishna Mohan Bannerji and Lal Behari Dey were Indian Christians, and Hume and William Wedderburn were British Christians who were among the early leaders of the Congress (Hume was the founder), and some of these became Congress presidents. There was a slackening of interest among Christians from 1895 because of the activities of the Arya Samaj and other causes already alluded to.[46]

With the partition of Bengal in 1905, the *Swadeshi* (national) movement was inaugurated. One way in which the Indian Christians responded to it was by developing indigenous leadership and freedom from foreign domination and dependence within the church. With this idea in mind, the National Missionary Society was founded.[47] The Society was founded on the principle that it will use only indigenous men, methods, and money for its work. The Society was never active in politics but, because it was purely Indian in its personnel and management, it continued to express sympathy for the national movement. A report presented to the Council meeting at Ranchi in 1923 expressed approval of the "Swaraj" idea.

> Swaraj or self-determination was recognized to be the legitimate goal of India and it was recognized that the task of the Indian Church was to enrich national aspiration with Christ's ideals.[48]

The Civil Disobedience Movement started under Gandhi's leadership attracted many Christians. J. C. Kumarappa and George Joseph were close associates of Gandhi. Both were entrusted with editing some of his publications during periods of his absence. S. K. George was another ardent follower. He could say without any reservation:

My politics begin and end with the following of Mahatma

---

46. E. C. Bhatty, "The Indian Christian Community and the Nationalist Movement," *NCCR*, 62, no. 11 (November 1942):446-48.
47. *Ibid.*, p. 449.
48. *Guardian*, 26 January 1923, p. 44.

Gandhi. To me he is God's great man raised up in the hour of India's great need to lead her to a fuller, freer life.[49]

Two other eminent Christians who were not followers of Gandhi but took an active part in politics were K. T. Paul and S. K. Datta. After a long period of service as National Secretary of the YMCA, K. T. Paul resigned that position so that he could be more active in politics. Paul, along with Datta, represented the Indian Christian community at the London Round Table Conferences (1930–1932) and there tried to bring reconciliation among the opposing leaders who took part. Paul knew Mahatma Gandhi intimately and was closely associated with most of the leading politicians during the troubled period between 1920 and his death in 1931. His biographer says that he was regarded by some British officials as "an extremist and a dangerous nationalist." But "he was a genuine believer in Indian freedom and was not prepared to barter India's right for any mess of pottage."[50]

Syrian Christians, as we have seen, were mostly concentrated in the former native states of Travancore and Cochin. Partly because of this, the community did not (with a few exceptions) provide national leadership in the freedom movement. But in the states of Travancore and Cochin they were among the foremost leaders of the freedom movement to achieve social justice and self rule. Of course, as in other parts of India, many Syrian Christians favored British rule in India. But large numbers of Syrian Christians actively supported the freedom movement.

Many Syrian Christians sympathized with and supported the famous Vaikom Satyagraha (campaign of nonviolent civil disobedience) of 1924 against untouchability, which had the blessing of Mahatma Gandhi, and through this movement many Syrian Christians came under his influence.[51] The Vaikom Satyagraha was primarily a social movement and the Temple Entry Proclamation of the Maharaja of Travancore in 1937 was a direct result of this.

The nationalist agitation for responsible government and political freedom became active in Travancore and Cochin only in the

---

49. *Guardian*, 19 January 1930, p. 293. Rajkumari Amrit Kaur, a Christian lady of aristocratic lineage, was another ardent follower of Gandhi. She later became the Health Minister in the Indian Cabinet.

50. H. A. Popley, *K. T. Paul: Christian Leader* (Calcutta: Y.M.C.A. Publishing House, 1938), p. 175.

51. C. P. Mathew and M. M. Thomas, *The Indian Churches of Saint Thomas* (Delhi: I.S.P.C.K., 1967), pp. 144-46.

late thirties and early forties of this century.[52] In the joint Political Congress that was formed around 1932 and in the State Congress (affiliated with the Indian National Congress), into which the former merged, Syrian Christians were among the foremost leaders.[53] T. M. Varghese, A. J. John, Vayala Idiculla, and other Syrian Christian leaders took an active part in the struggle against the repressive rule of C. P. Ramaswamy Iyer (Dewan or prime minister of Travancore) and for self rule. The Syrian Christian community played an important part in achieving responsible government for the states of Travancore and Cochin within the framework of the Indian Union.[54]

We should also recognize the political activities of the Indian Christian Associations in different parts of India (see next section) in this connection. The YMCA, the Student Christian Movement, and other Christian youth organizations also made their contribution indirectly toward Christian political participation by providing opportunities for discussions and political education.[55]

In reviewing Christian participation in the freedom movement, we see that Indian Christians have nothing much to be proud of. Large sections of the community had identified themselves closely with British administration and were lukewarm to the prospect of Indian independence. However, the educated class of Indian Christians, especially those who came under the influence of Mahatma Gandhi, made great contributions to the freedom movement, and the illustrious names already mentioned stand in proof.

History and Role of the Indian Christian Associations

Most Christians, especially the young and educated ones who took part in politics did so as followers of Gandhi in the Indian National Congress and its affiliated parties. But there were certain regional and national organizations within the Christian community itself that tried to work for the social and political rights of Christians in India. Even though they represented the more moderate and conservative voice of the community and often mere vested interests at local levels, they performed a useful function in giving public expression to an Indian Christian view-

---

52. *Ibid.*, p. 147.
53. Nayar, in D. E. Smith, ed., *South Asian Politics and Religion*, p. 187.
54. *Ibid.*
55. On YMCA and politics, see *ibid.*, pp. 118f.

point on different political and social issues of the day and in trying to safeguard the political rights of Indian Christians. The different Indian Christian Associations that were active in different parts of the country, mainly cities, and the All India Conference of Indian Christians (a national organization uniting these local associations in one organization) come under this category. As sociopolitical associations representing the non-Roman Catholic section of the Christian community in India, these merit our attention and study in the context of the investigation of Christian participation in Indian politics. In the absence of any published history of these associations, we must depend mainly on published reports in the *Guardian,* a Christian newspaper published for over a century in Madras, and in the *National Christian Council Review* (Nagpur), the official publication of the National Christian Council of India.

The twenty-eighth of December 1914 was an important day in the history of the Indian Christian community because the first All-India Conference of Indian Christians was held on that day.[56] Raja Sir Harnam Singh, President of the National Missionary Society (N.M.S.) since 1905, was also the president of the Conference. We have seen that the N.M.S. was partly an expression of the nationalist spirit among Indian Christians. There was close connection between the N.M.S. and the All-Indian Christian Conference. The Conference was held three days after the N.M.S.'s Tenth Anniversary in Calcutta, and the officials and the delegates were identical. Some of those who gave the principal addresses were J. R. Chitambar, J. C. Dutt, George Nundy, and K. N. Basu, all holding official positions with the N.M.S.[57]

The idea of founding an All-Indian Christian Council was first conceived by that "prince of Christians," Raja Sir Harnam Singh, when Lord Curzon was Viceroy and a wave of nationalism was sweeping the country. But the credit for bringing the Conference into existence belongs to the Bengal Christian Association.[58] This association was founded in 1877 under the leadership of the Reverend K. M. Banerji, K. C. Banerji, and J. G. Shome. It passed

---

56. Donald Fossett Ebright, *The National Missionary Society of India, 1905–1942. An Expression of the Movement Toward Indigenization within the Indian Christian Community* (Chicago: The University of Chicago Press, 1944), pp. 143–44.

57. *Ibid.*

58. All-India Christian Conference, Presidential Address by S. Balasingam Satya Nadar, 1945. *Guardian,* 5 April 1945, p. 108.

resolutions asking for merger of missions with Bengal churches and administration of these by the churches.[59]

Indian Christian Associations already existed in Bombay, Madras, Hyderabad, the Punjab, the United Province, and Burma. S. C. Mukherjee and his committee of the Bengal Association enlisted the support and cooperation of the above-mentioned local associations in convening the All-India Conference. It aimed at bringing different Christian associations to discuss matters of common interest.[60] In the Constitution passed in the second conference in 1915, the object of the Conference was defined thus:

> Its object shall be to watch over and promote the interests of the Indian Christian community. This object is to be achieved by loyal representations to government, by promoting cooperation and unity in the community, by fostering public spirit and by developing the intellectual, moral, economic, industrial and other resources of the community.[61]

It is clear from this that its political approach was moderate and based on making "loyal representations" to the British administration.

When Gandhi started his civil disobedience and noncooperation movement, the Conference could not agree with him. J. R. Chitambar in his presidential address in Bombay in December 1924 said that "the East and the West have met in India in accordance with the plan and purposes of the Eternal God" and that they were "for evolution, and not revolution." However, the resolutions called for repeal of laws restricting freedom in Bengal and also endorsing the "desirability of an immediate advancement in self-government for India."[62]

The Conference repeatedly, through its resolutions, spoke out against the principle of communal representation in the legislature and government. But the local organization did not always take this line. For example, in 1925 the U. P. Indian Christian Association passed a resolution favoring communal representation even though opposed by the representative from the All-India Conference, J. R. Chitambar.[63] According to comments by the *Guardian,* even though the Conference paid lip-service to non-

---

59. *Guardian,* 30 October 1924, p. 530.
60. *Ibid.,* 5 April 1945, p. 108.
61. *Ibid.,* 28 August 1924, pp. 415–16.
62. *Ibid.,* 1, 8, 15 January 1925.
63. *Ibid.,* 12 November 1925, p. 537.

communalism through its resolutions, "most of the speeches betrayed a desire to continue to press for 'privileges' for the community." However, there was a small group of persons who stood courageously for the policy of asking for no reservations.[64]

The official policy seems to have been to oppose communal representation in principle but at the same time request the government that if communal representation were accepted, the "legitimate rights" of Christians would be safeguarded. At the 24th Annual Session at Nagpur, the Conference, through a resolution, pointed out that the Christian community was being discriminated against in administrative cases and appointments. It also demanded of the government that since appointments were to be made for the Viceroy's Executive Council on a communal basis, the claims of the Christian community as the second largest minority should not be ignored. The Conference also passed a resolution asking for the appointment of a Christian as judge of the Madras High Court.[65] Resolutions in the same vein were passed in subsequent sessions.[66]

While the Conference did not approve of civil disobedience and the resultant mass violence, it condemned government repression and asked for self-government. It would seem that the Conference agreed with the Indian National Congress in its objectives but not with its methods.[67] The Conference congratulated the Congress ministries that came into power in the Provinces in 1937. It wholeheartedly supported the war effort of the government (in December 1939), and at the same time expressed its "full agreement with the determination of the country to obtain full self-government at the earliest possible time."[68] In 1942 it appealed to the Congress to reconsider its decision to launch mass civil disobedience, because it might lead to violence.[69] The Conference was opposed to the idea of partition of the country to meet Muslim demands.

In 1943 the Conference resolved to seek cooperation with

---

64. "Our Punjab Letter," in *ibid.*, 9 January 1930, p. 21.

65. *NCCR* 60, no. 2 (Februry 1940):101-2.

66. See Presidential Address in March 1945. It was noted that the Madras High Court had had no Christian judges since 1928 and that the situation should be remedied. *Guardian*, 5 April 1945, p. 107.

67. In 1930, B. A. Nag, the President, sent a telegram to the Viceroy conveying disapproval of civil disobedience and supporting government measures to check it. The *Guardian* took strong exception to this on 22 May 1930, p. 242.

68. *NCCR* 60, no. 2 (February 1940):101.

69. *Guardian*, 13 August 1942, p. 382.

Roman Catholics.[70] In 1944 M. Ruthnaswamy, the Roman Catholic leader, proposed that a joint council of Roman Catholics and Protestants be formed and this was approved in 1945. On 30 October 1945 representatives of the Catholic Union of India (a lay organization) and the All-India Conference of Indian Christians formed a joint committee to deal with public matters of common interest. The Committee passed a resolution suggesting that

> in the future constitution of India, the profession, practice and propagation of religion should be guaranteed and that a change of religion should not involve any civil or political disability.[71]

The National Christian Council of India warmly welcomed the formation of the joint committee after 25 years of attempts to bring the groups together. The Council suggested that the Protestants and Catholics should stand together to plead for the right to *propagate* their religion.[72]

The formation of the joint committee made it possible for the Christian community in India to take a united stand before the British Parliamentary Delegation. In their representation to the Parliamentary Delegation, the committee members unanimously supported the move for independence and expressed complete confidence in the future of the community in India. However, they desired proper constitutional guarantees regarding their right to practice, teach, and propagate their faith. They did not desire any special privilege or preferential treatment for the Christian community, but they desired that when the machinery for evolving a constitution was set up, the Indian Christian community should be recognized, as they knew other communities would be. A few members pleaded for reservation of seats.[73] An office for the joint committee (with M. Rahnasamy, Vice-Chancellor of Andhra University as President, and B. L. Rallia Ram of Lahore as General Secretary) was opened in New Delhi in 1947. Six Indian Christians were elected as members of the Minorities Committee of the Constituent Assembly.[74] A meeting of the Joint Committee was held on 16 and 17 April 1947 in New Delhi under the chairmanship of Dr. John Mathai, Transport Member of the govern-

70. *NCCR* 63, no. 5 (May 1943):202.
71. *Ibid.*, 65, no. 12 (December 1945):240.
72. *Ibid.*, 66, no. 1 (January 1946):3.
73. *Ibid.*, no. 4 (April 1946):120-21.
74. The National Christian Council of India complained that all the six belonged to one political party, namely, the Congress. *Ibid.*, 67, no. 3 (March 1947):104.

ment of India, and this committee presented a 13-point memorandum to the Constituent Assembly. The memorandum pleaded for guarantees for religious freedom both for the individual and religious organizations and institutions (very much as it is incorporated in the present constitution).[75]

The 27th session of the All-India Christian Conference was held in Bombay on 24 and 25 March 1947. The Honorable Dr. John Mathai, member of the Interim Government (under the prime ministership of Jawaharlal Nehru) presided. Messages were received from national leaders like Nehru, Mrs. Vijaya Lakshmi Pandit, Mrs. Sarojini Naidu, and Premier B. G. Kher of Bombay.[76]

India won her independence on 15 August 1947. Highly respected leaders of the Indian Christian community like H. C. Mukherjee, John Mathai, and Raja Sir Maharaj Singh advised the Conference that it should be completely disbanded as being unnecessary in free India. With the partition of India and the setting up of Pakistan, there was great opposition to all communal parties and most likely the Christian leaders did not want the community to be suspected of harboring communal sentiments and distrust of the majority.

The Conference was disbanded in 1947 only to be reorganized in 1953. Y. Santram of Delhi served as its general secretary until 1963. The present general secretary is David Shaw, an ex-member of the Legislative Council of Bombay.[77]

How did the Conference function at the local level? Even though the All-India Conference of Indian Christians was established only in 1914, local Indian Christian Associations did exist before that, as we have seen. The Indian Christian Association of Madras was established in 1880 and by 1914 there were Christian Associations in many places like Bombay, Delhi, Punjab, and U.P. They seem to have been mainly centered around towns and cities and did not have much (if any) membership in the rural areas.

In 1926 the *Guardian* commented that most of the Indian Christian Associations did not function properly and that they

---

75. *Ibid.*, nos. 6–7 (June–July 1947) :323.

76. *Ibid.*, no. 3 (March 1947) :104.

77. Interview with Y. Santram, December 1966. In 1966 some Christian leaders formed the "All-India Christian Union" for helping Christians to contribute more effectively for nation-building and strengthening Indian secularism. See *NCCR*, August 1966, pp. 324-62, for a report of the formation of this organization.

had little or no place in the community at large. "They . . . not infrequently consist of a small coterie of Indian Christians in towns, who in no way are representative of the community as a whole." These groups were often dominated by one or two families or even by a few individuals. The paper quotes the example of the ICA of U.P., which voted in favor of communal representation and suggested a list of names from among which one might be selected for the Legislative Council. But the panel consisted mainly of names from one family only![78] Many local associations did not follow the All-India body in its policy of repudiating communal representation and advocating joint electorates.

The All-India organization attracted the participation and leadership of many outstanding Indian Christians. B. L. Rallia Ram was its secretary for twenty-five years.[79] Many Indian Christian leaders of independent India like Raja Sir Maharaj Singh, H. C. Mukherjee, and John Mathai were active in the Conference and the Conference certainly gave encouragement and support to their leadership.

At present, Indian Christian Associations continue to function in several cities of India, including Delhi, Madras, Ahmed Nagar, and Calcutta. But in many other places, such as Bangalore, they have become defunct. The fact that the 1966 membership of the Association in New Delhi was only 300 shows that it is not very representative or active as an organization now. In Delhi and Madras, most of the activities are social. Occasionally they bring certain grievances of the community before government authorities.[80]

Christians and Communalism

In understanding the forces of *communalism* in India with reference to the Christian community, we may perhaps accept Smith's definition of the word as referring to the

functioning of religious communities, or organizations which claim to represent them, in a way which is considered detri-

---

78. *Guardian*, 11 November 1926, p. 518.
79. *Ibid.*, 12 April 1945, p. 119.
80. Interview with Indian Christian Association officials in Madras and Delhi, December 1966. Also see *Indian Christian Association, Delhi, Golden Jubilee 1911–1961, Souvenir.*

mental to the interests of other groups or of the nation as a whole.[81]

While the roots of communalism go back to the coming of the Muslim rule, and perhaps to the establishment of caste systems in India before that, its institutionalization in modern India's political history may be traced to the passage of the Indian Council's Act of 1909, which provided for separate Muslim electorates in most of the major provinces.[82] In 1906, Lord Minto had enthusiastically supported Muslim demands for the same.[83] In 1916, through the Lucknow Pact between the Indian National Congress and the Muslim League, the former accepted the principle of separate electorates. Even though the Montagu-Chelmsford Report of 1918 disapproved of communal electorates, the Government of India Act of 1919 provided for communal representation not only for Muslims but also for Indian Christians and some other minority communities. The Government of India Act of 1935 also provided for separate electorates, with a specified number of reserved seats, for Muslims, Indian Christians, and some other minority communities.[84]

What was the attitude of Indian Christians to communalism in general, and to the system of separate electorates and reservation in particular?

With certain notable exceptions, most Indian Christian opinion in 1918 was in favor of having communal representation in elections. It was felt that the community had special problems and rights that could be dealt with only by elected Christian representatives. Roman Catholics, on the whole, supported this position. There were also bickerings between Roman Catholics and Protestants regarding alleged breach of election pacts to the latter's advantage at the time of the election for the Imperial Legislative Council.[85]

K. T. Paul was one of the notable exceptions to those having this general attitude. He consistently opposed the principle of communal representation throughout his public career. His career illustrates enlightened Christian opinion regarding this problem.

---

81. D. E. Smith, *India As a Secular State*, p. 454.
82. *Ibid.*, p. 85.
83. See chap. 2 above, section on The Indian National Movement and the Establishment of the Secular State.
84. D. E. Smith, *India As a Secular State*, pp. 85-87.
85. "Indian Christians in the Council—Editorial," *Guardian*, 4 May 1923, pp. 207-8.

He and Datta are credited with changing Indian Christian opinion to one of opposing separate electorates. In 1914 he was telling young men of the harm that "the communal spirit has done for us in the past and what a revival of it in the present will mean."[86] In 1920 he gave evidence before the Joint Committee of the Houses of Parliament against communal electorates and favoring instead reservation of seats in a general electorate.[87] At the First London Round Table Conference also, he advocated reservation of seats in a general electorate rather than communal electorates. In this he was supported by the Indian Christian Association. But the other Christian delegate at the Conference, Pannirselvam, a Roman Catholic, supported communal electorates, in which he was but reflecting the opinion of the majority of the Indian Catholic community.[88]

At the time of his death in 1931, eminent national leaders praised K. T. Paul for opposing "demands for any special concessions for Christian Indians" (Gandhi) and for "nationalizing Christianity" (Rajagopalachari).[89]

The All-India Conference of Indian Christians, as we have seen from the last section, consistently opposed the principle of communal electorates. For example, in 1919 when provisions were made for separate electorates for Indian Christians where they were in considerable numbers, Madras Christians opted for the same. But in 1924 the Bangalore session of the All-India Conference said that the method of separate electorates would lead to unhealthy growth of sectarian feelings in the Christian community itself and urged the Indian Christian Associations in the Madras Presidency to take steps to rectify the situation.

The *Guardian* and the National Christian Council of India were both opposed to communal electorates. The *Guardian* wrote in 1926:

> How can we, *qua* Christians, ask for "representations" in the legislature? The legislature is not a religious congress or a "parliament of religions". . . . Communalism, we make bold to say, is the acid test of Indian Christianity.[90]

In an editorial, the *National Christian Council Review* (the offi-

---

86. *Intelligencer* 55, no. 8, quoted in Popley, p. 85.

87. *Ibid.*, p. 216.

88. *Ibid.*, pp. 191-92.

89. *Ibid.*, p. 242.

90. "Indian Christians and Indian Politics," Editorial, *Guardian*, 7 January 1926:5-6.

cial organ of the National Christian Council of India) said that

> the communal electorates . . . means that an Indian the mo-
> ment he enters into public life ceases to be an Indian and be-
> comes either a Hindu or a Muslim or a Christian. . . . For the
> growth of the political life of the country, it is clear that the
> present policy of grouping the followers of each religion as
> distinct political units should be given up and Indians of all
> religions, or of no religion, of a particular territory or area
> should be classified together as one unit for the exercise of their
> common civic and public rights.[91]

Even though most of the enlightened Indian Protestant leadership have been opposed to communal or separate electorates, there
have been suggestions that Christians should organize themselves
(apart from organizations for spiritual and religious purposes)
for their political, educational, and social welfare. The same editorial raises the question whether the Christian community should
organize itself to defend the rights of converts. This should be
studied, but the editorial cautioned: "We cannot as Christians lay
claim to any privileges to which we are not entitled as Indians."[92]
A correspondent from Delhi reminded the readers of the *Guardian*
that there was for Christians

> the imperative need for setting their [Christian community]
> house in order and of organizing themselves not for the purpose
> of opposing any other community but in order to fit themselves
> for rendering the best service to their country. They, along
> with others, have a contribution to make to the body politic.[93]

The All-India Conference of Indian Christians, the Indian Christian Associations, the Catholic Union of India, and similar organizations were organized with similar objectives in view. Some
were opposed to communal representation and communalism,
while others were for both. We shall consider later what place,
if any, such organizations have in a secular state.

The case of the Syrian Christian community in Kerala is interesting in this context. V. K. S. Nayar, a political scientist in
Kerala University, includes the Syrian Christians among the
"communal interest groups" in Kerala. Unlike the other communities in Kerala, which exercise political pressure through community associations, the Syrian Christians exercise it through

91. *NCCR* 46, no. 10 (October 1926):580.
92. *Ibid.*
93. "Our Delhi Letter" 20 March 1930, p. 140.

their church hierarchy and through newspapers controlled by the churches or members of the community.[94]

The Syrian community had followed communalistic policies from the beginning of the century. First they aligned with the Nair community against the Brahmin influence in the state administration in Travancore. But when the Nairs became well organized and dominant, Syrian Christians joined with the Muslims and the Ezhava (low-caste Hindu) community to fight Nair domination and form the Joint Political Congress. They demanded and got reservation of seats in the legislature and appointments to civil service on the basis of the numerical strength of each community. This led to the decline of Nair representation in these areas.[95]

With the merger of the Joint Political Congress in the State Congress, which became a unit of the Indian National Congress, Syrian Christians became powerful within the National Congress. Nayar explains the highly unsettled political history of Kerala since independence in terms of communal power politics, in which one of the most important groups has been the Syrian Christians. The Syrian Christian community, as a community, played a decisive part in the ousting of the Kerala Communist Government in 1959 through popular agitation. In the subsequent general election, the Syrian Christian bishops gave explicit directions not to vote for Communists.[96] However, there are no Syrian Christian community organizations that take a direct part in politics, and the hierarchy does not involve itself in politics directly except in extraordinary situations, such as when the Communist government came into power in 1957. The most recent example (early part of 1972) is the active participation of many bishops in the agitation of the governing bodies of private colleges (mostly Christian and Nair) against alleged attempts on the part of the state government to exercise more control over the institutions. Most Christian political leaders are members of different political parties. But the allegation has been that the Syrian Christians used the Congress Party (and now, the break-away Kerala Congress Party also) as the vehicle for Christian communalism through dominating it. Bishops are also accused of meddling in politics.

---

94. V. K. S. Nayar, "Communal Interest Groups in Kerala," in D. E. Smith, ed., *South Asian Politics and Religion*, p. 186.

95. *Ibid.,* p. 178

96. *Ibid.,* p. 189.

During the whole period of the national freedom struggle, Christians were generally praised by national leaders for squarely opposing communal electorates and for not demanding special rights. At the time of the writing of the Constitution, Christians, under the leadership of H. C. Mukherjee, not only renounced separate electorates but also reservation of seats. This, as we have already seen, brought forth unstinted praise from national leaders like Nehru and Patel and was a factor in the good will shown by the majority community in complying completely with the request of Christian leaders for guarantees of religious freedom, including the freedom to propagate religion and the freedom to conduct schools and have the right to impart religious instruction.

Therefore, as in the case of the freedom movement, Christians have a mixed score as far as their attitude to communalism is concerned. The recognized leaders of the Protestant community were opposed to the principle of communal representation and they carried on this tradition to the time of independence and after. Catholic leadership at first favored communal representation, but at the time of independence joined with the rest in renouncing such claims. But there have always been leaders and sections of the Indian Christian community that thought and acted in terms of narrow communal politics. This does not dim the luster of the Christian contribution to the evolution of a secular democratic constitution for India, that of renouncing all claims for separate electorates, reservation of seats, and any other special privileges.

Current Thinking of the Major Christian Bodies in India on the Secular State and the Role of the Church

The National Christian Council of India

The National Christian Council of India (NCCI) (organized in 1912) represents the major Protestant churches and missions in India. It is the most representative body of the non-Roman Christian community in India and as such has expressed itself on the nature of the secular state in India and the role of the Christian community and that of the churches in it. The NCCI has made representations before the government of India in matters of special concern to the Indian Christian community, and it also serves as liaison between the majority of Protestant foreign missionaries and missionary bodies in India and the government of India.

The NCCI, in cooperation with the Christian members of the Constituent Assembly, had worked for the acceptance of the principles of religious freedom and fundamental rights in the new constitution of India and it enthusiastically supported the emergence of the secular state in India.

According to the NCCI, the secular state is the only practical ideal in a land of many religions. It is also desirable because governments should recognize the authority of a higher moral law. When this is not recognized and the state assumes absolute sovereignty, then they may become instruments of injustice and tyranny.

> Enlightened citizens should therefore keep vigilant and courageously voice dissent when governments deviate from their essential *dharma* to serve the moral ends of men.[97]

The church and the state have different functions to perform in society, and they use different methods. The church is primarily concerned with the salvation of man and uses persuasion and love to achieve its ends. The state is concerned with order, justice, and civil liberty in society and has to exercise coercive power. Because of the differing nature and functions, there must be separation between church and state. Official relations between the two will damage both, and this is true of all religions.[98]

Religious freedom and fundamental rights bring responsibilities to the Christian community. First of all, there is a "Christian responsibility for supporting the state in its efforts to achieve social and economic as well as political justice."[99] The right to religious freedom and the responsibility toward the state are based on the claim that Christ has on all men. But Christian action does not ultimately depend on the permission of the state, even though "rights have their place in human systems as defining the recognition which man may legitimately expect from man."[100]

---

97. *The Secular State in India: A Christian Point of View* (Calcutta: Y.M.C.A. Publishing House, 1954), p. 3. This is the report of a "Consultation on the Secular State in India" sponsored by the NCC and the Study Department of the World Council of Churches.

98. *Ibid.*, pp. 3-4.

99. "Secular Rights and Christian Responsibility," Editorial, *NCCR* 69, no. 2 (February 1949):68.

100. *Ibid.*

It is in this context that the NCCI has constantly affirmed the right of Indian Christians, as well as foreign missionaries, not only to profess and practice their religion but also to propagate it, as is guaranteed by the Constitution. This propagation is part of the essence of the Christian religion. The church, on its part, should be above suspicion as to its motives in trying to convert. "Any taint of selfish proselytism ought to be removed from the fabric of our purposes."[101] Foreign missionaries should particularly respect the religious sentiments of those who are of other religions and should not preach indiscriminately before public audiences.[102]

Religious bodies should not infringe on the rights of others and disturb public order. The secular state naturally cannot allow

> the growth of communal organizations that seek to enhance themselves at the expense of the public welfare, or the security and freedom of other religious organizations.[103]

But the church is not a communal organization. As an institution the church has its place in the nation. The church has the responsibility to represent the interests of the Christian community "within the framework of the organized work of the government." This is necessary not only because large sections of the Christian community (like the Backward Class Christians) are inarticulate but also for the welfare of the nation as a whole. "A healthy public life can only be achieved by this active and responsible participation which Christian people believe they should exercise."[104]

In a "Call to Share in the Life of the Nation," an NCCI Commission recognizes the difficulty of Christians to take part in national movements which equate the nation with Hinduism. "The Christian can join movements whether secular or religious only so far as it does not mean a denial or compromise of his faith."[105] How should Christians share in the life of the nation? Not by forming a Christian political party or association to fight for Christian interests, but by entering secular democratic political parties. But there is a need for "organized effort which avoids the danger of communalism" to educate Christians in moral issues

---

101. *Ibid.*, p. 67.
102. *NCCR* 74, no. 9 (September 1954), p. 363.
103. "The Church and the Secular State—Editorial," *NCCR* 73, no. 11 (November 1953) :442.
104. *Ibid.*
105. *NCCR* 76, no. 12 (December 1956) :486.

in political and public life and offer responsible criticism to the state. It is deplorable that there are no organizations engaged in the political education of the Christian community.[106]

It is necessary for the state to take the initiative in achieving the social and economic welfare of the state through legislation and planning.

But ultimately it is only through voluntary religious, cultural and social agencies that the inner life of culture and community can be reformed and developed along healthy ways.

There is always a place for Christian educational and social agencies within society as voluntary organizations strengthening the moral fiber and democratic spirit of society.[107] It has also to be recognized that legislation is not a panacea for all social ills. Indiscriminate legislation can put unnecessary curbs on institutions that are functioning satisfactorily. For example, Public Trust Acts in some states have caused hardship to well-run Christian institutions.[108]

The Council recognizes the fact that the secular state came about largely because of Nehru's influence. But great numbers of people within and without the government do not understand the meaning of the secular state. This is particularly true about some state governments and some government officials at the lower levels. This, in effect, nullifies the provisions of the Constitution.[109]

As already stated, the NCC serves as a sponsoring authority for the majority of Protestant missionaries working in India. This is done at the invitation of the government of India.[110] The NCC is very much interested in preserving the freedom that foreign missionaries enjoy in doing missionary work in India. This is also the area where Indian public opinion and government authorities are most sensitive. Through direct representations and continuous contact with the Home Ministry, the NCC is involved in solving problems arising out of this and one finds a number of editorials and comments in the *NCCR* devoted to this problem.

The NCC, therefore, welcomes the secular state in India but is aware of the many practical difficulties that churches and re-

---

106. *Ibid.*, p. 487.
107. *Ibid.*
108. *Ibid.*, 73, no. 11 (November 1953) :443.
109. *Ibid.*, p. 442.
110. For the Roman Catholics, the same function is fulfilled by the Catholic Bishops Conference of India.

ligious organizations will face in the working out of its policies, particularly by those in the government who are not in sympathy with the secular-state ideal. The Council exhorts the churches and the Christian community as a whole to fulfill their responsibilities to the secular state. The churches and religious institutions should not demand of the government any special rights that they cannot claim for others also, or that may infringe on the rights of others. The Council sees for itself an important role in representing and being a spokesman for the non-Roman Catholics in their relationship with the government. At the same time the Council also urges the whole Christian community to take part in the social and political life of the country, and it supports the idea of the formation of Christian organizations, non-communal in nature, that would educate the community in its political rights and duties.

The Christian Institute for the Study
of Religion and Society (CISRS), *Bangalore*

The Christian Institute for the Study of Religion and Society (CISRS) in Bangalore has been widely recognized as one of the most important institutes of its kind in Asia. It has close affiliations with the National Council of Churches of India as well as with the World Council of Churches. Many of its publications are the result of consultations and conferences involving a large number of Christian (very often, also non-Christian) thinkers and leaders in India, and these publications may be considered as representing the more progressive social and theological thinking that is going on among Indian Christians.

The meaning of the secular state and its relationship to the Christian community in India have appeared as topics for study and discussion in the publications of the CISRS and have provided the theme for three issues of its Journal, in 1962, 1964, and 1971. Let us examine the major elements of the thinking of the CISRS on these subjects.

In India the word *secularism* is most often used in connection with the idea of a secular state. They are often used identically. Secularism or the secular state has three major components as understood in India: 1) the state is the organ of a national community comprising all the peoples of India, irrespective of differences in caste, creed, religion, language, and the like. All are equally entitled to certain fundamental rights, religious freedom, and to justice, equality, and freedom without religious discrimination; and 2) the state functions as the instrument of modernization of all traditional societies. In legislating for social reform, against, for example, caste discrimination, the traditional religious integration of society will be weakened. For introducing economic and social changes, the separation of social structures from religious sanctions becomes necessary. The state guarantees the right of religious minorities to preserve and promote their cultural identity by establishing their own educational institutions.[111]

In the Indian context, secularism is not an anti-religious dogma but a means of building a common political community where people belonging to different religions can cooperate and work together for common goals.[112] This is called *open* secularism, because it not only guarantees religious freedom but also welcomes useful insights from religion.[113]

The idea of the secular state presupposes the process of secularization. Secularism in society is both inevitable and necessary. It promotes scientific development and human freedom.

Secularisation has become necessary since it provides the basis for common humanity and citizenship in our culturally heterogeneous and class-conscious society.[114]

Secularization is also to be welcomed for the practical reason

that social unity and common objectives of social development in a nation of many religions, should be independent of religious creeds and exclusive religious communal interests.[115]

There are also specifically Christian reasons justifying secularization:

1) God has given a measure of autonomy to society and secular institutions. This should be recognized by religion. The sovereignty of God should not be thought of as the sovereignty of religion and its domination of society.

---

111. "Editorial: The Idea of a Secular State," *Religion and Society*, 9, no. 1 (1962):1. Also see P. D. Devanandan and M. M. Thomas, eds., *Problems of Indian Democracy* (Bangalore: CISRS, 1962), chap. on "Dynamic Secularism," pp. 79–80.

112. *Religion and Society* 9, no. 1 (1962):1.

113. *Ibid.*, p. 2.

114. Devanandan and Thomas, eds., *Problems of Indian Democracy*, p. 89.

115. P. D. Devanandan and M. M. Thomas, *Christian Participation in Nation-Building* (Bangalore: The National Christian Council of India and the CISRS, 1960), p. 153.

The church has no business to dominate or control the state, the university, the family and the arts, and when it has done so, it has perverted itself and stifled the fulfillment and growth of the natural purposes of secular society.[116]

2) The church has the responsibility of reminding civil society of its true nature and destiny, and of the sovereignty of God over society. This the church will be able to do only if it stands apart from society and when both are not completely integrated into each other.

3) Religious institutions (including Christian churches) often succumb to the temptation "to discover the unity of all things, and manifest it in a religious synthesis of society."[117] Religious institutions (or any pseudo-religious system or dogma) in themselves cannot represent the true nature of God's order in its complexity, order, freedom, truth, and so on.

There is a deep Christian truth in the secular protest, namely that the different spheres of human life have a real autonomy and must not be regimented into a narrow unity easily achieved through the religious integration of society.[118]

In endorsing the process of secularization we should be aware of the danger that secularism itself may become as closed and idolatrous as any religious system.[119] Secularism may be carried to the point of denying the religious nature and destiny of man. Communism is an example of this kind of extreme scientific secularism, which is not based on a spiritual foundation.[120]

Indian secularism should be based on

a synthesis of the positive and beneficial values of secularisation and the concepts and beliefs deeply embedded in our culture.[121]

The concept of "unity in diversity" and the composite character of Indian culture provide some basis for the development of such an open secularism.

Here the role of religion is not to dominate and control secular structures and society or to build a religious culture. The role of religions should be to inspire the secular culture from within,

---

116. *Ibid.*, p. 154.
117. *Ibid.*, p. 155.
118. *Ibid.*, pp. 155–56.
119. *Ibid.*
120. Devanandan and Thomas, eds., *Problems of Indian Democracy*, p. 89.
121. *Ibid.*

"so that it may not become self-sufficient but remain open to religious insights."[122] Here it is gratifying to note that some secular leaders are also aware of the need for an ethical and spiritual basis to make society genuinely human, and therefore welcome a secularism that is open to religious insights also.[123]

The working of the secular state has already created some problems. It has resulted in a "substantial loss in national integration and integrity." Secularization has destroyed many of the old loyalties and modes of spiritual integration but has not provided "an adequate alternative spiritual base." There is even a resurgence of old loyalties. A new philosophy of open secularism as described above is necessary to fill this vacuum.[124]

In India Christians too have had difficulty with secularism and for dissociating religion from its Western culture. Here they are on par with the other religions that have had difficulty in dissociating religion and society. But all religions and creeds in India have come under the influence of the Gospel.

Not only as a theological truth but also as an empirically acknowledged fact Jesus Christ is present as Judge and Redeemer in all religions and ideologies of India today.[125]

Christians and those of other religions should involve themselves in mutual dialogue and common confrontation of "problems and responsibilities of modern human existence."[126]

The Syrian Orthodox Church

The Syrian Orthodox Church in India, though it represents an important section of the Christian community, has not actively taken part in the general discussion on the secular state that has been going on in India, particularly in Protestant circles. But members of the Orthodox Church have contributed to the thinking of the N.C.C. and the CISRS, even though the church is not officially a member of either of these bodies.[127]

122. *Religion and Society* 9, no. 1 (1962):2.
123. *Ibid.*, p. 3.
124. Devanandan and Thomas, eds., *Problems of Indian Democracy*, pp. 83-89.
125. "Editorial," *Religion and Society* 11, no. 2 (1964):5.
126. *Ibid.*
127. Even though the Orthodox Church is an active member of the World Council of Churches, for several reasons it has not affiliated itself with the N.C.C. or the Kerala Christian Council. The Knanaya Diocese of the Orthodox Church has taken membership in the Kerala Christian Council.

However, two prominent members of the Orthodox Church have written about problems relating to secular state and secularization. Paul Varghese, formerly an associate general secretary of the World Council of Churches and presently the Principal of the Orthodox Theological Seminary at Kottayam (Kerala) has given a stimulating Orthodox rejoinder regarding the current discussion on these topics. The other member of the Orthodox Church to whose article I shall refer is C. I. Itty who is an associate secretary of the World Council of Churches. His views are very close to those of the CISRS and the NCCI.

Father Varghese, while agreeing with the need for secularization, warns that in recent discussions

> our "theology of the secular" comes perilously close to the "philosophy of the secular" which is being increasingly adopted by emerging nations like India and Ghana.

He continues:

> We assert the Lordship of Christ over the secular, but if we have nothing to say about the relationship between the secular and the transcendent, the Lordship of Christ means little that the average secular humanist could not also affirm.[128]

He asks the question whether "we need to abandon our awareness of the transcendent realm in order to be intellectually respectable in the eyes of our secular scientists."[129]

Rather than secularism, he sees "pluralism" as the right concept for India. He calls the ideal type of society in a secular state a "pluralistic human community."[130] For the Christian, this concept of "pluralism" comes not from social experience, but from the doctrine of the Holy Spirit. The Holy Spirit dwells in the community of the church but works in the whole creation. The Holy Spirit works in the individual. He is related to God and other persons. The work of the Holy Spirit is also characterized by freedom. It is this work of the Holy Spirit that gives unity to the plural society. The church manifests this unity. The Church is a channel for His work in the human society as a whole.[131]

---

128. "Why We Serve," *Frontier* 7 (Spring 1964):46.
129. *Ibid.*, p. 48.
130. Paul Varghese, "Secular Society or Pluralistic Community?", in Egbert de Vries, ed., *Man in Community: Christian Concern for the Human in Changing Society* (New York: Association Press, 1966), pp. 363ff.
131. *Ibid.*, p. 373.

Father Varghese makes a characteristically Orthodox contribution in affirming the importance of the transcendental dimension in secular society and in defining it in terms of the working and the gifts of the Holy Spirit.

Itty addresses himself to the problem of finding cultural unity in a pluralistic secular society, with particular reference to India.[132] He affirms the need for secularization. He sees a role for the Indian Christian community in three areas, namely,

> the secularization of culture, the development of common values
> and ethos for the national community and the building of a
> national, secular culture on spiritual foundations.[133]

Since his thought is similar to that of the CISRS and the NCCI, it need not be elaborated here.

In reviewing the Christian contribution to the Indian secular state, we see that there are both positive as well as negative points to make. Large numbers of Indian Christians at all times supported British rule as well as the communal approach in politics. The church hierarchy was on the whole conservative. On the other hand there were many Christians who were active in the nationalist movement from the beginning, and later many became ardent followers of Mahatma Gandhi and Nehru. The educated sections of the community on the whole supported the nationalist movement. In Travancore and Cochin, Christians were at least as enthusiastic as any other community in these states in agitating for self rule. We have noted the worthy contribution that Christian leaders in the Constituent Assembly made to the drawing up of a Constitution for India embodying the principles of a secular state. The contributions that the various Christian bodies are making to the continuing discussion on the secular state is also worth noting.

Protestant Christians seem to have made the greatest contribution toward the evolution of the secular state. This is evident from the fact that most of the nationalist Christian leaders were Protestants. H. C. Mukherjee, Raja Sir Maharaj Singh, K. T. Paul, and other such leaders are examples. This may be because Protestants were better educated and came more under the influence of Western liberal ideas. They were less constrained by the official

---

132. C. I. Itty, "Dynamics of a Pluralistic Society—The Indian Experience," in *ibid.*, pp. 308-29.

133. *Ibid.*, p. 326.

church hierarchy than was the case with the members of the Roman Catholic church.

The Syrian Christians were primarily influential only in Travancore and Cochin before independence. Here Orthodox and Roman Catholic as well as Protestant groups of Syrian Christians (even though not the churches as a whole) took active part in the freedom movement.

4

How the Churches Have Responded to the Challenges and Opportunities Provided by the Secular State—Some Instances

The secular state offers the churches and the Christian community many challenges and opportunities for service. The churches and the Christian community found themselves in a new context and atmosphere when India gained its independence in 1947. The overlordship of the British government was removed and the Christian community found itself a small but important minority community in independent India, her destiny to a great extent dependent on the actions taken by the majority community, namely, the Hindus. However, as we have seen, a liberal and secular Constitution was drawn up and the rights of all citizens and particularly those of the minorities were guaranteed by the Constitution.

The churches also found themselves freer than before of the charge that they were an appendage of British imperialism in India. The nationwide celebration of the Nineteenth Centenary of St. Thomas's visit to India and similar occasions provided Indian national leaders like Nehru and Rajendra Prasad (the first President of India) with opportunity to remind the nation that Christianity was as Indian as any other religion in India. The removal of the stigma of direct or indirect, real or imagined, connections with the British Raj gave the churches in India greater opportunities for serving India as a genuinely Indian church.

127

The transfer of control of church properties and of church administration from foreign mission bodies to Indian churches and the Indianization of the church hierarchy, which picked up even greater momentum after 1947, gave the churches in India a more genuinely Indian look. The Syrian churches in Kerala were autonomous and self-governing from the beginning, even though they had maintained ecclesiastical relations with the Syrian Patriarch of Antioch, as had the Roman Catholic section with the Pope of Rome. Since independence, Syrian Christians from the former native states of Travancore and Cochin (now Kerala) have gone to all parts of India in much greater numbers than before and have established congregations and built churches of their own. Individual Syrian Christians have come to occupy important positions in government, industry, educational institutions, and the like. This wide scattering of the Syrian Christians has afforded opportunities for Indians in general and leaders in particular to realize that Christianity has an old and respectable history in India and that Indian Christianity is not exclusively Western in character but also has an important Eastern counterpart.

The secular character of the Indian state and the newly affirmed Indianness of the Indian churches have offered new opportunities and challenges for the Indian churches. New forces are at work in India in the field of economic development, changing social structures and relations in the areas of education, industrialization, urbanization, politics, and so on. How are the churches responding to these new situations and opportunities for service? They also face challenges from situations and movements that are not always friendly. The rights of Christians as a minority to profess, practice, and propagate their religion and to maintain educational and other institutions—these and other rights have been challenged by the state and certain communal forces in the country. In accordance with its nature, the Indian secular state often takes the initiative in social legislation that may affect certain religious practices of religious communities. Laws affecting social evils like the dowry system have been passed. This affects certain Christian communities also. And there are other instances of legislation that affect Christians as a community. How have the churches and the Christian community responded to these? An examination of specific situations and instances where the Christian community had to make certain responses and took certain positions and attitudes in the context of the secular state will show us the direction in which the Christian community is moving. This will in turn help us to formulate our views regarding "new patterns for service and witness for Christians in the Indian secular state." For this purpose, we shall examine certain situations and issues to which the churches have responded. These instances cover different areas of the country and different groups of Christians as well as widely differing issues and problems.[1] An examination and appraisal of these varied situations will help us in our understanding of the involvement of the Christian churches in the Indian secular state.

Industrial Team Service, Bangalore

One notable feature of independent India is its rapid pace of industrialization. The old industrial cities of Bombay, Calcutta, Madras, Ahmedabad, Lucknow, and many others have become even greater industrial complexes. Cities that were comparatively unindustrialized have become new centers of industrialization. Bangalore in South India is a good example of this. In addition, completely new industrial complexes and satellite cities have come into being during the last two decades. Durgapur and Bhilai belong in this category.

Even in the West, where the process of industrialization is at such an advanced stage, the churches have been for the most part rurally oriented, or in any case have shown little interest in the specific problems of industry or of those involved in it as workers or at different levels of management. The Industrial Mission of Sheffield, the oldest mission of its kind in Great Britain, is only about 30 years old, and Detroit Industrial Mission, the oldest of its kind in the United States, is less than 20 years old. Hence it comes as no surprise that in a newly developing country the start of the industrial missions goes back only to 1963. Now there are industrial missions in industrial centers like Durgapur, Bangalore, and Madras. Bangalore Industrial Mission, known as the Industrial Team Service, is one of the most active and important of its kind in India, and we shall examine its activities to see the church's response to industry in one important city of India, namely, Bangalore.

1. Because the writer is a Syrian Christian, he is personally more familiar with the activities of the Syrian churches of Kerala. For making use of this experience, a larger number of examples dealing with the Christians of Kerala are used.

The growth of Bangalore as an industrial city began as late as the early 1940s.[2] As a result of this industrialization, the general population as well as the strength of the industrial workers grew dramatically. This may be illustrated by the fact that the general population has grown from 7.86 lakhs[3] in 1951 to 12.07 lakhs in 1961. The strength of industrial workers in 1961 was about 3.6 lakhs.[4]

The Industrial Team Service (ITS) grew out of the concern of the people of St. Mark's Cathedral in Bangalore and of its energetic Presbyter-in-Charge, H. F. J. Daniel, for those who worked in this city and surrounding areas at different levels in the various factories and firms. Interest was stimulated by the visit of Paul Loeffler of the World Council of Churches in 1961, when a group of managers and technicians met with him for discussion. The group continued to meet once a month and came to be known as the Loeffler Group. Daniel was connected with this group as well as the Christian Worker's Fellowship, formed a few months later. Soon, it became evident that Daniel needed assistance if he was to continue his ministry to the industry in addition to his ministrations in the Cathedral. The idea of a team ministry arose, and it came into existence in August 1963. It consisted of two clergymen—Harry Daniel and Alan Batchelor, an English presbyter; Mrs. Daniel; Paul Siromani, a layman, and his wife, who is a doctor. Mrs. Daniel was a trained sociologist.

The initial goals of the team were: 1) To give pastoral care to Christians who work in industry; 2) to help Christians working in industry to see themselves as servants of society and not refugees from society, 3) to engage in study and research to see what "Christian presence" means in the various centers of urban industrial life. The "ultimate" goal of the Team was described as follows:

The hope of the Team is that it may be used not only to help the Church serve industry, but to help renew the life of the Church itself. This is why it is initially based on a group of three congregations. Through this we wish to demonstrate that the concern for society should not merely be confined to a team of specialists, but be that of the whole Church. The service to

2. M. M. Thomas and H. F. J. Daniel, eds., *Human Problems of Industry in Bangalore* (Bangalore: CISRS and St. Mark's Cathedral Industrial Team Service, 1964), p. 1.
3. 1 lakh is 100,000.
4. Thomas and Daniel, eds., *Human Problems of Industry* . . . , p. 4.

industry is indeed an end in itself, but we hope that through learning to lose its life in the service of industry, the Church in Bangalore may find its true self.[5]

In addition to the congregation of St. Mark's Cathedral, two small congregations in two housing developments for industrial workers were involved in the work of the team. Even though the team members and the parish belonged to the Church of South India, it was an ecumenical effort insofar as the work had the backing of the Bangalore Christian Council and received cooperation from the (Roman Catholic) Indian Social Institute Extension Service, engaged in similar work.[6]

In practical terms, the three areas of service of the ITS were: 1) pastoral care of Christians in industry, 2) training of laymen and clergy in ministering to industry, and 3) service to industry as industry.[7]

The Team was responsible for the pastoral care of Protestant Christians who came to the industrial complex of Jalahalli, a few miles outside Bangalore, for there were no Protestant congregations already in existence. Later, this work was handed over to the City Mission Group. The Team was also involved in Christian Worker Groups which met in three areas of the city. At St. Mark's, the group, consisting mainly of men occupying supervisory positions in industry, was engaged in the study of certain books. At Jayanagar, a predominantly workers' Church group was particularly interested in organizing a Cooperative Credit Society. At Jalahalli the emphasis was on formal organization and a program of service for the community as a whole.

An Industrial Thanksgiving Service and May Day Service were annual events designed especially to express the church's concern and care for those in industry.

The ITS found that there was a general feeling among Christian workers that the church had nothing to do with the world and that it was against trade unions. They also understood duty in terms of merely obeying those in authority, and there was a horror of conflict. Their personal religion was not concerned with others. One member of the Team was specially responsible for organizing study groups among workers, and through this and other means,

---

5. *Ibid.*, pp. 63-64.

6. *Ibid.*

7. Most of the following information is taken from the ITS publication *Industrial Service News* 4 (May 1966) (Bangalore: Industrial Team Service, St. Mark's Cathedral).

helping workers see their proper place in industry as Christian laymen.[8]

As part of the training program for laymen and ministers for the church's ministry to those in industry, orientation courses for theological students and conferences for Christian workers are held in different parts of South India. Some are intended for local participants and are conducted in the local language. Others attract delegates from all parts of India and the proceedings are conducted in English.

One important part of the ITS program is service to industry as industry. This includes all workers, including non-Christians.

Siromani undertook a three month's course conducted by the Regional Workers' Education Center in Bangalore to become a certified Worker-Teacher. This enabled him to conduct unit-level classes in establishments where there was no Worker-Teacher, to accept invitations as guest lecturer for such classes, and to make some very useful contacts. The ITS also worked on setting up an Information Pool, with the cooperation of union leaders,[9] for the benefit of Trade Unions. An Information Pool with up-to-date comparative information regarding salaries, allowances, and conditions of service would be invaluable for unions at the time of making their Charter of Demands. Some research was also attempted by the ITS.

One member specializes in everything to do with the management. The 1965–66 report (mentioned above) shows that seminars were held for top managers and their wives. There was also a proposal for organizing a management training program on a regular basis. This may be a 4-year, part-time course for middle-managers. It was estimated in 1966 that in the following 5 years India would need 30,000 managers.[10]

Batchelor, the Team member specially responsible for work with managers has become an associate member of the Indian Institute of Personnel Management, which has an active branch in Bangalore. He is also a member of the Rotary Club of Bangalore and is specially active in the Employer-Employee Relations Committee of the Club. The ITS is a member of the Mysore State Productivity Council and has participated in a number of their programs. Members of the Team attended such conferences as

---

8. Notes taken by writer of a talk by the Reverend H. F. J. Daniel at United Theological College, Bangalore, June 1966.

9. The Communist-affiliated unions did not cooperate.

10. Talk by Rev. H. F. J. Daniel at United Theological College, June 1966.

Regional Workshop of the Indian Academy of Labour Arbitrations and Human Relations in Industry organized by the South India Textile Research Association (Coimbatore).

From the foregoing brief description of the origin and nature of the work of the ITS, it is clear that here is an attempt by the church in Bangalore to express its concern for those working in industry and for the problems of industry as such. This has been traditionally outside the pale of the church's concern and influence in India, and in the work of the ITS we have a dynamic example of responding positively to the rapid industrialization that is taking place in India. Even though the number of Christians in industry is comparatively small, this effort helps to show the secular society that the church and Christians in Bangalore are not merely interested in preserving their rights and privileges as a minority but are eager and willing to make their special contribution to the moral and spiritual welfare of those working in industry and to the progress of industry in general.

Reaction to the Niyogi Committee
Report in Madhya Pradesh

In 1954 the government of Madhya Pradesh, one of the state governments, appointed a committee to investigate the charges and counter-charges regarding the work of Christian missions, particularly among the aboriginals and backward peoples. The Christian Missionary Activities Inquiry Committee, as it was officially called (usually known as Niyogi Committee), was headed by M. B. Niyogi, retired chief justice of Nagpur High Court. The committee published its report in 1956.[11]

The activities of the committee and the publication of the report created widespread comment in the Indian press and by leaders both Christian and non-Christian. The report contained sweeping allegations against missionaries and Indian Christians in general. Extremist Hindu organizations like the Hindu Maha Sabha tried to raise anti-missionary and anti-Christian feelings in several parts of India.

A statement made by the Minister of Home Affairs in April 1953 in the Council of States to the effect that the freedom to propagate religion would be restricted to Indians only and denied to foreign missionaries had raised grave misgivings in the minds

11. D. E. Smith, *India as a Secular State*, pp. 207ff.

of Indian Christians. The number of visas granted to missionaries, especially Roman Catholics, was severely cut in 1955. There were also several incidents in the early part of the 1950s when Christian churches and institutions were attacked by fanatic Hindus in some parts of the country.[12] It was a period of crisis of confidence for the Indian church. It is instructive for us to examine how Indian Christians reacted to the activities of the Niyogi Committee and the publication of its highly unjust and provocative report.

After India became independent, within a few years almost all the princely states that were not directly ruled by the British were integrated into the different states of India. As the laws of the British administration did not apply to these princely states, some of them had followed a policy of not allowing missionary work in their territories. But with the incorporation of these states into the Indian Union, missionary bodies took advantage of the new freedom of religion to send missionaries into those erstwhile prohibited areas. Udaipur, Rajgarh, and Sarguja were such states to become part of Madhya Pradesh. Members of the Arya Samaj and other extremist Hindu leaders resented and opposed this missionary work, especially among the tribal people like the Oraons. There was also hostility to Christianity among local officialdom. Because of their partiality to Hinduism, the provincial government officials did nothing to modify the former laws that curtailed religious freedoms. To counteract Christian complaints, the officials sent adverse reports saying that Christianity was denationalizing the converts and that they were communists, and the state and central governments tended to believe them. It was in this context that the Niyogi Committee was appointed.[13]

At the very outset, the Catholic Bishops' Conference and other Christians opposed the composition of the Committee, which consisted of five Hindus and one Christian who had little connection with or sympathy for organized Christianity.[14] A Roman Catholic delegation waited on the Prime Minister (Jawaharlal Nehru) to oppose the appointment of the committee, but he advised that Christians should cooperate with the committee and tender evidence.[15]

---

12. Pothacamury, pp. 21-26.
13. G. X. Francis, "The Background of the Niyogi Report," in A. Soares et al., *Truth Shall Prevail: Reply to Niyogi Committee* (Bombay: Catholic Association of Bombay, 1957), pp. 121-29.
14. Pothacamury, p. 18.
15. Soares, p. 139.

Both Protestants and Catholics protested against the mode of inquiry that the committee followed. It toured different parts of the state and listened without cross-examination to witnesses who were mostly prejudiced. In addition to this, the committee invited written answers to a long questionnaire containing 99 questions. Regarding the prejudicial nature of the questionnaire, the Nagpur High Court made this statement:

> The questionnaire is, indeed, a very long and searching document. Every aspect of Christian life and missionary activity is subject to scrutiny therein. In many places it amounts to an accusation. Some of the questions border upon an inquisition, and may well be equated to a "fishing expedition" on the supposition that something discreditable may be discovered.[16]

The Catholics decided not to cooperate with the Committee in the enquiry. The National Christian Council, even though it protested against the method of the inquiry, still advised Christians to answer the questions so as to assist the committee.[17] In the opinion of most Christians, the inquiry was not conducted in an impartial and judicial manner.[18]

The Report, as was expected, proved to be sensational. It contained not only attacks on missionaries but, in the words of Asirvatham, also "gratuitous and sweeping attacks on the Christian church in India, and in the world as a whole."[19] I shall mention only a few points to illustrate the irresponsible and inaccurate allegations made.

It was alleged that most conversions were brought about by "fraudulent methods" and that conversion compromised the patriotism of the convert. The large influx of missionaries since World War II represented the result of a master plan for world conquest on the part of Westerners. Hospitals and orphanages, it was charged, were conducted merely to get converts, and money-lending was used as a means of conversion.[20]

As far as Indian Christians were concerned, it was alleged that the converts became "denaturalized" and strangers to their own country, and that Christians might one day demand a separate state. The Report stated that "missionary organizations seemed so

---

16. Quoted in Pothacamury, p. 20.
17. "The M. P. Questionnaire—Editorial," *NCCR* 75, no. 1 (January 1955):3.
18. Asirvatham, pp. 41-42. Cf. Soares, pp. 143ff.
19. Asirvatham, p. 42.
20. *Ibid.*, pp. 77-80.

widespread in the country that they seem to constitute a state within a state."[21]

The Committee recommended that foreign missionaries whose primary object was proselyting should be asked to withdraw. Conversions should be controlled severely and the right of propagation restricted to Indian citizens only, and "circulation of literature meant for religious propaganda without the approval of the state government should be prohibited." Social services for backward classes should be the sole responsibility of the state government, and nonofficial organizations should be allowed to run institutions for the benefit of only those of their own religious faith.[22]

The response of the Indian church to this report was not hysterical, as might have been expected, but restrained and rational. Soon after the publication of the Report, the National Christian Council of India sent a circular letter to heads of all member churches and organizations "suggesting that spectacular protests and public statements should be avoided and the Report carefully studied."[23] In August, an enlarged meeting of the Public Questions Committee of the NCCI was held at New Delhi. It was decided to make strong representations to the Madhya Pradesh and Central Governments.[24]

In January 1957, the Standing Committee of the Catholic Bishops' Conference of India made a statement addressed to Catholics. It pointed out that the suspicion against Catholics was not shared by all. It questioned the validity of the method as well as the conclusions of the Niyogi Committee. It cautioned Catholics against adopting an apologetic attitude. The church must defend its rights but it should also do greater service. Suspicion among non-Christians should be dispelled by works of charity and mercy. But the rights guaranteed by the Indian Constitution should be defended by concerted action.[25] The statement reflected not only quiet confidence in the good sense of the majority community, but also a stern determination to defend the rights guaranteed in the Constitution.

Two editorials were published in the *NCCR* on the Report and

21. *Ibid.*, p. 47.
22. "Conclusions and Recommendations of the Niyogi Committee," in Blaise Levai, ed., *Revolution in Missions* (Velore: The Popular Press, 1957), pp. 274-78.
23. "Report of NCC Triennial Meeting, 1956," in *ibid.*, p. 284.
24. *Ibid.*
25. Soares, p. 103.

its recommendations. They pointed out the shortcomings and discrepancies in the Report. They also examined the recommendations and showed that while they were highly impracticable and unlikely to be adopted, if accepted they would be "fraught with grave consequences—to the Christian church in India."[26] The editorials urged careful study of the Report and said:

> We would urge that a dispassionate approach, free from the kind of indignation which seldom promotes sound judgement, is desirable at this time.[27]

Comments were not wanting from responsible Christian laymen. John Mathai, former Finance Minister of the Government of India and then vice-chancellor of Bombay University, said that in the light of the declared policy of the Government of India and assurances from the prime minister, neither the secular character of the state nor religious freedoms were at stake. He praised the contribution of missionaries to India. But, he added, "It is no justification for the vast generalizations which are sometimes made against missionaries as a whole and against the Christian church here and abroad."[28]

M. M. Thomas (present Director of the CISRS), writing in the *NCCR*, commented on the totalitarian and anti-secular implications contained in the recommendations of the Report. He said that he was "more afraid of the political idea it represents and its effect on the future of the state in India than about the effect of the Report on Christianity." He added confidently: "Christianity is an anvil that has survived many hammers. It will outlive one more."[29] He defended the right of Indian citizens, including Christians, to have supranational loyalties, because without it "there is no criterion for judging national policies and the way is open for national imperialism and a totalitarian state."[30] Here we see the issue considered in its widest context.

I have referred to *Truth Shall Prevail: Reply to the Niyogi Committee*, a book by Catholic laymen. Direct and indirect com-

---

26. "The Niyogi Recommendations—Editorial," *NCCR* 76, no. 10 (October 1956) :368.

27. "The Niyogi Report—Editorial," *NCCR* 76, no. 9 (September 1956) : 321.

28. "Statement by Dr. John Mathai," in Soares, p. 104.

29. M. M. Thomas, "The State and Other Spheres of Life," *NCCR* 76, no. 10 (October 1956) :395.

30. *Ibid.*, p. 396.

ments on the subject matter are also contained in *Christianity in the Indian Crucible*[31] and *Revolution in Missions*.[32]

In reviewing the reaction of the churches and the Christian community in India to the Niyogi Committee Report, we might characterize it by listing the following points: 1) both Protestants and Roman Catholics took a united stand on the Report; 2) Christians were sensitive to the implications of the Report, which potentially threatened their religious freedoms guaranteed by the Constitution; 3) the response was not hysterical or tending to the exacerbation of communal feelings against the majority community. It was firm in defending its rights, but also recognized the shortcomings on their side; 4) the issues were understood and explained by Christian leaders in their national context as well, so that non-Christians also could join hands with Christians in opposing the anti-democratic and anti-secular character of the report.

The Christian community acquitted itself well in an extremely difficult and tense situation where the community could have given way to emotionalism. Instead, the community steadfastly held to its faith in Indian secularism and the good sense of the majority, and this response may be said to have further strengthened the secular character of the Indian state.

Christian Reaction to the Communist Government in Kerala (1957–1959)

Kerala Education Bill of 1957 and the Agitation against the Communist-Led Kerala State Government

The southern state of Kerala made history when in April 1957 it voted into power a Communist government under the leadership of E. M. S. Namboodiripad. It made history again when the same Communist government was dismissed from office by the Central government as a result of popular agitation in Kerala, wholeheartedly supported by and spearheaded by the Catholics in particular and the Christian community as a whole in general. Apart from members of the Communist party and its sympathizers, almost all other leaders and people in Kerala supported

---

31. Eddy Asirvatham, pp. 41-53, 77-88.
32. Blaise Levai, ed.

the "liberation struggle," known as *vimochanasamaram* in Malayalam.

In the 1957 election the Communists were the beneficiaries of widespread discontent with the previous Congress Party administrations in the state. They secured 60 seats in a House of 127 and they formed the majority with the support of five independent members of the State Legislative Assembly. The Government of India was anxious to give a fair chance to the first Communist administration in India at the state level.

The Communist government was in power for twenty-seven months, until 31 July 1959, when it was dismissed by the Central government. The Christian community played a key role in this development.

The opposition to the Communist government was centered around three of the four major communities in Kerala—the Nayar, the Muslim, and the Christian. The other major community, the Ezhavas, who belong to the lower economic and social level, on the whole supported the Communists. Thus Christian dissatisfaction was part of the general opposition to the government.

The popular opposition was based mainly on four factors: 1) poor administration; 2) corruption and misappropriation of funds, especially to benefit the Communist party; 3) the breakdown of law and order; and 4) the passage of the Education Act of 1957. I shall deal briefly with the first three factors and in greater detail with the last one.

In spite of the promise by the Communist government to implement the Second Five Year Plan with vigor and enthusiasm, this was not done. Out of nearly eighteen crores of rupees ($24 million) allotted for the second year of the Plan, the Communists were able to utilize barely five crores of rupees ($6.6 million).[33] An Inquiry Commission set up for the purpose found serious irregularities in the purchase of rice from Andhra by the Kerala government. It is believed that much of the money went to the Communist party.[34] The Communist-sponsored Labor Contract Cooperatives were given government contracts of Rs. 25,000 or less without any calling for bids. It was well known that the cooperatives were Communist cells in transparent disguise. The newly formed Toddy Tapper's Cooperatives soon controlled one-

33. Frank Moraes, *India Today* (New York: Macmillan Co., 1960), p. 124.
34. *Ibid.*, p. 128.

third of the toddy industry. The formation of these cooperative societies was one obvious method of strengthening the Communist Party financially.[35]

Soon after taking office in April 1957, the state ministry ordered the police not to interfere in "peaceful" strikes and picketing, but to intervene only in the event of violence. The Communists also encouraged the settlement of industrial disputes by what they described as "mutual consultations and negotiations," rather than by compulsory adjudication when conciliatory efforts failed. The police having first been paralyzed, this was the green light for the Communist Labor Unions to intimidate the management to accede to their demands. The safety of life and property was at stake, but the police interfered in only a few cases. The local Communist leaders virtually dictated to the police, and anybody who was in the bad books of the party leadership was unsafe. Communist cell courts were active in many villages.[36] Political murders and attacks in particular and crime in general increased by leaps and bounds. Murder increased by 47% during 1957–58.[37] Protection of the law was difficult for non-Communists to obtain. In many places they had to band together for self-defense. It was the breakdown of law and order in the state that finally forced the Central Government to intervene.

However, it was the education bill that the Communist government brought forward to curb the role of the private agencies in the education of the state that precipitated the final move against the government by the people. Out of 11,000 educational institutions in the state in 1957, 7,000 were under private management. Of those 7,000 private institutions, about 3,000 were operated by Christian agencies and about 3,000 by Hindu caste organizations.[38] The decision of the Christian managers not to reopen schools after the long vacation in 1959 accelerated the momentum of the popular movement against the government.

The major Christian churches, perhaps for the first time in the history of Kerala churches, took a united stand against the government on the matter of the education bill. They had made representations to the government for two years since the bill

35. *Ibid.*, p. 126.
36. Kainikara Padmanabha Pillai, *The Red Interlude in Kerala* (Trivandrun: Kerala Pradesh Congress Committee, 1959), p. 165.
37. *Ibid.*, p. 159.
38. D. E. Smith, p. 366.

was first introduced in 1957, but their objections were not taken into consideration.[39]

The stated purpose of the Act was

to provide for better organization and development of educational institutions in the state, providing a varied and comprehensive educational service throughout the state.[40]

Many of the provisions of the bill merely codified previous practices or replaced executive orders and were beneficial, especially to the teachers. But there was general skepticism regarding the bona fides of the ministry, and the Christian managers took strong exception to some of the provisions of the bill.

The key provisions of the bill were as follows: teachers' salaries to be paid directly by the government and all fees collected to be remitted to the government; conditions of service of government schools to be applicable to aided schools also; appointment of teachers only from a state register prepared by the state public service commission; power granted to the government to take over the management of any school for five years in case of mismanagement of schools; local people to be associated with the administration of schools.[41] The bill as originally passed contained clauses empowering the government to take over any category of aided schools if this step was considered necessary in order to standardize general education or improve the level of literacy. But these clauses were found unconstitutional by the Supreme Court of India and were modified.[42]

The fundamental objection of the Christian managers to the Education Act was that it took away the freedom of the management to appoint qualified teachers of their choice to their schools. According to the new Act, the public service commission of the state (a government-appointed body) was to prepare a list of teachers for appointment to the government schools and the private aided schools indiscriminately, having in view the probable number of vacancies in the year and that on a district basis. Forty-five percent of the posts were to be reserved for the backward communities and the remaining posts were to be filled ac-

39. C. P. Mathew, "Churches in Kerala and the New Education Act," *NCCR* 79 (August 1959):270.

40. S. C. Joseph, *Kerala the "Communist" State* (Madras: The Madras Premier Co., 1959), p. 156.

41. *Ibid.*, p. 157.

42. D. E. Smith, pp. 366-67.

cording to a communal ratio in open competition. Since almost one third of the total number of schools were Christian, this would drastically have limited their choice in the selection of teachers. They would have been obliged to appoint teachers who were not in sympathy with Christian values, even those who were opposed to them. A former member of the parliament and an eminent Christian educationalist, the late C. P. Mathew, asked:

> May not, however, one expect reasonably that there would be agreement on one point, namely, that the teachers in Christian schools must be largely those who have a Christian sense of values, a Christian outlook on life, a Christian estimation of the significance of man in the universe and a sense of Christian dedication?[43]

All the conditions laid out by the Act had to be fulfilled if the private schools were to receive aid from the government. The Act, however, allowed private schools to appoint teachers from outside the list provided by the government if they did not receive any aid from the government. But conducting such schools (except a few to cater to the children of the rich, who could afford it) would be a practical impossibility, for most of the population would not be able to pay the high fees necessary to run such schools without aid from the government. In government-aided schools, in the lower grades no fees were collected, and in the upper grades fees were very small compared with the expenses involved.

"Vimochana Samaram" or the "Liberation Struggle"

Opposition was mounting against the Communist government during its two-year rule, not because of any one particular legislation or misdeed only, but because of the whole record. But the decision of the State Ministry to implement the Education Act in spite of the popular opposition, led to the decision by the opposition to close down all nongovernmental schools as a protest. The opposition demonstration reached its zenith in June 1959, when the schools were to be reopened after the summer vacation.

Yet, as Nehru declared in the Lok Sabha (lower House of the Parliament) in the debate after the dismissal of the Communist government of Kerala on 31 July 1959, and establishment of the President's rule under Article 356 of the Indian Constitution,

---

43. Mathew, "Churches in Kerala and the New Education Act," p. 271.

the Education Bill in itself did not spark the massive and unprecedented popular agitation against the ministry that began on 10 June and ended seven weeks later on 31 July when the Communist government was suspended.[44] The United Front of Anti-Communists, comprising all the non-Communist political organizations in the state under the leadership of the late Mannath Padbanabhan, fought the government tooth and nail but sticking to nonviolent methods. It is widely believed that V. O. Abraham, President of the Christian School Manager's Association, scored a tactical victory when he was able to persuade the respected Hindu leader to assume leadership of the agitation. The hierarchy and members of the different churches gave wholehearted support to the movement.

As the agitation gathered momentum, the late Prime Minister Nehru advised the state Chief Minister to resign and seek the verdict of the people again at the polls, but the suggestion was not accepted. The movement gathered momentum from day to day, especially with mass arrests and four police firings. Some 10,000 people were imprisoned and more than 80,000 were arrested and then released and 15 people shot dead by police firings. One remarkable feature of the agitation was the mass participation of the highly conservative women of all communities in the demonstrations.[45] Finally the central government bowed to the public will and dismissed the State Ministry. Thus ended the remarkable experiment in reconciling Communist rule with parliamentary democracy.

Two consultations, one held soon after the Communists came into power and the other after they were dismissed, were organized by the Kerala Christian Council in association with the National Christian Council of India and the Christian Institute for the Study of Religion and Society (Bangalore). The papers and findings of the Second Consultation are helpful in evaluating "how Kerala Christians failed or succeeded in responding to a concrete situation."[46]

That the Christian community in Kerala did respond to the extraordinary situation of Communist rule in Kerala is obvious from the way in which most Christians participated in the oppo-

---

44. Moraes, *India Today*, p. 133.
45. Jitendra Singh, *Communist Rule in Kerala* (New Delhi: Diwan Chand Indian Information Center, 1959), p. 135.
46. *Church, Society and State in Kerala: Papers and Findings of the Alwaye Consultation, October, 1959* (Bangalore: CISRS, 1960). Preface.

sition to the Education Act and in the "Vimochana Samaram" ("liberation struggle"). The 1957 Alwaye Consultation had expressed the view that the Communist government ought to be given discerning support. That such support was given in at least some cases is evident from the fact that there was no opposition in the Legislature to the Agrarian Relations Bill. But not much support was given to the Kerala Anti-Dowry Bill and the Christian Succession Act (Repeal) Bill 1958, which was to have extended to Kerala the provisions of the Indian Succession Act.[47]

The opposition against the Education Act seems highly justified and warranted. The enforcement of the Act would have resulted in complete loss of freedom of the Christian minority in conducting schools of their choice and maintaining their Christian character. The Act also contained provisions for indoctrinating children through government control of the production of text books.[48] If the churches and the community had been quiet and had meekly accepted the situation for fear of being branded as communalists, they would have lost their freedom to conduct schools without undue interference from the government. In saving this freedom, they, along with other communities, prevented the government from, in effect, nationalizing education. This would have been injurious to both education and democracy.[49]

This is not to say that Christian schools are run in an exemplary way or that the motives in the opposition to the Bill were completely unmixed. Many so-called Christian schools had nothing distinctively Christian about them except ownership by Christian bodies, and many malpractices, such as asking for special donations from teachers for appointments, were present. Ownership of educational institutions brought prestige, power, and influence to the churches concerned. Many were also merely communal in fighting for the "loaves and fishes" of the privilege to appoint large numbers of members of their own churches to their schools whether they were committed Christians or not. In spite of all this, certain basic principles were involved and the Christian community did great service to the state and the country by standing up for them.

In the case of opposition to the Education Act, the decision

not to re-open their schools unless the Act was withdrawn or

47. *Ibid.*, p. 56.
48. Moraes, *India Today*, p. 131.
49. *Church, Society and State in Kerala*, p. 31.

suitable modifications made therein was taken by the important churches in the state in their responsible councils, committees or assemblies.[50]

But the agitation to remove the Communist government, which involved most members of the different churches, has to be distinguished from the official policy and actions of the churches as churches. This was political action by Christians in the capacity of citizens. The leaders of the churches in their individual capacity also supported the movement. The vast majority of Christians were convinced that the Communists were not practicing democracy in the state and that it was legitimate to agitate to convince the Central Government that the state ministry should be dismissed by the President, using powers that the Constitution bestowed on him for this purpose. As the Second Alwaye Consultation said, "The church should always uphold democratic values and proclaim the principles that ought to govern the different issues facing the country." It adds a caution that

> though the Bishops and clergy, as citizens of the state, have a right to express their opinions on political issues, great care should be taken by them in the use of their official position.[51]

Regarding the method of the agitation, which was "direct action" or "mass satyagraha" directed to paralyze the government so as to force it to resign or be dismissed by the Central Government, many observers outside Kerala, among them many Christians, were opposed to this method. They contended that this would weaken the democratic process in the country.[52] However, public opinion in Kerala and responsible Christian opinion within Kerala justified it on the basis of the extraordinary situation that prevailed in the state. M. M. Thomas wrote during the time of the agitation:

> the "liberation" movement is not the result of political engineering, but represents a spontaneous popular upsurge against the Communist denial in idea and practice, of the common good.[53]

Even though the *status quo* interests of the Christians played a

---

50. *Ibid.*, p. 33.
51. *Ibid.*, p. 58.
52. *Ibid.*, p. 50.
53. *Ibid.*, p. 36.

part in the agitation, he said that the democratic interest dominated the communal and it would be eminently "communal" for
Christians to cut themselves away from the general movement.

The response of the Christian community could only be justified
because of the extraordinary circumstances described above. On
this occasion the major communities sank their communal differences and fought for the preservation of democracy in the state
and Kerala Christians have to be commended for contributing
their full share toward the movement.

But this praise, too, has to be tempered by the fact that the
leadership of the "liberation movement" also represented to a
great extent communalists and traditionalists, including those of
the Christian community. The major "backward" community of
the state, namely Ezhava community, supported the Communists.
In the name of the movement in some places there was repression
of members of the Ezhava and other backward communities. This
cannot be justified. Within the Christian community itself there
are the "backward" and the "advanced" sections. These sections
have not been integrated with each other. So the churches would
seem to favor the maintenance of the *status quo* regarding the
position of the backward classes and hence align themselves with
the reactionary forces in society.

In conclusion it might be said that Kerala Christians have set
a good example in vigorous political action at a time of crisis.
They have fought for democratic values and the defense of their
legitimate rights, which are also in the interests of the nation.
But the same zeal for working for democratic values is not seen
in normal times. Their opposition to the Education Act and the
Communist government would have had greater moral authority
if their educational institutions were not open to the criticisms
of corruption and if they had a better record in integrating
"backward" Christians into the general Christian community.

The crisis that took place in 1972 in university education in
Kerala may be considered a sequel to the situation in 1957 regarding secondary school education. In June 1972 the government
of Kerala decided to lower the tuition rate in private college in
Kerala to the level of fees in colleges run directly by the state
universities, but without compensating the managements for the
loss. The government offered to pay the full salary of the teachers,
but it wanted, in return, more control in the appointment of
teachers and in the admission of students.

The different churches and the Nair Service Society, which run most of the private colleges in Kerala (sixty-eight of them), refused to reopen the colleges after the summer vacation in July and a statewide agitation was launched against the government to protest what the managements considered as undue interference in the conduct of the colleges. Leaders of the Christian churches considered the demands of the government for control over appointment of teachers as infringement of their fundamental right (guaranteed by the Indian Constitution) as a minority community to establish and manage educational institutions of their choice. Bishops of many churches, particularly those of the Roman Catholic church, took the unprecedented step of leading protest marches in person and speaking at public protest meetings. For two-and-a-half months the agitation and counter-agitation by the Youth Congress, many teachers, and leftist-oriented students, produced a grave situation in the state. It was interesting that while most of the official leadership of the churches was against the government policy on this, several Christian members of the State Legislature who were members of the different parties forming the ruling coalition sided with the government or kept silence on the issue.

There were protracted negotiations between the government and the leaders of the communities concerned, but they broke down several times. However, finally a compromise was worked out with the help of some leaders of the Central Government who were particularly anxious to have this issue resolved, since it involved minority rights also. According to the compromise formula, a five-member committee will be constituted for each college to make teacher appointments. The management will choose two members directly and three from panels of names to be supplied by the government and the University. All appointments are to be based on merit, but fifty percent of the jobs are to be reserved for members of the community that runs the college. Admissions of students are also to be on the basis of merit, but with some reservation of seats for members of the particular communities to which the colleges belong and for Backward classes.[54]

Even though both sides claimed victory, it was only a victory of sorts for the private-college managements. They had to concede the principle of some government control over the matter of appointment of teachers. The government also had to settle for much less than what they had bargained for, but having

---

54. *The Malayala Manorama,* 18 August 1972, p. 1.

established the principle of government control it is more than likely that eventually it will find ways to exercise more control over the management of private colleges.

Here the issues involved were those of the autonomy of private educational institutions and to some extent that of the rights of minorities to manage the affairs of their institutions without government control. The government demands more control, alleging corruption in the management of private educational institutions, including those run by the churches. It is only legitimate that the government be concerned about this problem, and that it demand some control insofar as it provides huge subsidies for the running of these colleges. However, these controls should not lead to the elimination of private agencies from the field of education and to government monopoly in the area.

The growing pressures for more state control over education make it imperative that the churches radically rethink their role in the educational field and see how they can make it more relevant, meaningful, and in line with the changing but just aspirations of society. But the attitude of the churches in Kerala, on the whole, is one of defensiveness rather than willingness to reform and innovate new ways of witness and service, and to purge itself of corruption where it is present.

The Role of the Christian Churches in the
Kerala Election (1965)

The general election held in Kerala on 4 March 1965 was fought more vigorously than usual even for Kerala, because of the special circumstances under which the election was necessitated. The leaders of the Christian churches in Kerala took an active part in the election through their various public statements and pastoral letters issued to the faithful.

The Indian National Congress was in power in Kerala before the election, and the election was caused by the fall of the Congress ministry. The history of the fall of the ministry is interesting, and typical of Kerala. The Chief Minister (the chief executive of the state) was R. Sankar, who belonged to the low-caste Ezhava community. P. T. Chacko, a faithful member of the Roman Catholic church and a popular Christian political leader, was the next most powerful minister in the Cabinet. He was forced to resign on certain charges of personal misdemeanor, which some people claimed were false. Those who followed Chacko's leadership in the party in turn accused the Chief Minister of corruption, and they demanded that proper inquiry should be made regarding the charges and that he should resign. Since their demands were not met by the Congress High Command, fifteen Congress members of the Legislative Assembly withdrew their support of the Chief Minister. The majority in the House was lost and the Chief Minister was forced to resign. The dissident members of the Congress party were expelled from the party and they formed the Kerala Congress party.

The people of Kerala, on the whole, had long been dissatisfied with the internal wranglings of the Congress party, which led to the fall of several ministries. Those opposed to the Communist party, especially Christians, were afraid that the democratic forces of the country would be utterly defeated in another election unless there was unity within the Congress party and they desired that the Congress party should form an election front with other democratic parties. But the many attempts at bringing unity between the two factions of the Congress proved a failure. Meanwhile, P. T. Chacko met with sudden death while on a business trip to the northern part of the state. He had already become a hero to a large section of the people in the Travancore-Cochin area, since it was felt that he was dismissed on trumped-up charges and because he had proved himself an efficient minister in office. His body was taken ceremoniously to his home near Kottayam and people gathered by the thousands at different places to pay their last respects to him. His burial was a grand affair in which many of the Christian bishops and political and social leaders took part, along with a vast concourse of people. Since Chacko was already identified with the new Kerala Congress party, it gained much strength during this period.

The Kerala Congress had the backing of a large number of Christians who opposed the policies and leadership of R. Sankar. The party gained much strength and power from the support it got from Mannathu Padbhanabhan, the undisputed communal leader of the Nair community (high-caste Hindus) in Kerala. He may have had his own reasons for opposing the party led by an Ezhava leader. Sankar was wholeheartedly supported by Kamaraj Nadar, the President of the Indian National Congress. He publicly stated that the poorer and less-fortunate communities of Kerala were pitted against the richer and high-caste communities. A class color was given to the tussle between the two parties.

As the date of the election drew closer, it became even more apparent that unless the National Congress and the new Kerala Congress parties could join together and fight in the election with the cooperation of as many smaller democratic parties as possible, the beneficiary would be the Leftist Communist party, which was the more militant and "pro-Peking" wing of the Communist party of India. Only about six years before, the people of Kerala had gone through the historic "liberation struggle" by which the Communist party, which had come into power in Kerala in 1957, was forced out of office because of the encroachments they had made on the religious and social freedoms of the people.[55]

It is in this context that we have to understand the role played by the Christian community in the 1965 election. In previous elections, too, the Roman Catholic bishops and other Christian leaders had played an important part, but in 1965 bishops from all the major Christian denominations in Kerala and some lay representatives met at Kottayam on 5 January to discuss the political situation in Kerala. It was the practice, in previous years, for the heads of different churches to act independently. The Roman Catholic church was politically the most powerful and it acted through its Bishops' Conference without consulting leaders of other churches. But in 1959, bishops from all the major Christian churches in Kerala had met to discuss how best they could fight against the Communist government. This precedent, and the growing influence of the ecumenical movement, made it possible for the bishops to meet on this occasion. The bishops (ten Roman Catholic and six others) met and discussed the political situation in Kerala and made an appeal to the democratic parties to maintain unity in their ranks.[56] The Conference also appointed a committee to negotiate with the democratic parties to achieve this end. It was very clear that their main objective and hope were the reconciliation between the Indian National Congress in Kerala and the dissident Kerala Congress party. The statement was given wide publicity in the daily newspapers of Kerala. The Committee, under the leadership of the late C. P. Mathew, a former M.P. and a reputed Christian lay leader of the Mar Thoma Syrian church, met Kamaraj Nadar, the President of the Indian National Congress, but nothing came of it. The Congress and the Kerala Congress leaders claimed that the failure of the mission

55. See above, section on Christian Reaction to the Communist Government in Kerala.
56. *Malayala Manorama*, 6 January 1965.

of the committee was due to the stubbornness and intransigence of the other party. Abraham Mar Clemis, one of the bishops, complained that the failure of the mission was reported to the press even before the committee could report back to the Christian Bishops' Conference and so the opportunity for a new attempt was lost.[57]

The Roman Catholic church is the biggest Christian denomination in Kerala and they have 16 Archdioceses with a membership of three million people.[58] The Catholic Bishops' Conference met at Ernakulam on 23 February and issued a statement. The bishops exhorted all the Catholics to use their right to vote and to vote in such a way that a "stable democratic government . . . will work for the good of all the people in the state." For this to happen, it was important that democratic votes should not be allowed to split. Catholics were asked to say special prayers during the period before the election.[59]

As soon as the statement of the Catholic Bishops' Conference came out, Christian leaders in the National Congress and the Kerala Congress parties interpreted the statement as an endorsement of their own party. While the National Congress leaders emphasized the term "stable government," saying that only their party had any hope of forming such an administration, the other party emphasized the fact that the bishops had called for a government that would work for the good of all, and claimed that the National Congress had proved unfit for the same and hence they should be given a chance now. Statements and interpretations came from different leaders. All the major Christian daily newspapers except the influential *Malayala Manorama* were openly in favor of the Kerala Congress, and a general impression was created that the Christian Bishops were, on the whole, in favor of the Kerala Congress, since, according to them, the National Congress had spurned the bishops' efforts at reconciliation between them and the dissidents.

Juhanon Mar Thoma, Metropolitan of the Mar Thoma church and a former President of the World Council of Churches, who had consistently taken an active interest in politics by putting out forthright and fearless statements on previous elections, did the same during this election too. He affirmed the right of Christian religious leaders to give advice and leadership in political

---

57. *Deepika*, 3 March 1965, p. 2.
58. *Ibid.*, 20 February 1965, p. 1.
59. *Malayala Manorama*, 24 February 1965, p. 3.

matters. It was meaningless to say that religion and politics should not be mixed. It was the duty of the church to raise its voice for the good of the country and the people. Christians should eschew communalism and work in politics as a unified body. He exhorted all to use their voting rights and prevent the Communist party from coming into power.[60] He did not endorse either the Congress party or the Kerala Congress.

As the date of the election drew closer, statements attributed to different bishops and leaders were published in the newspapers, endorsing one party or the other. Early in January the head of the Orthodox Church (the second largest Christian denomination in Kerala, with a membership of about 1½ million people), Catholicos Mar Ougen Baselios, had made a press statement (before going to Ethiopia for a church conference) saying that it was his belief that if the democratic administration nurtured by Gardhiji and Nehru was to continue in India, then the National Congress should be strengthened and should win.[61] Since he was away from the country during the time of the election, there were no more statements from him. On the eve of the election, fifty-four members of the Managing Committee of the Orthodox Church (including laymen and clergy) put out a statement strongly endorsing the Congress party.[62] Two bishops also stated that they personally would be voting for the National Congress. Mathews Mar Athanasius, Assistant to the Catholicos, stated that the statement of some members of the Managing Committee did not represent the official position of the church since no decision on this had been made in the Holy Synod. Another bishop, Mar Clemis, also stated that since many church members were ardent supporters of one of the two parties, it would be inappropriate for the church to take a partisan attitude toward either.[63]

Different Catholic bishops had also sent pastoral letters to the people of their dioceses mainly on the lines of the statement of the Catholic Bishops' Conference. In addition, the Archbishop of Changanacherry exhorted the faithful that when there were two acceptable democratic candidates to choose from, they should vote for the candidate most likely to win, so that a Communist would not be the beneficiary of a split in democratic votes. Taking this instruction seriously, one might guess, representatives of

---

60. *Ibid.*, 5 February 1965, p. 3; 11 February 1965, p. 3.
61. *Ibid.*, 4 March 1965, p. 2.
62. *Ibid.*, 3 March 1965, p. 1.
63. *Deepika*, 3 March 1965, p. 1.

thirteen Catholic organizations in the Changanacherry archdiocese met and issued a call to vote for the candidate of the Kerala Congress, since he was the one most likely to win of all the democratic candidates in the constituency. On the other hand, according to the *Malayala Manorama,* Archbishop Attippetty of Ernakulam, who was also Chairman of the Catholic Bishops' Conference, made a statement specifically asking his people to support the National Congress candidate. It was alleged that this was done (in spite of the previously stated neutral stance of the statement of the Catholic Bishops' Conference), because the Congress candidate at Ernakulam was a Latin Catholic belonging to his diocese. In other places also, it was alleged that candidates were supported on communal and personal bases rather than on consideration of any principles.

The statements and reactions of the bishops of the major Christian churches in Kerala are important to be considered, because these people are the main spokesmen of the churches concerned. Prominent Christians are members and leaders of the different democratic parties (and some of the Communist party) and they of course worked for their own parties. Out of the four major Christian dailies of Kerala all except the *Malayala Manorama* supported the Kerala Congress. Both the *Malayala Manorama* and the *Deepika* wrote editorials justifying the right of bishops to give advice and leadership in political matters so long as they were not advocating narrow communal policies. The *Manorama* said that the bishops had expressed their opinions as individuals and that as individuals and as citizens they had the right to give guidance to those who were going astray.[64] Some of the non-Christian papers and leaders had protested against the statements made by bishops as unwarranted meddling in politics by church leaders.

As we review and try to evaluate the role of the Christian community, the first thing that strikes us is that the "role" was played almost exclusively by the hierarchy. Of course, Christian members of different political parties were active in and for their own parties. The fact that a great number of Christians are active in politics is commendable. However, there is little evidence that many of them were conscious of their special Christian responsibility as politicians. The fact that the policy statements of the churches were put out without discussion in bodies including lay representatives is not encouraging.

---

64. *Malayala Manorama,* 4 March 1965.

That almost all the bishops did take a lively interest in the 1965 election is commendable. The ecumenical approach to the problem, though in a limited way, was very refreshing. This is a breakthrough from the traditional pattern of Kerala politics, where not only each religious group but also each sub-caste and sub-group acts independently of the others. It was good that Christian representatives met together to evolve a common policy for the good of the state.

The main effort of the Christian Bishops' Conference was to effect a reconciliation between the National Congress party and the dissident group, the Kerala Congress party. Under the given situation in Kerala, it was essential that the rift should be healed if any democratic party was to come to power. But in this they were unsuccessful. Prominent laymen who were devoted Christians and active in politics were invited to the Christian Bishops' Conference, and the contact committee appointed by the bishops consisted entirely of laymen.

It is a debated question whether the bishops have the right to make public statements or issue pastoral letters to their constituencies regarding the way the people should vote. In an interview, Juhanon Mar Thoma, Metropolitan of the Mar Thoma church, defended the right of the bishops to issue pastoral letters enunciating general principles of action at election time, which should be binding on the people. This they do as the heads of the churches. In addition, they have the right to make public statements in an individual capacity, expressing their personal views about current political issues. Even though some people might mistake it for the official voice of the church, this risk had to be taken. Religious leaders should, for example, speak against the Communist party, since statements made by non-Communist political leaders are not always taken seriously, especially when they speak about other parties. As disinterested leaders who have the trust of their people, bishops should speak out on general issues.[65]

While one may agree with the necessity to speak out against anti-democratic parties, the statements of bishops can very often mean, and were interpreted to mean, that they supported one particular democratic party. In the past the hierarchy gave tacit support to the National Congress on the whole, to the detriment of the growth of democratic opposition parties. In the 1965 election, the Kerala Congress was a serious rival to the National

65. Metropolitan Juhanon Mar Thoma, interview with the writer on 5 October 1965.

Congress and it got support from many of the bishops. However, other democratic parties, though quite insignificant in this election, were not given any support at all. Perhaps this was inevitable in this election and such a position was necessary since only the Communist party would have benefited by further splitting of democratic votes. But churches and bishops have to be careful that they do not always just support the *status quo* and thereby discourage the possible emergence of other vital democratic opposition parties.

Where members of both the National Congress and the Kerala Congress parties were candidates from the same constituency, some bishops seem to have favored one of the two. This inevitably estranges members of his church who support the other candidate. It is advisable that bishops and other official church leaders avoid partisan politics.

There seems to be feverish action by the bishops and Christian leaders at the time of an election or during a crisis. But this is not done in the context of continuing interest and involvement in the political processes of the country, which discontinuity impairs the effectiveness of the activities of church leaders at times of political crises.

The churches have not succeeded appreciably in motivating church members of deep Christian convictions to enter into politics and work through different parties. The churches have not made any real attempt to give guidance to those Christians who are in politics, except in times of crisis. The church should encourage them to apply Christian principles in their thinking and actions, and to maintain high ethical standards in their political activities. It is the inability of the church to inspire many Christians to be thus active in politics that necessitates the involvement of the hierarchy as such in direct political activities. While the church leaders have every right to try to influence the course of political decisions and elections, particularly in times of crisis, ideally this should be done through lay Christians who are active in politics. Institutional involvement of the church in direct political action may make the church seem partisan and impair its capacity to speak to all its members and to all citizens of the state.

Evaluating the performance of Christians and Christian leaders in the 1965 election, Juhanon Mar Thoma said that Christians have not acted according to any principle, but that selfish communal interests and loyalty to particular personalities were the dominant determining factors of their behavior. Christians, he continued, have been the cause of much communalism, and the situation has not changed.[66] Christians have to be exhorted to be active workers in the different democratic parties, and make them strong and healthy, devoid of communalism, factionalism, and parochialism, so that there will be no lack of strong healthy parties contesting the election in a healthy way. They can encourage the polarization of parties into two or three major ones by acting as a reconciling force in the event of a breakdown within parties, even as they did, if unsuccessfully, in the 1965 elections.

Moral and Religious Education in Christian Colleges

Christian higher education has been an important part of Christian missionary work in India and it has made significant contributions to the development and growth of higher education in India. Beginning with the establishment of Serampore College in 1818, the missions and churches started many colleges. Regarding the contribution of the Christian colleges, Richard Dickinson says that in terms of quality and numbers, Christian colleges were prominent before World War II and that they have continued to maintain an enviable record.[67] Dr. Dickinson was the Asia director for the ISS-FERES Project, a joint venture of the World Council of Churches and the Vatican, which made a two-year study of "the role of Christian higher education in national development in India today."

During 1966–67 there were 130 Christian colleges in India offering courses leading to the bachelor's degree or beyond. Of these, 78 were Roman Catholic, 45 Protestant, and 7 under non-Roman Syrian Christians. Approximately 117,000 students studied in these colleges. Forty percent of the students and fifty percent of the full-time faculty in these Christian colleges were Christians. The majority of the Christian colleges are in the south and thirty percent of all colleges in Kerala are under Christian auspices.[68] In India at present, there are 67 universities and 2,700 colleges affiliated with them.[69] The total number of uni-

---

66. Interview, 5 October 1965.
67. Richard D. N. Dickinson, "Indian Christian Colleges: Do They Have a Future?" *NCCR* 88, no. 4 (1968) :193.
68. *Ibid.*, p. 194.
69. *Ibid.*, p. 201.

versity students was about a million, compared to only 300,000 in 1950–51. From these figures we can see that the Christian colleges still make a sizable contribution to higher education in India in that more than ten percent of India's university students are being educated in Christian colleges.

The Christian colleges occupy an esteemed position for their high quality compared to non-Christian colleges. The recent research of Dickinson and his associates shows that Christian colleges have a higher percentage of passes in the university examinations, have better hostel and library facilities, have a higher percentage of women students, and are "appreciated by their alumni for moral and spiritual values they are claimed to impart and for the sense of discipline they inculcate."[70] The compliment given by the Sri Prakasa Report is also worth noting. Referring to the Christian educational institutions it says:

> On the other hand, schools and colleges run under Christian auspices educate students of all classes. Though from the outside they may resemble other institutions, yet the atmosphere inside these institutions is different. . . . We would like to see the atmosphere of these institutions extended to all schools and colleges in the country.[71]

Some of India's greatest leaders have come from Christian colleges, which still attract many good students and faculty.

Noting the place of Christian colleges in the university educational system of India, we may look at the specific question of moral and religious education in Christian colleges. Christian colleges were traditionally considered a part of the evangelistic outreach of the churches. According to a survey conducted in the early 1930s, Christian education was supposed to have had four aims: training of Christian leadership, direct evangelistic influence, the leavening of social life, and the demonstration of new types of education.[72] But now the context in which the Christian colleges fulfill their function has changed radically since independence. How have the Christian colleges met the challenge for providing moral and religious education in the Indian secular state?

---

70. *Ibid.*, p. 203.

71. *Report of the Committee on Religious and Moral Instruction* (New Delhi: Ministery of Education, Government of India, 1964: first published, 1960), p. 10. The Report is usually known as Sri Prakasa's for he was the chairman of the committee appointed by the Government of India.

72. *Guardian*, 46, no. 32 (8 August 1968) :251.

Article 28 of the Indian Constitution stipulates that no religious instruction shall be provided in any educational institution completely supported by state funds. But religion may be taught in schools run by religious minorities and supported in part by the government. Three important educational commissions, appointed by the Government of India since independence, have recommended strongly that some form of education in moral and spiritual values should be given in all educational institutions. The Sri Prakasa Commission Report concluded that

> the teaching of moral and spiritual values in educational institutions is desirable, and specific provision for doing so is feasible within certain limitations.[73]

The Commission quoted with approval the recommendations in this regard of the University Education Commission (1948) (Radhakrishnan Commission). The Radhakrishnan Commission had suggested that in the university students may study the lives of great religious and spiritual leaders, a "selection of a universalist character" from various Scriptures, and central problems of philosophy of religion.[74]

The highly acclaimed Kothari Commission Report of 1966 emphasized the "need to pay attention to the inculcation of right values in the students at all stages of education." It notes that the recommendations of the two previous commissions in this regard have not been acted upon, which will adversely affect the character of the new generation, and states that "It has, therefore, become necessary and urgent to adopt active measures to give a value-orientation to education." Hence, it recommended that the central and state governments arrange for giving instruction in spiritual, moral, and social values in the schools under their direct control. The recommendations of the University Education Commission on religious and moral instruction should be followed. These courses should be taught not by specially recruited teachers but by general teachers, preferably from different communities. The privately managed institutions should also follow the same pattern.[75]

The response of Christian educationalists was on the whole negative to the recommendations of the Sri Prakasa Report. It

73. *Report of the Committee on Religious and Moral Instruction,* p. 17.
74. *Ibid.,* p. 21.
75. *Report of the Education Commission 1964-66* (Delhi: Ministry of Education, Government of India, 1966), pp. 19-20.

was felt that the approach of teaching moral and spiritual values through teaching comparative religion was syncretistic. It was also felt that because of a superficial approach to the study of various religions that this would involve, due to limited time available for such a course, it would not serve its purpose.[76] A Christian study group, which met in Bombay, approved the recommendation that the lives of great religious teachers should be taught before the doctrines about their teachings. For this it was suggested that a life of Christ suitable for non-Christian teachers and students should be prepared.[77] But the group also found the approach of the Sri Prakasa Report syncretistic. There was a lack of appreciation of the distinctive nature of Christianity as well as of other religions.[78] The group also raised the question whether "spiritual values [can] . . . be effectively taught in the liberal humanistic spirit which pervades much of the Report." It was not merely a matter of training teachers only. They must have "faith" as well.

As we look at the history of religion men have always seemed to be religious and value spiritual things in terms of specific traditions and communities.[79]

It was also felt that in the Sri Prakasa Report, the emphasis was on the personal and not on the community, and that the idea of serving the community was not supported by the conception of spiritual values found in the Report.

We see that in India Christians and the state readily agree that religious and moral values should find an important place in any educational scheme, but how this should be given practical form in a multireligious secular state without hurting the sensibilities of various religions is a more difficult problem to solve. While reacting negatively to the current proposals, Christians do not seem to have come up with any alternative plan applicable to all colleges in India.

As far as religious and moral instruction in Christian colleges is concerned, it can be reported that the majority offer religious instruction or Bible teaching to their Christian students and some

---

76. John B. Carman, "The Place of the Study of World Religions in a College's Religious and Moral Education Programme," *Journal of Christian Colleges in India* 1, no. 2 (1968) :65-66.

77. Rev. John Langdon, "The Sri Prakasa Report: A Christian Appraisal of the Committee's Recommendations," *NCCR* 81, no. 1 (January 1961) :21-22.

78. *Ibid.*, p. 22.

79. *Ibid.*, p. 24.

form of special moral instruction to students of other religions. In one survey covering forty-eight Protestant and Mar Thoma Christian colleges, it was found that forty offer religious instruction courses and thirty give courses in moral instruction. But the quality of the courses and the commitment to them leaves much to be desired. Both students and teachers are dissatisfied with the current state of affairs regarding moral and religious instruction. Most students "attend only in order to get attendance or to please the Principal" and the teachers also were apathetic about these subjects.[80] From his acquaintance with conditions in more than a dozen colleges in Kerala and Madras (through personal experience or through friends who are former students or teachers in these colleges), the present writer can corroborate the situation described above.

The causes for the general disarray in this field are many. First there is a lack of Christian teachers who have the interest and who feel competent to teach courses in moral and religious instruction. Even where there is interest, training is lacking. Few textbooks that could be used for these classes are available. One very important reason for the lack of interest on the part of students and teachers is that these courses are not part of the degree requirements, so there are usually no examinations or grades given in them. In recent years, the number of Christian colleges has multiplied to satisfy the institutional ego of the churches or Christian communities concerned, rather than to serve a specifically Christian purpose, and these courses are offered merely as a matter of tradition.

However, there are also creative and positive attempts to improve the situation. There have always been some colleges that honestly attempted to make moral and religious instruction a meaningful exercise, and have to some extent succeeded in doing so. I shall briefly refer to some of the more creative experiments being made to improve the quality and appeal of moral and religious education.

William A. Kelly, in an article already referred to, reports on a training course for college teachers of moral and religious instruction held at Ootacamund (Madras State) during May–June 1967. The course was sponsored by the South India Board of Christian Higher Education and the Student Christian Movement

---

80. William A. Kelly, "Religious and Moral Instruction in Christian Colleges: An Appraisal," *Journal of Christian Colleges in India* 1, no. 2 (1968) :8-9.

of India. The group defined the purpose and aims of moral and religious instruction. It also recommended that religious instruction should be offered to Christians as well as other interested students, and that Christian students should take moral instruction along with other students at some stage in their college course. Teachers of moral instruction should be selected for their conviction of the value of the course, willingness to teach, and their competence and impartiality, irrespective of religious affiliation. The group also emphasized the need for special training for teachers of both moral and religious instruction.[81]

Materials have been prepared by different Christian agencies in recent years for use in religious and moral instruction classes. These include those prepared by the Christian Education Council of South India, those published by Wilson College (Bombay), and the Tambaram Series of Religious Instruction materials. Some of them are meant for use in non-Christian colleges as well. The Xavier Board of Christian Higher Education (Roman Catholic) has also prepared a three-year Moral Science syllabus.[82]

Even though many Christian educationalists have reacted negatively to the recommendations regarding moral and religious education by the Radhakrishnan Commission, and its reaffirmation by the Sri Prakasa and Kothari Commissions, which advocated a comparative study of religions, some leaders have been dissatisfied with this response. John B. Carman persuasively argues that it is not reasonable for Christians to expect non-Christian students to grow to ethical maturity without proper grounding in their own religion. Christians also should study the traditional religious background of India along with non-Christians.[83]

There are a few colleges that have departed from the dichotomy of religious and moral instruction and are offering several courses in the field that both Christians and non-Christians may take. At Isabella Thoburn College in Lucknow and Christ Church College in Kanpur, several courses like "A Comparative Study of Graeco-Roman, Hindu and Hebrew Ethics," "Seeing God through Art Forms," and "Science and Religion" are offered. Every student must take some of these courses and Christian students are required to take some specifically Christian courses in some year

---

81. *Ibid.*, pp. 8-9, 23-25.
82. *Ibid.*, p. 15. See also Mother Anita Horsey, "The Xavier Board Draft Syllabus for Moral Instruction in Colleges," *ibid.*, pp. 71-74.
83. Carman, pp. 67-68.

or years. The Baring Union Christian College in Batala provides a single unified curriculum as a program in General Education. A survey of different religions is taught, usually by followers of the particular religions. Christian students have additional weekly Bible study under the auspices of the Student Christian Movement. Some Roman Catholic colleges require all students to take "Moral Science." Roman Catholic students are given an additional course in Catholic doctrine. A much more informal approach is being attempted at American College at Madurai, which has a Department of Religious and Ethical Studies. The course is meant to be "student-centered" rather than "content-oriented."[84]

In reviewing the problems and prospects for religious and moral instruction in Christian colleges, we should notice the recent establishment of the National Board of Christian Higher Education in India. It is highly significant in that it represents the Roman Catholic, Protestant, and Syrian churches in India, and has the potential to provide significant leadership to Christian colleges in India. The second issue of its Journal was devoted to the problems regarding moral and religious education.[85]

Even though the opportunity and challenge to provide moral and religious education in Christian colleges have always been present since their start, they are presented with these in a more urgent and dynamic way since independence and the establishment of the secular state. The problem is not only how best to provide this instruction in Christian colleges to both Christian and non-Christian students, but also how to provide instruction in moral and spiritual values to all university students in India. The response of Christian colleges to the first part of the challenge is on the whole tradition-bound and ineffective. However, some bold new approaches are being experimented with, and with the organization of the National Board of Christian Higher Education, there is hope that more meaningful solutions will be found and implemented in this area. The lethargy and lack of interest of many Christian teachers and leaders, as well as the lack of adequate purpose and goal in the running of many colleges are, however, major obstacles standing in the way of achieving this objective.

Christians have not so far contributed much to solving the problem of offering instruction in moral and spiritual values in all schools. Christians have, on the whole, been suspicious of any

84. *Ibid.*, pp. 68-70.
85. See references above.

attempts to teach Hinduism and other religions through the media of government-run schools. They are afraid that communal forces will use this opportunity to strengthen their forces and that religious syncretism will become the official ideology of the state. While these and similar fears may be legitimate, Christians should not merely be content with the negative reaction. Here again, it it encouraging that at least some of the colleges are experimenting with new forms of offering such courses, and this may provide some lessons for the nation as a whole in this field.

The Dowry Prohibition Act, 1961, and the Response of Kerala Christians

The payment of dowry has long been a social evil in the Indian society. Because the British government was unwilling to interfere with the personal laws of any religious community in India, no law was passed against it during the British period. But after independence, some of the state governments legislated against the payment of dowry.[86] As a measure of social reform, the Indian parliament enacted the Dowry Prohibition Act in 1961. The Act prohibited the giving of any property or valuable security to either of the parties in marriage (including parents) "as a consideration for the marriage."

The evil custom that the Act tried to prohibit was the common practice of "purchasing the bridegroom" by giving dowry. It often happens that the bridegroom, his parents, or a broker demands the payment of a large amount by the bride's father if the marriage is to be settled. The parents of the girl, who desire to arrange a suitable match for their daughter, are thus forced to give to the prospective son-in-law or his parents an amount that very often they cannot afford. When a father has several daughters and is not very rich, his plight becomes intolerable. Many girls are forced to remain unmarried because their parents are not able to raise the dowry necessary for a match with a suitable youth. Parents often go greatly into debt or have to sell their property to meet this situation, creating much unhappiness and misery.

It is well known that a similar situation exists also among the Syrian Christians of Kerala. Most of the marriages are "arranged

86. The Andhra Pradesh Dowry Prohibition Act, 1958, and the Bihar Dowry Restraint Act, 1950.

marriages," as elsewhere in India, and an important part of the marriage negotiations is to determine the amount of dowry that will be paid to the bridegroom or his parents at the time of, or shortly before, marriage. When a bridegroom is supposed to have highly desirable attributes such as a higher education, well paid job, social status, and the like, the amount of dowry that he will ask is much greater than what a bridegroom with lesser qualifications can aspire to get. Thus marriage often degenerates into a financial transaction. "Nowadays a marriage is sometimes thought of as much as a business deal to increase capital as anything else. . . ."[87] All the evil effects mentioned in the previous paragraph are the result.

This is not to ignore the fact that many young men and their parents refuse to give undue importance to financial considerations when arranging marriage. In those instances the dowry, when it is given and received, represents a voluntary gift from the parents of the bride to the couple. Here the dowry does not entail hardship for the parents of the girl, for only an amount (in cash and/or in ornaments) that they can afford is given.

There are also some advantages to the dowry system. It enables parents to find a suitable partner for a daughter, even when she is not very good-looking.

If the daughters are not well educated and

if they are below average in their physical appearance, it is rather hard for the parents to find a suitable husband without payment of a good sum as dowry.[88]

Under the prevailing system of arranged marriage among Syrian Christians, the dowry system assures that almost all girls will be married. The dowry can act as social security. Among Syrian Christians the dowry is paid in lieu of the daughter's share in the father's property. Since this is often given in cash, it prevents fragmentation of property and also forestalls disunion and enmity between brothers and sisters regarding the division of the paternal property. It can also provide a good start in life for the couple, in many cases.

During their rule from 1957 to 1959 in Kerala, the Communist government proposed legislation to abolish the dowry system. (The reform never came into force.) A study done among middle-

87. L. W. Brown, *The Indian Christians of St. Thomas*, pp. 178-79.
88. George Kurian, *The Indian Family in Transition* (The Hague: Mouton and Co., 1961), p. 81.

class, well-educated Syrian Christians living in rural and in urban areas (outside Kerala-Bombay) showed that most of the former considered it as "interference in the private life of citizens." The majority of those who lived in the city (Bombay) considered the law "progressive and good but difficult to enforce." Many of those who were opposed felt that the Communist government had proposed the legislation as "a strategy to bring down the social and economic position of Christians." The negative reaction of the Syrian Christians resident in Kerala may have been colored by the general antipathy toward, and mistrust of, the Communist government.[89] From general observation it may be said that, more and more, educated young people even in Kerala are against the dowry system.

While the Dowry Prohibition Bill was being discussed in the Parliament, representations made by leaders of several Syrian churches that the Syrian community should be exempted from the purview of the Bill were successful.[90] No specific exemption was needed because it was argued that the Syrian Christian practice of giving *Streedhanam* was different from *dowry* as defined in the Act. However, no attempt was made to incorporate clauses in the Bill by which the Syrian Christian practice of giving dowry, by whatever name it is called, would come under the working of the Act. When one member of Parliament enquired whether the government would think of amending the Christian Succession Act on which the practice of giving *Streedhanam* was based, the Law Minister stated that he would not undertake any legislation concerning a minority community without first consulting that community.[91] It may be noted that the Act excluded *Mahr* (dower, in English phraseology), which is a "sum of money or other property which the wife is entitled to receive from the husband in consideration of the marriage" in the case of persons to whom the Muslim Personal Law (Shariat) applied. It is government policy to leave alone personal laws of minority communities as far as possible until they themselves ask for change.

In his article referred to above, V. O. Abraham (a Syrian Christian lawyer) persuasively argues that from a legal point of view *Streedhanam* is to be distinguished from dowry. The former

---

89. *Ibid.*, pp. 79–80.
90. E. V. Mathew, "Towards a Uniform Law of Succession," *Guardian*, (22 February 1968), p. 59.
91. V. O. Abraham, "The Dowry Prohibition Act and the Payment of Streedhanam." Typed MS, p. 13.

is in effect an amount in lieu of the daughter's share of her father's property, and not something that is paid as "a consideration for the marriage." *Streedhanam* is a right of the woman and not a *quid pro quo* for the marriage. Furthermore, it is the absolute property of the Christian wife, whereas dowry is not. Abraham also shows that *Streedhanam* is recognized as such in the Christian Succession Acts of Travancore (1916) and Cochin (1921), which are still operative as far as Syrian Christians in these former native states (now part of Kerala) are concerned.[92] It should be noted that according to the Christian Succession Acts referred to above, the daughters are not entitled to any share of the father's property except the *Streedhanam*.

To understand the response of church leaders to the prohibition of dowry, we should also refer to the connection between *Streedhanam* and a tithe (known as *pasaaram*), equivalent to ten percent of the *Streedhanam*, which was given to the church.

> This convention represented a voluntary gift from the bride who on her marriage became a member of her husband's church, and was thus separated from her own parish church.[93]

The percentage given to the church varied somewhat, but in the past this marriage tithe constituted one of the main sources of church income. Church authorities were afraid that if the payment of *Streedhanam* was prohibited, the custom of giving a percentage of it would also vanish. Abraham argues that *pasaaram* is not inextricably connected with *Streedhanam*, that even when the latter is not paid, the former is paid to the church on the basis of a conventional sum considered suitable for the family.[94] Even now there are certain Syrian churches in which *pasaaram* has no relation to *Streedhanam*. However, it should be admitted that in most Syrian churches the payment of *pasaaram* is closely linked to the payment of *Streedhanam*, and the removal of the latter might adversely affect the former. The opposition of the church leaders to the Dowry Prohibition Act as it applied to their community may in part have been motivated by the institutional interests of the churches they represent.

E. V. Mathew also claims that this opposition shows the upper middle-class orientation in the thinking of the leadership. He says that within the organizational set-up of the churches, the voice of

---

92. *Ibid.*, pp. 4–8.
93. Pothan, p. 66.
94. Abraham, pp. 17–18.

the poorer sections of the community, which suffer most from the dowry system, is not heard.

> [The] churches cannot but reflect their essential upper-middle class characteristics because of its organizational set-up. Due to a built-in conservatism of the vocal middle-class, the churches have missed their true role and sensitivity.[95]

The church may be too middle- and upper-class oriented, and the needs of the poor are not given proper consideration.

I have already suggested that part of the opposition to the Act may be attributed to the fact that in Kerala it originally was proposed by the Communist-led government. Some leaders may have felt that anything proposed by the Communists should be opposed.

Church leaders are not uniformly blind to the evils of *Streedhanam*. Some bishops have made appeals to the membership not to demand as *Streedhanam* an amount that the girl's parents cannot afford to pay. Bishop Abraham Mar Clemis of the Knanaya diocese set Rs. 3000 ($400) as a ceiling for the highest *Streedhanam* to be paid. Even though not strictly followed, this has had a moderating effect on the amount of *Streedhanam* given and received in the diocese. He has also set up a fund to help the poor members of the church who found it difficult to raise any amount for *Streedhanam*. Recently a nonprofit organization has been set up under Christian auspices, to help poor people in this regard.

In evaluating Christian response to the Dowry Prohibition Act, we may say that, even though *Streedhanam* among Syrian Christions, when properly understood and practiced, does not represent an evil custom and does have positive values, as generally practiced it has all the evils of the dowry system as a whole. Hence the churches have been insensitive to the needs of social reform in their midst. They have been motivated more by the narrow economic and institutional interests of the churches than the welfare of the people, especially the poor.

It is unfortunate that the churches have not realized the implications of Article 35 of the Indian Constitution, which directs that India should have a uniform civil code. Even though the government of India has been very cautious in suggesting changes in personal laws affecting minority communities, the communities concerned should themselves take the initiative in getting these

---

95. Mathew, p. 59.

laws changed to conform to the law as it applies to the majority of the people of the country. The Syrian Christians could also have set a good example to other minority communities in this respect.

The picture of the churches that emerges from this situation is the church as the defender of the status quo. Because society changes rapidly, unless the church also learns to change and even give leadership to change, it will became an anachronistic institution in the secular Indian state.

Organizations of Christian Professional Groups

The vast majority of the Christian community are lay people. The clergy and the professional leaders of the churches form a very small percentage of the total membership of the Christian community. Their prime duty and calling is to help in equipping the Christian community spiritually as well as in other ways so that they will be able to fulfill their role as individuals, as churches, and as a community in India. The Christian community consists primarily of the laity, and only through their active participation can the Christian community's role in the secular state be fulfilled.

One Indian Christian conference made the following statement about the church's responsibility to the laity in training them for service to the world:

> Since the strong conviction is now growing in the church that informed and committed participation by laymen in the so-called secular areas of profession and civic life is the most significant factor for transforming society in Christ, we should urge laymen and women to equip themselves with the Christian insights for their various avocations and consciously to plan out Christian witness in their work both as individuals and groups.[96]

How far have the churches acted upon the discernment of the importance of organizing Christians in various professions and walks of life and equipping them with Christian insights so that they are able more effectively to discharge their duties not only to the church but to the community at large? Let us examine briefly the work of one well-established and two new Christian

---

96. "New Patterns of Christian Social Witness in India—Nasrapur Findings III," *Religion and Society* 7, no. 1 (1960) :61.

professional organizations. The well-established organization is the Christian Medical Association of India; the new ones are the Kerala Seminar for Christian Writers and Journalists and the Kerala Seminar for Christian Lawyers. The first is an all-India organization, whereas the other two are state organizations.

The Christian Medical Association of India (referred to henceforward as CMAI) can be said to be the medical wing of the National Christian Council of India. It is an organization of Christian doctors. It has a Para-Medical workers' section and a Nurses' Auxiliary. Some of the objects for which the Association is established, according to its constitution, are to prevent and relieve human suffering in the Christian spirit, to promote mutual help and greater efficiency among Christian doctors, and to hold conferences and to publish relevant literature.[97]

In 1967 the CMAI was associated with the Christian medical work carried on by about 250 hospitals, 120 rural health centers and dispensaries, 16 tuberculosis hospitals, and 51 leprosaria. The Association has regional units in different states and is affiliated to similar organizations in West Pakistan and Burma. Through the National Council of Churches in India, it receives help from the World Council of Churches and different mission boards in the West. In 1967, the donations from India were Rs. 29,353 and the donation from foreign sources, Rs. 21,935 ($1 = Rs. 7.50). Some of the recent activities of the CMAI have been the following:

1) The Family Planning Project. This was started in 1966 with the help of the Church World Service, Oxfam, and other agencies. More than 120 hospitals associated with the CMAI are taking part in the Project. The Project includes maternal and child care and a comprehensive education program with competent field teams touring various regions. On 5 February 1968 a Conference on Family Planning of the Christian Hospitals was held in Delhi at the invitation of Chandrasekhar, the Minister for Family Planning in the Indian Cabinet. All expenses for the conference were met by the government of India.

2) During 1967–68, a survey of Christian hospitals was undertaken on an interdenominational basis by a team of Indian and overseas representatives. This was to enable the Indian and overseas church bodies to decide upon new strategies for medical mission work in India in the future.

---

97. *The Christian Medical Association of India: Constitution, By-Laws and Memorandum of Association.* As Revised January 1963, p. 7.

3) The Central Board for Training of Auxiliary Medical Workers has continued to do good work in training laboratory technicians, radiographers, physio-therapists, and medical social workers. The program is to be enlarged to include hospital administrators and hospital chaplains. The Nurses' League, with its Examination Boards, is associated with the training of nurses in about 80 hospitals.

4) The Joint Tuberculosis Fund distributed Rs. 70,000 worth of anti-T.B. drugs to 131 hospitals, and indigent beds have continued to be maintained in 13 sanatoria in 1967.

5) Biennial conferences were held in 1966 and 1968 (the last one being the 20th biennial conference) and regional conferences are also held. Delegates also attended international conferences.

6) A secretary for preventive medicine was again appointed in 1967 and has been active.

7) One Sunday is set apart as Hospital Sunday, and cooperating churches are requested to send the collections on that day for the work of the CMAI. Since 1967, a Week of Prayer for Christian Medical Work is also observed in February.

8) The Journal of the Christian Medical Association is published monthly.[98]

From the foregoing survey we see that the CMAI is engaged in organizing and helping those Christians in the medical and paramedical professions. It is commendable that the Association is engaged in charitable as well as nation-building activities. Under the former category comes its work in hospitals and sanatoria, providing funds for the upkeep of indigent patients (in the T.B. clinics), distributing medicines, and so forth. In the latter category, it is involved in training para-medical workers, providing examination and accreditation services for a number of nursing schools, and working in preventive medicine. Perhaps the most important task that the CMAI is involved in in this category is the Family Planning Project, for India is engaged in a mammoth program in family planning. The fact that the Union Minister in charge of family planning invited the CMAI members for a conference is indicative of the fact that it is doing important work in this field.

The CMAI seems to be aware of the need for modifying the

---

98. The above information is from the following leaflets published by the CMAI: "The Christian Medical Association of India: Annual Appeal for Donations, July 1968," "Hospital Sunday 12th February 1967," and "Week of Prayer for Christian Medical Work 1st December 1967."

strategy in medical mission work in India so as best to serve the changing needs of India, evidenced in the recently conducted survey of hospitals. It may help churches and the Christian community as a whole to rethink their role in this field.

While the CMAI seems to be involved in vast institutional projects, from the present survey it is not clear how far it is catering to the needs of the Christian doctors and medical workers as individuals. Only insofar as they are helped to see their Christian responsibilities and to fulfill them will the CMAI be truly effective.

The CMAI is primarily a Protestant organization, just as the NCCI is. The Executive Secretary of the NCCI points out that

> the CMAI mostly organises those who are serving in Christian hospitals, but not those doctors or nurses who are working under secular auspices.[99]

This curtails the effectiveness of the Association. Christian doctors and nurses working under secular auspices too have to be helped to see their duties as Christians in the profession and to discharge the same to the fullest extent possible. The CMAI is still very much dependent on foreign financial aid and this too will have to be changed. The government may control the inflow of foreign aid by way of finance and personnel, and the Association will have to become self-supporting.

I shall now briefly refer to the two other organizations already mentioned.

The Kerala Christian Writers and Journalists Fellowship was jointly sponsored by the Roman Catholic Journalists' Association and the Kerala Christian Council in 1965. In the third annual seminar held at Kottayam (Kerala) in May, 1968, sixty participants of different churches, representing daily newspapers, church magazines, and weeklies, took part and discussed the topic: "Social Justice and the Role of Christian Writers and Journalists in Promoting It." Through a resolution, the Seminar appealed to journalists and writers "to wield their pens to quicken social conscience and to put down corruption in the institution of the church and in public life." Regarding Christian magazines, it was suggested that in order to foster the ecumenical spirit, they should accept articles from writers of other denominations than their own. The Seminar also passed resolutions condemning actions of the Orissa and Maharashtra governments restricting religious

---

99. Letter of M. A. Z. Rolston dated 21 August 1968.

freedom. Another important action of the Seminar was to present merit awards to six eminent Christian writers in recognition of their special contribution to Malayalam literature.

While the Fellowship is still in its beginning stages, it seems to have great possibilities in organizing Christian writers and journalists, whose numbers are considerable in Kerala, and to encourage new people to enter the field. These writers and journalists represent those who work both for secular and Christian publications and those who are independent writers. Regarding the Fellowship, K. A. Mathew, secretary of the Kerala Christian Council, says that it can be an effective force for "the renewal of the church and reconstruction of society."[100]

Another example of a Christian professional organization is the Seminar for Lawyers organized by the Kerala Christian Council in December 1967 at Ernakulam, the seat of the High Court of Kerala. About thirty, including some nonlawyers, discussed the topic "The Role of Law in the Service of Man in the Changing Society in India." Papers were presented not only by those who subscribed to the traditional Christian faith but also by a Christian who is a Marxist advocate and an official of the Communist-led government of Kerala at that time. Some eminent non-Christian lawyers also took part in the discussions. The seminar emphasized the educative role that law can play in the context of radical changes taking place in society. It was also pointed out that Christians should take an active part in the making and improvement of laws.[101]

The Seminar appointed two committees for continuing work. One was for studying from the angle of people's welfare the social enactments of the different legislatures in the country as well as the judicial judgments upon them. The second committee, consisting of the Christian advocates of the Ernakulam bar, was for taking steps to initiate an organization of lawyers to render free legal aid to poor people, who may fail to get justice for lack of funds to engage legal counsel. Even though this is not clear from the report, it may be inferred that the seminar was the first step in the formation of a Christian Lawyer's Association.[102]

It is significant that Christian lawyers met together to discuss

---

100. "Kerala Seminar for Christian Writers and Journalists," *Guardian* 46, no. 23 (6 June 1968) :183-84.

101. K. A. Mathew, "Lawyers' Seminar held by the Kerala Christian Council at Ernakulam," *Religion and Society* 15, no. 2 (1968) :73.

102. *Ibid.*

their special responsibilities as Christians, and in doing so they met with theologians as well as men of other faiths and no faith. They have also taken steps to give practical shape to some of their conclusions and recommendations.

Christian professional organizations may become an important means of helping the Christian laity to fulfill their responsibilities to the Christian community and the nation. I have referred to organizations in the medical, legal, and literary fields. Two of these are only regional organizations in their beginning stage. There are a number of vocations and occupations where Christian organizations may help the Christian laity in these areas to think through their Christian responsibilities to the nation and act effectively as a group.

There are two inherent dangers in the formation of exclusively Christian organizations. One is that they may become parochial in their outlook and define the purpose of their organization merely to foster their own interests or that of the Christian community. But a true understanding of the Christian mission should make such organizations outward looking and open-ended.[103]

The other danger is that Christians may withdraw from involvement in secular professional organizations, where they also have a duty to be involved and through which they may be able to wield greater influence in serving the interests of the nation. Christian professional organizations should not demand exclusive loyalty and commitment from their members so that they cease to be effective members in their secular professional organizations.

While much needs to be done, it is good that the churches are showing an awareness of the possibilities in this area. Now such organizations seem to be limited primarily to the educated professions. But there is still need for such Christian organizations among farmers, factory workers, artisans, and the like. This is not to say that in every field Christians should organize themselves separately. But in many instances, such organizations could perform a useful function.

Planning in the Syrian Orthodox Church

In a secular state, both religion and state should be open to creative influences from each other. We may look at the idea of

---

103. See below, chap. 5, section on Service.

planning that has been accepted within the Syrian Orthodox church as a result of the direct influence of the concept of the five-year economic plans accepted and practiced by the government of India since independence. The government of India first established a Planning Commission in March 1950 and the First Five Year Plan was put into operation in 1951.[104] Since then, two more Five Year Plans have been implemented and the country now is in its fourth.

Among the hierarchy perhaps the first person to introduce the idea of long-term planning in the Orthodox church was Metropolitan Abraham Mar Clemis. When he was consecrated and took charge of the Knanaya diocese (one of the several dioceses in the Syrian Orthodox church in India), he announced a five-year plan for the spiritual, social, and economic improvement of the diocese. The idea of long-term planning was well received by the people, and with the help of the Knanaya Association (elected representative body of the diocese) he was able to achieve many of the goals that had been outlined in the five year plan.

There were no five-year plans in the diocese since then until recently. The Knanaya Association discussed and approved a three year plan on 10 August 1968. Some of the programs then outlined are the following: 1) put greater emphasis on the religious education of the people; 2) each parish should build at least one house and give it to a family that does not own its own; 3) build a student's hostel at Kottayam; 4) publish a history of the diocese in English; 5) found a religious order for women; and 6) enlarge the educational loan fund.[105] From previous experience it may be expected that with such focused planning, more of the objectives will be achieved than without a plan. We may also notice some of the socioeconomic programs that are in tune with the nation-building activities of the state.

The Syrian Orthodox church as a whole had been wracked with internal divisions for almost five decades and it was only in 1958 that peace was established between two rival parties in the church. One of the early actions of the reconstituted Malankara Association Managing Committee (elected by the Malankara Association, which is the most representative assembly of the Indian Orthodox church) was to appoint a Planning Committee for the whole

104. Chester Bowles, *Ambassador's Report* (New York: Harper and Brothers, 1954), p. 159.

105. "Pastoral Letter from Abraham Mar Clemis Metropolitan," *Edessa Magazine* (Malayalam) (15 September 1968), pp. 10-11.

church under the presidency of Metropolitan Abraham Mar Cle-mis. A number of laymen prominent in different walks of life, including politics, were appointed to the Committee, along with priests. The Planning Committee appointed three subcommittees: on education, theological seminary, and organization. These sub-committees, again consisting of eminent priests and laymen of the church, drew up reports on how to improve the administration of the church, the educational institutions of the church (like primary and secondary schools, colleges, etc.), and the theologi-cal seminary of the church.[106]

In spite of the excellent suggestions given in the reports, no long-term planning was undertaken by the church as a whole. The main reasons were the conservatism of the church leadership and the organizational disarray at the level of the denomination as a whole. The constituent dioceses were better organized, and as in the case of the Knanaya diocese, were better able to implement such plans. But the idea of planning is something that has ap-pealed to the people and it is possible that, as the church gets more efficiently organized at the interdiocesan level, the Planning Committee may become really active.

These attempts at long-range planning by setting up a plan-ning committee and drawing up five-year plans show the inter-action of ideas between church and state. Even though the idea of long-range planning in itself is by no means a new one, the fact that the attempts at planning coincided closely with the five-year plans of the Indian government lead us to believe that the inspira-tion has come from this source. Since the Orthodox church has had little direct contact with the Western churches, the idea was not imported through them. Even though the Orthodox church has not succeeded markedly in this area, the very attempt shows the possibilities of being open to insights from the state.

Conclusion

We have examined some instances of how the churches have responded to the challenges and opportunities provided by the secular state, also varied situations under which the churches have acted. In many instances the churches have acted positively and creatively so as to further the best interests of the Christian com-

---

106. Malankara Association Managing Committee, *Planning Committee Reports on Education, Theological Seminary and Organisation*, n.d.

munity as well as the state. The work of the Bangalore Industrial Mission and of the organization of Christian professional groups is a good example.

In other instances the churches were more concerned with their institutional self-preservation than with the greater interests of the nation. Some of the reactions of the Kerala churches to Communist rule in Kerala and their response to the Dowry Prohibition Act betray this. Most often, the motives are mixed. Sections on religious education in Christian colleges and planning in the Orthodox church show that often beginnings have been made in the right direction but that the churches must still travel a long way before it may be claimed that adequate responses have been made.

The churches and the Christian community should always be undergoing a process of growing up into their full potentialities. The reaction to the Niyogi Report has shown that the community can react firmly to a serious situation without getting hysterical or unduly defensive. The community and the churches have to develop concepts of themselves that are theologically and sociologically adequate, because their responses to the opportunities and challenges presented in the environment of the secular state will depend on this to a great extent. Having examined some of the ways in which the churches have actually behaved in the past, we may now explore some of the principles and patterns that should guide Christian action in the Indian secular state.

5

New Patterns for Service and Witness for Christians in the Indian Secular State

In the previous chapter we examined some instances of Christian participation in the national life of India. Having seen how the churches reacted in a few instances, we may now survey some of the areas in which the churches should be involved in the life of the Indian secular state, and the principles that should guide it in this involvement and participation in national life, noting the need for and principles of Christian participation in politics. It is being belatedly recognized that if Christians are to make their rightful contribution to national life, it can be done only in cooperation with non-Christians. We shall observe some of the issues involved. In the Western secular democracies, minorities have played an important part in the evolution and preservation of religious liberty. We shall explore the special role of the Christian community as a minority in India in strengthening the secular nature of the Indian state. Christian service is of the essence in the practice of the Christian Gospel. Perhaps the greatest impact that the Christian community has made on the Hindu community is through service. It is important to discuss the place of service in the strategy of Christian action in India today. We shall also note some of the emerging patterns of church-state consultation and cooperation in India. In the discussion of these various aspects of Christian service and witness in the Indian secular state, I shall make particular reference to Indian Christian thought in these areas.

Christian Participation in Politics

What are the distinct contributions that Christians and the

177

Christian community of India have to make to nation-building in this country? Why should Christians soil their hands with the business of politics? Do Christians in India have any special contribution to make to national politics, apart from their being Indian citizens like every other citizen of India? In our secular state, can any special role be allowed for a religious group in politics or in other spheres of life? These and similar questions arise constantly and have to be answered from time to time.

Why Christians Should Participate in Politics

It is axiomatic, though not always in the focus of our attention, that all citizens of a democratic state have a responsibility to take part in the political life of the country. Despite this, there are many who fail to act on this principle. Among these are Christians, who strive for the salvation of individual souls alone, considering that to be the proper calling of Christians, and hence politics remain outside their field of concern. What is the Christian insight that will meet the objection of such Christians to involvement in politics, and that will reinforce the genuine interest that all the citizens of a democratic state, including Christians, are expected to take in the political life of the country to which they belong?

The biblical understanding of God's action in history belies the thesis that Christians should have nothing to do with politics. Like the Communists, Christians take a lively interest in history and the historical processes because of their understanding of the nature of God and the Incarnation, which should impel them to take a more-than-casual interest in politics and programs of social welfare and reform.

Loyalty and obedience to God, and love of neighbor are of the essence of Christian social and personal ethics. A wholehearted commitment to both these principles would thrust a Christian headlong into politics, using the term in its widest sense.

God is the Lord of history and this is the biblical understanding of the involvement of God in history. In the Old Testament, Israel's history may be viewed as a political drama in which God and the Israelites were co-actors. As Bishop John A. T. Robinson (of *Honest to God* fame and also an eminent biblical scholar) says in one of his essays, entitled "The Gospel and Politics," that recognizing God as the God of history meant taking responsibility *for* history. The Israelites considered history as purposive.

To them, "historical absenteeism was simple atheism."[1] Moses and Nehemiah may be considered as much political leaders as religious, and the Prophets made many pronouncements that were nothing if not political—all this in obedience to God. Christ, the new Moses did not follow the way of violence but chose the way of the "Suffering Servant," but he announced the coming of the Kingdom of God *within history*. St. John's declaration, "The word was made flesh and dwelt among us," is an indication of the process of God's identification with history. Such understanding is most inclusive and comprehensive.

Love of neighbor ought to involve a Christian in politics. It means being concerned for the poor, the stranger, the sick, and the suffering. This love of neighbor is a corollary to loyalty to God as the Lord of history. Responsibility for history should mean concern for persons.[2] Nathan protested to David when he sent Uriah to the battlefront merely to get rid of him so that he could marry Uriah's wife, and Elijah the prophet of the Lord could not keep silent when Ahab the king became greedy for Naboth's vineyard and unjustly wrested it from him. Jeremiah said of king Josiah, "He judged the cause of the poor and needy. . . . Is not this to know me? says the Lord." Here to act justly is to care for the poor; i.e., right politics is equated with true religion. To know the God of history means just this.

In the life and teachings of Jesus there is an even stronger connection between loving God and loving one's neighbor, for Jesus says, "whatever you have done to the least of these, you have done to *me*." "I was hungry, thirsty, naked, sick, a stranger and in prison." Being concerned for one's neighbor in our day and age means being concerned with food production, water supplies, housing, hospitals, prisons, refugees, and so on.

> And if in our day you really think you can be concerned for these things, or rather for your neighbor in them, namely, at the level of personal kindness and without being drawn into politics, you are simply being escapist.[3]

Both love of the Lord of history and love of neighbor involve one who is committed to the biblical faith deeply in political activities.

---

1. John A. T. Robinson, *On Being the Church in the World* (London: S.C.M. Press, 1960), p. 112.
2. *Ibid.*
3. *Ibid.*, p. 114.

Recent ecumenical Asian theology has placed a great deal of emphasis on the Christian basis for social concern in general and political action in particular. Several aspects of God's work in Christ in the world are stressed in this connection.

Most important here is the understanding of the scope of Christ's redemptive work as social as well as cosmic. It is a Gospel of redemption of not only the whole human race but also of the whole created world. Christ reconciled "all things to Himself." So the church's witness to Christ's redemption should include the message of the renewal of society. Christ's message of salvation calls not only for conversion of the individual but also the renewal of society.

The Church must be active in promoting an atmosphere in which individuals can grow and mature spiritually:

> Man is a unity of body and spirit and his true nature is realized in society. The life of the person is deeply influenced by his material environment and by his membership in the community. The church and the Christian must be concerned about any threat to the welfare and dignity of persons arising from particular economic, social and political situations.[4]

Now, as never before, political decisions control the economic, social, and other aspects of the life of a nation, and no effort should be spared to create an atmosphere of spiritual freedom in which persons can grow and develop to their full capabilities. This is possible only when Christians take a deep interest in politics.

A narrower but equally important question, that of safeguarding religious liberty, not only for Christians but for all, should induce Christians to take an active interest in politics. This is especially urged in a situation where Christians are in the minority, as in India. They have a right and duty to work to safeguard the interests of the community, especially of sections that suffer because of economic and social disabilities. This is the *raison d'être* of Christian participation in politics.

Christian Attitudes toward the Functions and Goals of the State

Men have oscillated between two views of the state—1) the

---

4. East Asia Christian Conference, Inaugural Assembly, Kuala Lumpur, Malaya, 1959.
The Witness of the Churches in the Midst of Social Change: A Survey of Ecumenical Social Thought (Kottayam, India: C.M.S. Press, 1959), p. 8.

state as an institution ordained by God, and 2) the state as a necessary evil that should be got rid of in course of time. Romans 13 has been used to justify the theory of the divine right of kings and to absolutize the authority of the state. The proponents of *laissez-faire* capitalism want the state to provide a framework of law and order with minimal interference in the life of the people so that people may freely pursue their economic, social, and spiritual ends. To the Communist the state "is the product and the manifestation of the irreconcilability of class antagonisms,"[5] and the state is to be finally abolished. But while it exists, the state is to be an instrument of social change.

In Roman Catholic theory

> the state is viewed 1) as a "perfect" society, 2) as an order embracing and respecting a hierarchy of ends under the common good, and 3) as a moral organism.[6]

This implies that the state is autonomous within its own sphere, subject to the fact that the ultimate end of man, which is his salvation, is beyond the governance of the state and that each state is a member of a community of nations. The theories of state of Continental Protestants range from the depreciation or denial of the state to its deification.[7]

A balanced and realistic view is found in the pronouncements of the Oxford, Tambaram, Amsterdam, Evanston, and other ecumenical conferences of the Protestant and Orthodox churches. The "message" of the Oxford Conference said:

> We recognize the state as being in its own sphere the highest authority. It has the Godgiven aim in that sphere to uphold law and order and to minister to the life of its people. But as all authority is from God, the state stands under His judgement. God is Himself the source of justice of which the state is not the Lord but servant.

As early as 1938 the Tambaram Conference called upon the church "to take an attitude toward the state which is positive and constructive, not merely negative and critical." The later conferences, including those of Asian churches, recognized the important role of the state in promoting social justice and human

---

5. Walter G. Muelder, *Foundations of the Responsible Society* (New York: Abingdon Press, 1959), p. 103.
6. *Ibid.*
7. *Ibid.*, p. 106.

welfare in general. The Bangkok Assembly of the East Asia Christian Conference (1964) endorsed and amplified the previous statements, which lay down as fundamental the basic goals that the Christians should set before the newly independent nations of Asia.[8]

Modes of Christian Participation in Indian Politics

1. By Christian churches. I have already referred to the Christian imperative to be active in politics. But what about the church as a religious body? The church as the body of Christ is to be the instrument of Christ's will on earth. It is the inescapable duty of the church, therefore, to obey Him in all fields of human activity, including politics. The church is bound to "interfere" in politics "because it is by vocation the agent of God's purpose, outside the scope of which no human interest or activity can fall."[9] The church's mission transcends mere political action while including a genuine concern for politics. The church should seek to influence the life of the country in all its aspects, including political life.

The main avenues along which the organized churches may act in politics lie in indirect action. Since the churches include all kinds of people, belonging to different political parties, the church should not identify itself with any single political party. It may, on the other hand, be necessary for the official spokesmen of a church to warn against certain parties because of their essentially anti-Christian and anti-national character. But this right has to be judiciously employed. The church or the Christian community may lend active support to a specific program of one political party when such a program is deemed necessary to secure the larger interests of the country.[10]

The most important arena for the church and church leaders is, however, not in politics but in theology and Christian ethics. The churches have a right to speak on the *moral and ethical aspects* of political issues. They should observe restraint in passing opinion about technical and strategic issues, except where these

---

8. See *The Christian Community within the Human Community* (Containing Statements from the Bangkok Assembly of the E.A.C.C., February-March 1964, Minutes, Part 2), pp. 21-24.

9. William Temple, *Christianity and the Social Order* (London: S.C.M. Press, 1950; Penguin, 1952), p. 21.

10. Devanandan and Thomas, eds., *Christian Participation in Nation-Building*, p. 49.

involve grave moral and religious questions. A continuous interchange of ideas between theologians (both lay and clerical) and Christian leaders on the one hand, and lay technical experts and political leaders on the other, could be very productive in evolving national policies that give due consideration to moral values without sacrificing national interests. The church has a great responsibility always to warn the nation against a moral complacency that absolutizes the nation's values and policies at critical times. At the same time it should not fall into the temptation of giving merely idealistic but irrelevant answers that do not deal with the real dilemmas of the nation.[11]

Several Asian ecumenical pronouncements have given specific suggestions as to the methods of political witness that the church may employ.[12]

In the United States, the Roman Catholic church and the major Protestant denominations maintain agencies in the nation's capital for influencing the government in social action and legislation. Raymond Wilson of the Friends Committee on Legislation gives the following as the main reasons for denominational representation in the nation's capital: 1) To support the government on right policies; 2) To oppose the government on wrong policies; 3) To urge necessary government action; 4) To help churches to take action where government action is unnecessary or inappropriate.[13]

Regarding the Methodist church in the United States, Stotts and Deats suggest that the Methodist senators and representatives in Congress (they numbered nineteen and seventy-four respectively in the eighty-sixth Congress) should be in regular communication with Methodist church leaders in Washington to learn what their church believes about the principal social issues they have to deal with. The church, by maintaining representation in the Capital, can give encouragement and moral support to the

---

11. John C. Bennett, *Christians and the State* (New York: Charles Scribner's Sons, 1958), pp. 270-72.

12. In this connection, attention may be drawn to pp. 24-29 of the E.A.C.C. booklet, *The Witness of the Churches in the Midst of Social Change* (cited above), where the methods of political witness are dealt with under six heads: a) Relevant Preaching, b) Prophetic Ministry, c) Life of the Local Congregations, d) Teaching Ministry and Political Education, e) Strengthening the Roots of Democracy and f) Political Participation of Christians.

13. Herbert E. Stotts and Paul Deats, Jr., *Methodism and Society: Guideline for Strategy* (New York: Abingdon Press, 1962), pp. 261-62.

Christian legislators in their effort to promote social action consistent with Christian principles.[14]

Major Christian churches in India, separately and/or through ecumenical channels (e.g., through the National Christian Council of India) should maintain agencies in New Delhi as well as in state capitals through which the churches may influence the government in the right direction on relevant issues. They should particularly keep in touch with Christian legislators and give them the assurance of the church's support in fighting for social justice, human dignity, and freedom. A committed Christian legislator is stronger if he has the moral backing and support of the church. The same discriminating support should be given to non-Christian legislators, leaders and groups who are fighting for goals consonant with Christian principles. Preliminary steps have already been taken by some Christian agencies for representation in New Delhi.[15]

2. *By individual Christians.* This leads us to understanding the duty of individual Christians in politics. It is through their direct involvement in politics that Christian principles are brought to bear upon the life of the Indian nation. Since we have and believe in a parliamentary democracy, Christians are morally obliged to join such political parties as are working for the welfare of the people and for international peace and good will. Each Christian should exercise his franchise responsibly and help in the political education of the less politically conscious fellow citizen.

He should also support all the progressive policies and programs of the government and not hesitate to oppose, through legitimate means, measures that are oppressive and opposed to the welfare of the country or any section of the community. At present it may also be the duty of a Christian to help in the building up of responsible democratic opposition, so that the democratic processes become meaningful and there is possibility of a change of government when it becomes desirable.

Politics is an area of moral ambiguities, not only because of the forms of corruption often associated with it, but because the choices are limited. Politics is said to be "the art of the possible." Thus there is never one particular "Christian line" that an individual Christian may follow. He should act in a manner consonant with ethical principles consistent with Christian norms.

14. *Ibid.*, p. 250.
15. See below, section on Emerging Patterns of Church-State Consultation and Cooperation.

Here Christians might differ in their evaluation and appraisal of political parties, programs, and issues. In any case, the ambiguities of political decisions should not keep one away from active participation in politics.[16]

3. By the Christian community. This may be distinguished from the churches in that, apart from their specifically religious role and functions, members of the Christian community may be viewed as a group of citizens of the country having a common cultural, social, religious, and sometimes economic background, and they as a cohesive group may act jointly for the welfare of the nation as well as that of the community. In this, they do not necessarily act under the direction or at the behest of the religious hierarchy or church organization.

We frequently ask ourselves whether the Christian community should act as a separate group in politics, and whether they should form a Christian political party for this purpose. In India ecumenical opinion has been vehemently opposed to the formation of a political party or even acting as a *pressure group*. It was adherence to this principle that impelled Christian members of the Constituent Assembly to renounce the offer for reservation of seats and separate electorates for the Christian minority for elections to the Parliament and State legislatures. Christians preferred to throw in their lot with all other communities in India on an equal basis.[17] In doing this the Christian community gave laudable leadership to all minority groups in India.

The forming of a Christian political party is bound to give the wrong impression that Christianity implies a particular political program. But the Christian Gospel does not provide any ready-made political program, and no political program can claim to be absolutely Christian. The forming of a separate Christian party would also drain other parties of Christian leadership.

In a country like India, where negative communal forces are very powerful, the forming of a Christian party could be construed as the further strengthening of reactionary forces and tendencies.

Even though a minority, the Christian community now has the opportunity to work through several all-India parties, which are pledged to work for the national welfare and to guarantee the rights of minorities. The forming of a "minority front" by itself or in association with other minority communities to safeguard

---

16. Bennett, p.. 286.
17. See above, chap. 3, section on Christians and Communalism.

its interests serves only to inflame the suspicion of the majority community. What ought to be done is to cultivate confidence on both sides. As the late illustrious Home Minister G. B. Pant once said,

> Our aim is to secure a secular state in which there should be no feeling of minority or majority and all would live together happily as equal citizens.[18]

The minority communities as well as the majority community have the responsibility not to act in any way that would undermine the mutual confidence and tolerance between the different communities in India.

While renouncing the efforts to form a Christian political party, Christians should not forget that as a community they have the responsibility of making their contribution to nation-building especially through political action. The present level of Christian involvement in Indian politics leaves much to be desired. The Bombay follow-up study of 1959 expressed the opinion that a lay organization for Christian political education and social action may be desirable. It said, after having made suggestions regarding church action and study,

> Apart from this top-level study and limited action under the auspices of recognized Christian organizations there is need also for some other organized means of educating Christians politically and enabling them to take social action—something between expressions of general concern in politics by the churches as organized bodies, and the individual Christian's participation in party politics. Organized Christian effort which avoids the danger of communalism is what we are looking for.[19]

The study offered strong reasons why an All-India Civil Organization of Christians was necessary.

Recently there have been some attempts to form All-India Christian organizations,[20] not as political parties but as sociopolitical organizations to work toward strengthening the secular democratic character of the Indian state, to help Christians discharge their political responsibilities, and to promote the rights

---

18. *Hindustan Times*, 18 March 1950, p. 8. Quoted in Luthera, p. 161.

19. Devanandan and Thomas, eds., *Christian Participation in Nation-Building*, p. 55; see also pp. 57-58 for reasons favoring the formation of such an organization.

20. For a report on the formation of the "All-India Christian Union," see *NCCR* 86, no. 8 (August 1966), pp. 324-26.

of Christians, especially those sections within the community that are backward.

In the past, there have been a few lay Christian organizations like the Indian Christian Associations, the Catholic Union, the Masihi Sangh, and so on. Before independence, some of them, like the Indian Christian Associations, were quite active as spokesmen of the Christian community in political and social matters, and had good leadership in men like the late Raja Sir Maharaj Singh and the late H. C. Mukherjee. None of these organizations became truly all-India organizations and none can claim to have been particularly successful in helping the rank and file of the Christian community in exercising its political rights and discharging its political duties. After independence, and with the adoption of the Constitution, which affirmed the secular character of India and guaranteed fundamental rights and religious freedom to all citizens, these organizations became defunct.

Recent attempts to form the Christian Union of India for sociopolitical action and education are sure to raise questions in the minds of Christians as well as non-Christians. It is quite likely that many will dub them as purely communal and a retrograde step for the Christian leadership to take. Others, however, will see in them a legitimate expression of the political concern of the Christian community for the welfare of the nation as well as that of the community. Ultimately these attempts have to be judged by the way they operate. One can never overlook the fact that these nascent organizations may be used by vested interests for narrow communal goals. But on the other hand there is the possibility that vigorous organizations could be built up from the grassroots level, and that they could be of great help in making Christians really alive to their political and social responsibilities, contributing their full share to the building up of a national community in India and an international community based on order, freedom, and justice. They could also serve as media of dialogue with other communities in the matter of defining national goals and in promoting them.

The Christian should consider participation in politics as a religious obligation. Moreover, "even as his entry into politics is the result of Christian commitment, his political activity should reflect Christian obedience."[21] Christians can be active in the political sphere as churches, as a community, and as individuals.

21. Devanandan and Thomas, eds., *Problems of Indian Democracy*, p. 207.

The role of the churches must mainly be indirect, trying to influence the "spirit and ethos, the moral sensitivities, and the value systems" of the national community as well as preparing their members spiritually and socially for responsible political action. The Christian community may have a greater direct role in politics, even though it would be inadvisable for Christians in India to form a Christian political party. However, the church's witness in political life is articulated principally as its members, i.e., individual Christians, become involved in the responsibilities of citizenship at the local, national, and international levels. Here the obligations of all the citizens of the country are equal, but it is hoped that the biblical teaching regarding the love of God, the Lordship of Christ over history, and the love of neighbor would make the Christian citizen particularly sensitive to discharging his political duties conscientiously. But the effectiveness of the individual Christian and Christian political leaders can be strengthened by the moral support that the church and the Christian community should give them in applying Christian principles in politics.

Need for Dynamic Cooperation between the Christian Community and the Non-Christian Religions and Secular Bodies in India

In the secular state of India, the Christian community is set amidst men of different faiths and no faith. It is only in dynamic cooperation with them that Christians can fulfill their destiny as responsible citizens of secular India.

In the past, the Christian community had very much isolated itself from the other communities in India. In churches founded by the Western missionaries, Christians were accused by others of being identified with the British administration. By their adoption of Western patterns in dress and social customs, and by putting themselves under the patronage of the missionaries, they separated themselves from the larger community socially, culturally, and spiritually. The old Syrian churches of Kerala also, though not intimately connected with the Western missionaries, have kept themselves isolated from the rest of the community. The Syrian community had for centuries taken its place in the caste hierarchy of the Kerala society and was effectively insulated from the rest of the community regarding social and religious contacts. Christians in India generally tried to avoid any contact with Hindu culture for fear that these "pagan cultures" would have a pernicious effect on the doctrinal purity of the church.

Speaking about the Christian community in Delhi, Alter and Jai Singh say that they look upon themselves as a separate and distinct community—a *qaum*, an Urdu term meaning race, people, or nation.[22] According to the same authors, the Christian *qaum* in Delhi has three characteristics: a) it is an ethnic community with a membership determined mostly by birth; b) it is an ingrown community primarily concerned with its own welfare and suspicious of outsiders; c) it is a community like other communities in India having its own symbols, beliefs, and ways of worship.[23] The *Samudayam* (caste-community) consciousness of the Kerala Christians with their closed social structure parallels the *qaum* consciousness of the Delhi Christians. Both cases, representative of the situations in the Indian Christian community as a whole, show that the Christian community is tainted with communalism and casteism, as the previous chapter also noticed.

The Christian *qaum* mentality as described above is contrary to the views of the New Testament regarding the church.[24] Membership in the church should not be determined primarily by birth; it should be defined by response to God in Jesus Christ (John 1:12–13, 3:3). The church should not be an ingrown community but should be a universal community transcending all barriers of race and culture. The church is not one community among many communities, but the "new humanity," drawing its distinctiveness from Christ (II Cor. 5:17, 1 Peter 2:9–10, John 14:6).[25]

One of the urgent problems that India is faced with is building national unity and integration. Religious pluralism has been one of the causes of division in India. Political groupings are often based on religious and caste divisions. The relationship between the different religious and caste communities has been marked in the post-independence period more by conflict and competition than by cooperation and uniting in a national community. The

22. James P. Alter and Herbert Jai Singh, "The Church in Delhi," in Victor E. W. Hayward, ed., *The Church as Christian Community* (London: Lutterworth Press, 1966), p. 79.

23. *Ibid.*, p. 130.

24. The sociological "givenness" of the Christian community has to be measured against the theological "ought" of the church.

25. Hayward, ed., pp. 130-31.

Christian community is not very different in this respect from any other caste or communal group. However, apart from Kerala, Christians, because of their small numbers, have not been able to play a large role as a communal body. In Kerala, however, the Christian community often acts as a communal group.

How can Christians promote cooperation between and among different sections of the population of India and contribute toward the building up of national unity? What should be the basis of this cooperation, and what are its goals?

Much thinking is being done in India regarding cooperation (and dialogue as a prerequisite of the same) between Christians and men of other faiths and no faith. Some of the most creative thinking in this area has been done by, among others, the late P. D. Devanandan.

The Indian society consists not only of men of various religious persuasions but also those of no religion. The common goal of everyone should be to

> evoke a secular society in India in which the common endeavor of men of all faiths would be the achievement of true community—being based on considerations of social justice, personal values and human rights.[26]

The basis for our cooperation with those of faith and no faith is the "common humanity" that everyone shares. Regarding this, Devanandan says:

> We are all involved in a common social crisis, tied together by a community of interests; our common humanity serves as a common denominator; and on the frontiers of renascent faiths, doctrinal barriers no longer foreclose religious commerce.[27]

In the past there has been some attempt to promote a "united front" of religions against "anti-religious" forces like Communism and closed secularism, and there have also been attempts to evolve a world religion as a means for religious cooperation. One of the earliest attempts in this direction was the Parliament of Religions, which met in Chicago in 1920, at which Swami Vivekanandan made a profound impression by his appearance. But this approach has not met with any degree of success, and reli-

---

26. P. D. Devanandan, *Christian Concern in Hinduism* (Bangalore: CISRS, 1961), p. v.

27. P. D. Devanandan, *Preparation for Dialogue* (Bangalore: CISRS, 1964), p. 190.

gions are as far apart from each other as they were before. Here the attempt was to find unity on the basis of religion itself.

But religion itself need not be a good thing. Dietrich Bonhoeffer has spoken of "religionless Christianity" because of this. Since man is sinful, even his religion expresses his sinfulness; and religions, including the Christian religion, can be as corrupt as any other human institution. But all religions are under the judgment of God. Hence common humanity, rather than religion, provides a common point of contact and conversation; here one can meet not only the religious but also the nonreligious. The conversation about Christian faith can often be carried out best in the secular context.[28]

M. M. Thomas says that this common humanity is given through Christ and can express itself both in religion and in revolt against religion. Moreover, an alliance of religions can lead to syncretism. So it is common humanity given through Christ rather than common religiousness that should serve as the basis for dialogue and common action.[29]

The traditional religions of India, as well as the secular humanism of India, are characterized by a new ferment. The renaissance of Hinduism has already been referred to. The Ahamadiya movement is a good example of resurgent Islam. Cheragh Ali Khan, the founder of Aligarh Muslim University, and Mohammad Iqbal, the reformer, laid the foundations for reinterpreting Islam in modern terms.[30] I have also referred to the secular humanism of Jawaharlal Nehru. Devanandan saw secular humanism as having a special significance in "awakening the ancient religions to the dimension of responsible personal and interpersonal existence of the world."[31] He also saw the renewal of traditional faiths as a result of the Holy Spirit's working through them. He asks:

Can Christian faith discern in such renewal the inner working of the spirit of God, guiding men of other faiths than ourselves, as well as men of no faith, into a new understanding of God's ways with the world of men today? If all "New Creation" can only be of God where else could these "new" aspects of

---

28. *The Christian Community within the Human Community*, p. 10.

29. M. M. Thomas, *The Christian Response to Asian Revolution* (London: SCM Press, Ltd., 1966), p. 95.

30. C. I. Itty, "Dynamics of a Pluralistic Society—The Indian Experience," in DeVries, p. 325.

31. Herbert Jai Singh, ed., *Inter-Religious Dialogue* (Bangalore: CISRS, 1967), p. 27.

other beliefs in the thinking and living of people have sprung from?[32]

More specifically, the newness of life in non-Christian religions may be due to the impact of Christian ideas. Many Christian truths provide the basic philosophy for much non-Christian religious practice.[33]

So, in seeking to cooperate and enter into dialogue with men of other beliefs, Christians are not entering into an area where God is not at work. It is the duty of Christians to discern and affirm the presence of God whenever it is found. Theophane Mathias, S.J.,[34] recently said:

> Much as it may go against the grain to say so, God is also present in the dedication of the Communist worker who strives to uplift the lot of the working class or the burning zeal of the Black Muslim who may be misled but sincerely wishes to make the life of his race more human, in the Hindu or Buddhist who endeavors to spread contentment and peace around him.[35]

Thus there are sufficient grounds and an urgent imperative to cooperate and enter into dialogue. What are the goals of this dialogue and cooperation? The most important goals are 1) nation-building, 2) promoting national integration by developing a composite culture, 3) providing a spiritual basis for the Indian secular state, and 4) de-alienation of the Christian community.

Nation-building. Communalism and casteism have been the bane of Indian politics.[36] This is clearly seen in the political history of Kerala since independence. Communalism has developed, partly because of the isolation of different religious groups from each other. In the context of social and religious isolation from each other, many political and religious leaders fan up mutual suspicions and then exploit them for personal and communal ends. The big task of nation-building of the country, of finding solutions for its vast economic and social problems, cannot be achieved in such an atmosphere. The active cooperation of all citizens, irrespective of religion, caste, color, creed, or sex is necessary to

---

32. Devanandan, *Preparation for Dialogue*, p. 177.

33. *Ibid.*, pp. 190-91.

34. Fr. Mathias, an Indian, is the director of the Jesuit Educational Association of India.

35. "Christian Missionary Role Found in Non-Christian Religions," *Christian Science Monitor*, 16 December 1968, p. 11.

36. See definition of communalism in chap. 3, section on Christians and Communalism.

achieve this end. Cooperation and dialogue between members of different faiths in the secular context of their work and common issues can help break down the walls that separate religious communities from each other. This is also essential for the secularization of politics and the maintenance of the secular character of the state.[37]

Promoting national integration by developing a composite culture. Religious pluralism is one of the basic reasons for the lack of national integration in India. However, national unity is not to be achieved by forcing everyone to conform to one religion or by doing away with all religions.[38] The process of secularization that has been going on in the various religious communities of India provide a basis for unity. Dialogue and cooperation between followers of different religions on the basis of their common humanity can contribute toward the unity of India. According to Itty:

> There is a strong possibility of evolving a national culture in a pluralistic society if the people share a common heritage from the past, a common involvement in the present and common goals for the future.[39]

There already exists the common heritage of participation in the freedom struggle, which is the basis of Indian nationalism. What is needed now is involvement with each other and development of common goals for the future.

Even though eighty percent of Indians are Hindus, the unity of India cannot be based on the Hindu religion, for there are significant minorities like Muslims, Christians, Sikhs, Parsees, and those who do not belong to any religion. Such a religious integration of society would be against the spirit of the secular state. However, the Hindu culture cannot be ignored in evolving a composite culture for India. This composite culture should be "inspired by a common humanity with openness towards different faiths and their different contributions to the common pool."[40] According to Devanandan, Indian unity should be

> based on common nationality and not on common faith . . . a common culture into which not only the various elements of the diverse, historic patterns of culture in our country can be inte-

37. See Jai Singh, ed., *Inter-Religious Dialogue*, pp. 32-34.
38. Devanandan, *Preparation for Dialogue*, p. 121.
39. DeVries, p. 320.
40. Jai Singh, *Inter-Religious Dialogue*, p. 30.

grated, but also a culture in which can be contributed both "old" traditional values and "new" revolutionary gains of modern technology and social advance.[41]

It is only as those of different religious traditions study and understand the cultural traditions and bring into a common pool their best cultural insights that a new composite culture can be developed.[42] In this connection, the possibility of secularizing certain Hindu religious festivals so that they could be celebrated as national festivals, thus creating a sense of national community, could be explored.[43]

Providing a spiritual basis for the Indian secular state. The composite culture that is to be evolved in India should have a spiritual basis, an ethos, to give it inner direction. No culture can remain dynamic for long without this inner spiritual resource. Even a secular one should have spiritual foundations to be stable.[44]

As was said earlier, a secular culture that is not open to spiritual values and insights from religion becomes a closed culture and may be identified with integral secularism. Cultures, whether based on the classical traditions of one's own country or the result of a synthesis of many modern strands such as science and secular humanism, may become absolutistic in many ways. It may be an ethnocentric absolutism, which assumes that one's own culture is superior to all others. Second, it may be a classical absolutism, which considers one period in history as the "summit of human achievement." The attempt then is to recover the golden age. Third, there is historical absolutism, which regards whatever is at present as representing the highest progress possible.[45]

In India, as in any other country, these dangers are present. On the one hand there is the attempt to integrate Indian society based on classical Hindu culture, and on the other to see in absolute terms modern democracy and the socioeconomic goals of the ruling government. It is the duty of Christians, in cooperation with those of other religions and those with no religion who are concerned with ultimate goals and meaning of life, to provide a basic perspective for culture on which the culture can be judged and reformed continuously.

---

41. Devanandan, *Christian Concern in Hinduism*, pp. 138-39.
42. Devanandan and Thomas, eds., *Christian Participation in Nation-Building*, pp. 263-64.
43. Devanandan, *Preparation for Dialogue*, p. 125.
44. DeVries, p. 322.
45. David Bidney, *Theoretical Anthropology* (New York: Columbia University Press, 1954), pp. 422-23.

M. M. Thomas believes that there is a new awareness in Asia "of the personal dimension of individual and collective behavior."[46] Three cultural movements are instrumental in opening up traditional Asian cultures, which lacked such emphasis on this new dimension of the personal. They are, 1) the resurgence of Asian religions with their will to reform themselves, 2) the movements of secularization and secular humanism that are still open, and 3) Christianity expressing itself in mission and new ways of service.[47] These are movements that are concerned not only with the immediate political and economic ends of man but also with the more ultimate dimensions of human life, even though secular humanism is a philosophy that ignores man's relationship with God. Christians should be in dialogue with all individuals and movements that contribute toward providing to the emerging, hopefully composite and secular culture of India, with a spiritual ethos. Mutual interaction among these progressive movements may lead not to religious syncretism but to

> a cultural synthesis which can be open enough for a constant dialogue at depth on the nature and destiny of man, a synthesis secular in its framework and personal in its orientation and increasingly becoming personal in content.[48]

Dealienation of the Christian community. Christians have for long been isolated from the rest of the Indian society. If Christians are to be able to contribute vitally toward the building up of a secular society in India, this situation has to be remedied. They should enter into conversation with non-Christians on fundamental aspects of their faith so that there is mutual understanding and appreciation, as well as interpenetration of values. Christians should also embark on a program of indigenization,

> whereby the creed and cultures of other religions in whose midst Christians are placed [are] reinterpreted in the light of the fundamental core of the Christian faith and integrated into the style of living and communication of the Christian religion.[49]

Christians should discard foreign customs and manners and also mix socially with non-Christians. Only by "re-establishing their cultural kinship" with others in the country, and presenting Chris-

---

46. M. M. Thomas, *The Christian Response to the Asian Revolution*, p. 67.
47. *Ibid.*, p. 75.
48. *Ibid.*, p. 92.
49. Jai Singh, ed., *Inter-Religious Dialogue*, pp. 30–31.

tian truth in forms, symbols, and institutions that are more familiar to the people, can Christian truth be more effectively con-
veyed.[50]

The Role of the Christian Community as a Minority— Championing the Cause of Religious Liberty and Defending Legitimate Rights

We have earlier explored the role of Christians in politics.
Christians in India also have a special role, as the second largest
minority community, to contribute toward the furtherance of
the ideals of the secular state and particularly of maintaining
separation between religion and state and religious liberty as
well as defending the legitimate rights of its disadvantaged members.

In Europe and in America, religious minorities have played a
decisive role in maintaining separation between religion and
state and in enlarging the area of religious freedom. They have
acted as catalytic agents in this process of separation.[51] Stokes
and Pfeffer conclude from their study of church-state relationship
in the United States that "the convictions and interests of non-
conformist religious groups, among which the Baptists and Qua-
kers were prominent," formed one of the two main historical
factors that contributed to "the constitutional religious freedom
and actual separation of church and state" in the United States.[52]
The part played by the Catholic minority in seventeenth-century
England and the Baptist minority in New England to secure
religious freedom is pertinent in this connection.[53] The Jewish
community as a minority community in the United States has
been very sensitive to any infringement on the principle of separation between religion and state and religious freedom, and
frequently registers protests against alleged transgressions by the
government in these areas.

In any country dominated by a large religious majority, the
temptation is always present to throw away the ideals of the
secular state and to make encroachments on the freedom of religious and other minorities. If Christians staunchly defend their

50. Devanandan, *Preparation for Dialogue*, pp. 174–76.
51. D. E. Smith, *India as a Secular State*, pp. 41–42.
52. Stokes and Pfeffer, p. 578.
53. D. E. Smith, *India as a Secular State*, p. 41.

rights as citizens of India, they will not only be defending their own rights but fighting for the principles of the secular state on which the Indian constitution is based.

In fulfilling this duty, the Christian community should not develop a "minority consciousness" and act as a communal body in a defensive way. This may be a natural reaction against Hindu communalism. But the "minority psychology" will only harm the Christian community as well as the nation. It can make them too sensitive to the reactions of the majority and timid in their actions to defend their rights. This can hurt the nation as a whole.[54] The community should study the relations between itself and the Hindu community with a view to preventing typical majority and minority reactions to issues.[55]

The answer to this problem is not to enter into a minority pact with other communal bodies to present a united front against any conscious or unconscious discrimination that may originate from the majority community. This step would only create adverse reaction among the majority community and create a spiraling process of mutual suspicion and recrimination. There should be dissemination of correct information, and ways and means should be found to educate the majority community regarding the interests of the minority communities, and appeal should be made to the good will, patriotism, and sense of justice of the majority community.[56]

However, this approach has its limitations. Political structures may not always be amenable to persuasion and may need the prodding of pressure groups to get them into action. Christians, being a small group, may not be able to make their voice heard in the various political parties. Regarding the Muslim community in India, Theodore P. Wright, Jr., says that it should organize pressure groups to lobby in the legislatures and administration, as is done by different groups in the United States. The distinction between political organizations and social welfare organizations should not be drawn too narrowly. The latter also will have to be somewhat political to be powerful and effective.[57] Wright recognizes the added difficulties of such pressure-group politics in India

---

54. M. M. Thomas, "Christian Citizens and Minority Consciousness," *NCCR* 79, no. 11 (November 1959) :425.

55. Devanandan and Thomas, eds., *Christian Participation in Nation Building*, pp. 51–52.

56. Thomas, "Christian Citizens and Minority Consciousness," pp. 426–27.

57. Theodore P. Wright, Jr., "The Effectiveness of Muslim Representation in India," in D. E. Smith, ed., *South Asian Politics and Religion*, p. 135.

because individual law makers are less easily swayed by extra party considerations than is the case in the United States. But even though more difficult, this is being done by big business and such other groups.[58]

That Christians should be well organized, so that their voice will be heard and felt in administrative circles, is a plea that is more insistently being made by some Christian leaders. Protesting against the allegedly arbitrary order of expulsion of Father Ferrer, a Roman Catholic missionary, by the Government of India, Eddy Asirvatham wrote:

> If Indian Christians were as well organized or had as much of a political nuisance value as certain other minorities, they would not be treated in the nonchalant way in which they are treated today. Our Christian leaders and councils should busy themselves in doing something concrete in vindicating the rights guaranteed to us under the Constitution, instead of merely passing pious resolutions. They have made inaction buttressed by theological jugglery almost a virtue.[59]

Since independence, the Christian community has by and large eschewed direct political action. The CISRS and other more "progressive" Christian bodies have maintained that the Christian community should not organize themselves merely to safeguard the political and religious rights of the community and that this should be done only through the nonsectarian political parties. A 1956 study condemned any effort to revive the defunct Indian Christian Associations.[60] It would be readily conceded by all that the formation of a Christian political party would be highly inappropriate and disadvantageous to the community and to India. But there seems to be greater acceptance of the necessity of organizing the Christian community to serve the nation better. The Christian Union of India, formed in 1966, proclaims its policy to be the following:

> The Christian Union of India stands for doing away with the image of Christians as a community seeking political power for its own advantage, and, instead, for endeavoring to build up the image of a community dedicated to serve the nation. There is, therefore, the need to mobilise the whole Christian

---

58. *Ibid.*, pp. 135-36.
59. "Letter to the Editor," *Guardian* 46, no. 22 (30 May 1963):170-71.
60. Chandran and Thomas, eds., *Political Outlook in India Today: A Pre-election Study*, pp. 130-32.

community so that their sense of solidarity is reaffirmed, leading to effectiveness in serving the nation.[61]

Efforts are being made to merge some of the surviving Indian Christian Associations with the Christian Union of India. It has also registered its opinions on several matters that affect the Indian Christian community, even though it is primarily concerned with Indian Christian contribution to nation-building.

There is no contradiction in working for the interests of the community and those of the nation if the former are not defined narrowly and selfishly. Christians should not demand any rights merely because they are Christians. If they are vigilant regarding fundamental rights as they pertain to themselves, they will be defending the rights of all citizens of India. Some sections of the Christian community are particularly weak and socially disadvantaged. The Christian community as a whole has special responsibility to look after the interests of such groups and to champion their rightful causes.

The Christian community as a minority has a special responsibility to ensure that the religious freedom guaranteed in the Constitution is practiced both in letter and in spirit. This is necessary so that the state itself will not become autocratic and control all areas of one's life.

> The state must express in its own structure its recognition that man has ends and loyalties beyond the state. The state's guarantee of religious liberty as a fundamental right of the human person is one such expression. But the right to accept, practice and propagate the religion of one's choice, and freedom from discrimination between citizens on the basis of religion, are fundamental for the health of the state itself.[62]

So Christians should be ever vigilant to promote the belief in and practice of religious liberty in the country, and should evolve effective organizations for this purpose.

In this connection we may note the need for an effective all-India civil liberties organization made up of prominent members of all communities. Minorities can press for their legal rights through this without being branded as "communal." It can more effectively appeal to the sense of justice of all sections of the

---

61. "Christian Union of India—Policy and Programme," *Guardian* 46, no. 1 (4 January 1968) :5.
62. *The Christian Community within the Human Community*, pp. 21-22.

country, especially the educated sections of the majority community.[63]

Forms of Christian Service in the Indian Secular State

The Christian community in India has traditionally involved itself in social service activities aimed at the Christian community as well as the community at large. The numerous educational institutions and also institutions for medical help—hospitals, dispensaries, and the like, and social assistance—orphanages, homes for the handicapped, and so on—testify to this fact. Particularly with the coming of the missionaries and the vast resources at their command, schools, colleges, hospitals, and such institutions were started in various parts of the country and non-Christian leaders have often commended the high standards of excellence maintained by many of these institutions. I have referred to the high praise given to Christian educational and philanthropic institutions by some leaders in the Constituent Assembly.[64]

Christians have pioneered in women's education, English education, and education in general. Even now, some of the best-known educational and medical institutions in India are those run under Christian auspices. The Christian church is the largest educational agency in the state of Kerala. But with the attainment of independence and the expanding services of the Indian welfare state, a rethinking is taking place as to the place of Christian service in the new Indian secular state. In many of the areas of service where the churches have traditionally been involved, the state has become more and more active. As in Kerala, under the Communist government in 1959, there have been attempts to completely eliminate Christian participation in education. As the government expands its services in some other areas, the service being rendered now by some Christian institutions may become superfluous.

Traditionally, social service was considered as "a preparation for the Gospel" or as "instrumental to evangelism." But recent Indian Christian thinking is that service (*diakonia*) is an end in

---

63. Chandran and Thomas, eds., *Political Outlook in India Today*, pp. 132–33. See also D. E. Smith, ed., *South Asian Politics and Religion*, p. 135.
64. See above, chap. 2, section on The Debates of the Constituent Assembly.

itself. It *is* an end in itself. It is not a bait for Christian expansion. At the same time, as Devanandan says,

> We dare not deny . . . that even in such *diakonia* God's redemptive power is at work in our day-to-day life, liberating the individual and renewing human society.[65]

Worship, evangelism, and service go together, but they are not dependent on each other.

> These three elements constitute together our witness to Christ. Each stands on its own right and neither is to be subordinated to the other or regarded as instrumental to the other. But they must be held together in the fellowship of the common life which the Holy Spirit creates.[66]

Service should not be an instrument of evangelism.

> At the same time, evangelism which does not spring out of the church's common life in which love is visibly expressed in service will become merely empty sound. Both must be recognisably rooted in the Fellowship of the Holy Spirit.[67]

Fr. Paul Varghese avers that "only a worshipping community can render true Christian service."[68] So we see that in present-day Indian Christian thinking, Christian service is still seen to have an important and integral place in the work of the Christian community. But the forms of Christian service and even its rationale have to be expressed in new ways to meet the changing understanding regarding *diakonia* and the changing needs of the nation.

Traditionally Christian service was aimed at the Christian community itself. Of course, because of its evangelistic emphasis and the sheer numerical preponderance of non-Christians, Christians were not the only, or even the primary beneficiaries of Christian service. But now with the new understanding that Christian service should be rendered without any ulterior motives

---

65. P. D. Devanandan, *The Gospel and Renascent Hinduism* (London: SCM Press Ltd., 1959), pp. 43–44.

66. "Findings of the Nagpur Theological Study Conference, 1957," *Religion and Society* 4, no. 3 (December 1957):44.

67. *Ibid.*, p. 55.

68. "Why We Serve," *Frontier* 7 (Spring 1964):47.

69. *Christian Service in the Revolution*. Report of Sukabumi, Indonesia Consultation (1962) (East Asia Christian Conference, 1963), p. 32.

and on the basis of common humanity, the objects of service should not merely be the Christian community but the local and national community as such.[69] The church's social service should express concern for the total humanity.[70]

Recent Indian Christian thought has emphasized the need for integrating social service with the programs of nation-building that the Indian welfare state undertakes whenever this is in line with Christian values. It is also envisaged that the church may have to vacate areas of social service where the state is able to provide adequate services. The church will have to give up its work in fields like education, medical service, and industrial training as the government undertakes more and more of these services.[71] But there will always be a place for Christian agencies, even in fields that are primarily catered to by the secular state, because voluntary associations and agencies may serve as pilot centers and serve as models. Because of their voluntary and Christian character they may preserve many values that may not always be present in a government agency.

However, when we examine Christian institutions for service, such as Christian schools, colleges, and hospitals, many of them either overlap the services rendered by the state or do not have any distinctively high quality of service to justify their existence now. But because these institutions bring prestige to the particular Christian communities concerned or are looked upon as agencies to provide employment for Christians, they are maintained and often multiplied. Many of the Christian schools and colleges in Kerala come under this category.[72]

As the welfare state takes over more areas of service where the Christian community has been active, many areas are still left uncared for by the state and new avenues are opened up because of processes like urbanization and industrialization taking place in India. There is great need for the Christian community to do pioneering work. As Bhatty says: "Consecrated imagination is required to launch out in these spheres where as yet the government is not able to do much." In order to do this "it may be

---

70. Bengt R. Hoffman, *Christian Social Thought in India: 1947-1962. An Evaluation* (Bangalore: Christian Institute for the Study of Religion and Society, 1967), p. 145. See chap. 4, *The Role of the Church in Social Service and Social Action*, pp. 143-69, for a critical summary of Indian Christian thinking on this topic.

71. *Ibid.*, p. 147.

72. See above, chap. 4, section on "Vimochana Samaram" or the "Liberation Struggle."

necessary to close ineffective hospitals and educational institutions so that finance and personnel can be released to face the challenge."[73] Dr. Bhatty lists rural schools and hostels, mobile dispensaries and preventive medicine, work among beggars, work in Red Light areas, care for the aged, pre-primary schools and student hostels as areas of pioneering work.[74] Another study suggests that "the churches should pioneer with new institutional patterns in industrial urban areas." Christian ashrams and communities in city slums, social service centers, and institutes for the development of better labor management relationships are some of the new avenues suggested for Christian service.[75] The Bangalore Industrial Mission is an excellent example of this type of pioneering service by the Christian community responding to the needs of modern India.[76]

Institutional patterns of service are not the only forms of Christian service. The number of Christian institutions for service will always be small in relation to the need, and the number of professional Christian ministers and full-time Christian workers is very small compared with the Christian population. If the Christian community is to be fully mobilized for service in the secular context, and made more effective, it has to be equipped for this. They should acquire Christian insights and consciously plan Christian witness in their work, both as individuals and groups.[77] The various organizations of Christian professional groups that have been referred to represent attempts of the Christian community to fully utilize their lay constituency for service. But here only small beginnings have been made.[78]

If the goal of Christian service is helping anyone in need, this objective can be achieved only in collaboration with non-Christians. In cooperating with non-Christians for service, certain criteria have to be followed. It is evident that Christians cannot cooperate in activities that plainly contradict the Christian understanding of the nature of man and society and the purpose of God for man. Christians should seek cooperation on the basis of

---

73. C. E. Bhatty, "The Church's Contribution to Social Development in India," *NCCR* 81, no. 4 (April 1961) :144-45.

74. *Ibid.*

75. "New Patterns of Christian Social Witness in India—Nasrapur Findings—III," *Religion and Society* 7, no. 1 (April 1960) :59.

76. See chap. 4 above, section on Industrial Team Service, Bangalore.

77. "New Patterns of Christian Social Witness in India," p. 61.

78. See chap. 4 above, section on Organization of Christian Professional Groups.

Christ's command to love one another as He has loved. This means that in all things we should seek the neighbor's good.[79]

Christian collaboration with non-Christians poses certain problems, also. There may be many specific Christian values and goals that non-Christians may not share with Christians. For example, in running a college, non-Christians may not share the Christian enthusiasm (when it is present) for imparting Christian education. Here it would be difficult to share the management of such an institution with non-Christians, who naturally do not share the same specific values and goals. However, in the Christian college there are many areas where non-Christians would have the same goals as Christians; for example, in maintaining academic standards and promoting the spirit of enquiry and community. In all areas where cooperation is possible, it should be aspired to. This would keep Christian service institutions from becoming parochial and narrow minded (as they very often are) and help those Christians involved in such activities to become more sensitive to the needs and wishes of their non-Christian compatriots.

Many Christian institutions of service, particularly educational and philanthropic institutions, are run with government subsidy. In the case of Christian schools in Kerala more than 90 percent of the current expenses of the schools are met by such a subsidy. As we have seen, during the Communist rule in Kerala, the state government tried to restrict the freedom of the Christian management to appoint qualified teachers of their choice. This was vehemently protested, because it was felt that without the freedom to appoint teachers imbued with Christian ideals, the running of Christian schools would not serve its purpose. All private institutions receiving government aid are to some extent restricted by the rules laid down by the government. Often they do not interfere with the Christian purposes and goals of these institutions, but sometimes they do. When they do interfere seriously, either the institutions will have to be closed or have to be run without aid from the government. The Christian Medical College at Vellore is one example where a Christian institution has declined aid from the government because it was thought to have exerted undue restriction on the college's freedom of action with regard to its Christian purposes and goals.

79. "The Theological Basis of Christian-non-Christian Cooperation in Social Thought and Action," Nagpur Theological Study Conference, October 1957, *Religion and Society* 4, no. 3 (December 1957):55.

Christian service should be concerned not merely with charity, meeting individual needs, but also aimed at achieving justice in society.[80] This idea has become particularly prominent since independence. Christians should give leadership in reforming social structures, and provide a critique of society and the social programs of the state through careful research and study. In these areas it would be most feasible and important to be in collaboration with men of other faiths. Christian institutions like the recently formed All-India Christian Union and the well-established Christian Institute for the Study of Religion and Society are particularly active in these areas and seek to cooperate with men of other faiths in achieving these goals.

An important aspect of Christian *diakonia* or service is the ministry of reconciliation. In the Indian secular state there is great need for this type of service, for the cleavages in society have been accentuated since independence. The spirit of unity that prevailed in the country immediately after independence seems to have vanished. Conflicts between classes, communal groups, and political parties, and between the central and state governments seems to have gone beyond healthy limits. In Kerala, as well as in many other states, the main reason for political instability is the personal vendetta among politicians often of the same party.

> Hence the need for reconcilers between persons and parties if politicians are not to be allowed to dismember and destroy the nation to spite one another.[81]

During the last 25 years since independence, many Indian leaders have lavished high praise on the Christian community for the educational and philanthropic work that it has done.[82] In spite of the fact that there have always been those who criticized the community for using educational and philanthropic work for proselytism (the criticism was justified in some cases), the overwhelming feeling in the majority community has been that of good will and appreciation. The compliment given by the anti-missionary Madhya Pradesh Inquiry Committee (Niyogi Committee) report is particularly interesting.

---

80. Paul Abrecht, "Rapid Social Change and Human Need," *NCCR* 80, no. 12 (December 1960):453-54.

81. D. A. Thangasamy, "The Church's Diakonia in the Present Political and Economic Situation in India," *NCCR* 88, no. 1 (January 1968), p. 19.

82. See Pothacamury, pp. 20-21.

The contribution of Christian missionaries to the shaping of Indian life in modern times has, indeed, been very impressive. Apart from the controversy on the point of proselytization, they merit high appreciation as pioneers in the fields of education and medical relief.

The report further praises the missionaries for the establishment of schools, colleges, hospitals, orphanages, and institutions for the maimed and handicapped. It further notes that they were instrumental in elevating the position of the depressed classes and the status of women, and in stimulating many social and religious reforms in the Hindu community.

The Community Centers and Industrial Schools opened by them are, like other institutions, the best of their kind. India will ever be grateful for the services rendered by them.[83]

During the debates in the Constituent Assembly regarding freedom to "propagate" religion, which clause was particularly desired by Christians, Hindu members praised the Christian community for its philanthropic and educational contributions to the country.[84] The fact that this and other clauses guaranteeing religious freedom were willingly incorporated into the Constitution may partly be attributed to the fact that Christians renounced claims for special privileges as a minority and the general good will that the leaders of the majority community felt toward Christians because of the community's excellent record in philanthropic service to the country.

More recent recognition of this fine record is not wanting. A few years back, Mother Teresa, a Roman Catholic nun, was honored by the government of India by having conferred on her the title "Padma Shri" for her noble work among the aged and the dying in Calcutta. Two children of the Communist Chief Minister of Kerala (E. M. S. Namboothiripad) were students of Christian colleges. Recently the eminent Sarvodaya leader, Jaya Prakash Narayan, chided the local press for blacking out his remarks regarding the great service rendered by Christians in helping the villagers during the Bihar famine of 1966–1967.[85]

I have given these examples at some length to show that Christian service should have an important place in defining the role

83. Quoted in *Ibid.*, p. 80.
84. CAD 7:831-32 (Pandit Lakshmi Kanta Maitra), 837-38 (T. T. Krishnamachary).
85. *Guardian* 46, no. 10 (7 March 1968), p. 79.

of the Christian community in the Indian secular state. Only as Christians demonstrate their loyalty to Christ and love toward humanity through disinterested service to fellow human beings will India take seriously the message of the Gospel that is preached by Christians. This Christian service should not be thought of merely in terms of charity but in all its different and new forms as described above. But charity should remain an important element in Christian service in India for many more years because of the poverty of the country and the inability of the state and social agencies to provide for the needs of all the people.

Emerging Patterns of Church-State Consultation and Cooperation

We can readily see that very different forms of religion-state relationships exist in Southeast Asian countries. In Pakistan, Islam is the established religion and theoretically speaking all state laws are to be based on Islamic principles. In Indonesia, the government is based on the idea of *"gotong-rojong*—mutual cooperation for harmony." In the Indonesian "guided democracy," along with political parties, regions, and different functional groups like farmers, laborers, businessmen, and so on, the priests of the various religions are also represented in the policy-making body of the state. Thus religion is officially represented in the government.[86]

In the Indian secular state there is separation between religion and state, though not in the absolute sense. As we have seen, the state reserves to itself the right to interfere with the secular aspects of religious activities and to promote social reform, even when it touches spheres of religious activity. But there is no official connection between the various religions and the government. (This is not to ignore the fact that in some states like Kerala, there is a department—the Devaswom department—dealing with the management of Hindu temples. But this is not owing to any establishment of religion but because the state had to assume certain responsibilities that the previous rulers—in the case of Kerala, the maharajas of Travancore and Cochin—had fulfilled as a condition for these areas joining with the Indian Union after independence.)

---

86. Peter D. Latuihamallo, "The Search for Consensus Democracy in the New Nations," in Z. K. Matthews, *Responsible Government in a Revolutionary Age* (New York: Association Press, 1966), pp. 221-22.

Even though there are no official connections between the Christian church and the government, the latter has to deal with the Christian churches as institutions and the Christian community as a whole in several areas. For example, the Catholic Bishops' Conference of India and the National Christian Council of India are the official agencies through which applications for visas for foreign missionaries desiring to work in India have to be submitted to the government of India. Individual denominations are also allowed to submit applications from missionaries directly.

It has been the practice of the government of India to consult the communities before legislation that exclusively affects them is introduced in the Parliament or the state legislatures. The National Christian Council of India and other Christian bodies have submitted memoranda when legislation such as the Christian Marriage and Succession Act were introduced. In the preceding chapter we saw that the Syrian Christians of Kerala were excluded from the purview of the Anti-Dowry Act, as a result of the representations that some members of the community made.[87]

As far as the Christian community is concerned, the official channels of contact with the government of India are the National Christian Council of India (NCCI) and the Catholic Bishops' Conference. While the latter is fully representative of the Roman Catholic part of the Christian community, the NCCI is not fully representative of the non-Roman Catholic Christians. For example, the Syrian Orthodox church of Kerala is not a member of the NCCI. Efforts should be made to make the NCCI more fully representative. It would be ideal if all the Christians in India could speak through one representative organization, so that there would be greater unanimity and hence forcefulness in the opinions expressed and the representations made.

There is also the problem of making sure that the opinions expressed by the hierarchy and the official leadership of the Christian community represents the opinions of the rank and file of the Christian community. Some critics of the practice of the dowry system among Kerala Syrian Christians accuse the hierarchy of representing the views of only the upper-class Christians in opposing the application of the Anti-Dowry Act to the Syrian Christian community. The same accusation is also made regarding the proposed Kerala Christian Marriage and Succession Act.

---

87. E. V. Mathew, "Towards a Uniform Law of Christian Succession," *Guardian* (22 February 1968), pp. 59-60.

Much of the official leadership seems to oppose the proposed provisions for equal share in the father's property for both sons and daughters. The status quo, on the other hand, is opposed by more radical thinkers within the community.[88] The community and the churches have to recognize the fact that opinions expressed by different socioeconomic groups tend to reflect their own backgrounds and interests. There should be an interplay of these different opinions so that more balanced and objective opinions will evolve. Christians of different social classes should be engaged in the process of making social judgements.[89]

Of the three major religious bodies in India, the Christian community is the best organized. The Muslim community is less organized and the Hindu community is the least organized. In the Western countries, the institutional separation between church and state is possible because both entities are highly institutionalized. The Christian churches in the West are organized well enough to look after their own institutional needs. The high degree of secularization in the West has also made it possible to have civil codes free of religious control. In India, the Christian churches are well organized and they are able to manage by themselves matters pertaining to their religion. In the area of personal law, customs vary somewhat from one Christian community to the other; for example, the special practices of Kerala Syrian Christians regarding inheritance and the giving of "streedhanam" (as we have seen, similar to, but claimed to be different from, dowry). But these special practices do not have any strong religious sanctions to back them up and Christians may not have much difficulty in accepting a uniform civil code.

The Muslim community is organized enough to manage its own religious institutions. But the matter of personal law is closely related to their religion. The policy of the national government is to have a uniform civil code for the whole of India, but since it wants to achieve this goal without estranging the minority communities, particularly, its general policy is to wait until the demand for reform comes from the community concerned. If this is not forthcoming, there is no guarantee that the government will wait indefinitely for it. Progressive leadership within both the Muslim and Christian communities has a responsibility to educate the rank and file of the communities to accept a uniform civil code.

88. *Ibid.*
89. Bennett, *Christians and the State*, p. 277.

We have seen how the government of India under British rule became involved in the management of Hindu temples and festivals. The government had either inherited these functions from previous rulers or undertaken the overseeing of institutions to prevent mismanagement. The present federal and state governments are also involved in the management of Hindu religious institutions of various types. Unless the Hindu religious community is better organized, this may have to continue perpetuating a situation that compromises the essential nature of the secular state. Hence, encouragement from the government, as well as contacts with other communities, may help the Hindu community in this respect. In the matter of personal law, in spite of opposition from conservative elements, the government of India under the leadership of the late prime minister Jawaharlal Nehru did enact the Hindu Code Bill, which secularized many of the religiously controlled personal laws. Here the government acted with greater confidence, since it could not be accused of persecuting a minority.

While the state may not give special recognition to any one religious community, it may cooperate with various religious groups and organizations in their capacity as voluntary service organizations working for the welfare of society. In their capacity as voluntary associations, they should not be discriminated against because of their religious sponsorship. It should be the policy of the government to promote the growth of voluntary associations, including religious organizations. Such associations, by their very nature, give their respective membership the satisfaction of meaningful relationships and give vitality to a democratic society.

> It is only through voluntary religious, cultural and social agencies that the inner structure and spirit of the culture and community can be reformed, and developed along healthy lines. Hence the state initiative in the reconstruction of any social institution should be exercised in cooperation with voluntary groups. . . . It will also ensure sensitivity to the human aspects of social change.[90]

The state should appreciate and support the considerable contribution that Christian institutions in India are making in the educational, medical, and philanthropic fields.

---

90. Devanandan and Thomas, eds., *Christian Participation in Nation-Building*, p. 17.

The Indian secular state is not anti-religious. Some states, like the Communist state, "den[y], a priori, the validity of any institution based on man's concern with the ultimate or his encounter with the Infinite."[91] This is not true of India. But as a welfare state, the Indian secular state interferes with many aspects of an individual's life. This cannot be avoided, but it involves the danger that the welfare state (the idea of the welfare state is an integral part of the Indian secular state) may destroy the freedom and dignity of individuals by exercising absolute control over all aspects of their lives and over the community. Only vigilance on the part of the public can prevent such an encroachment on personal freedom and the rights of the individual, including his religious freedom.

Religious freedom for the Christian is essentially based on the biblical injunction that one should obey God rather than men. The state should recognize that man has loyalties that transcend his loyalties to the state. As one Asian study points out,

> the state must express in its own structure its recognition that man has ends and loyalties beyond the state. The state's guarantee of religious liberty as a fundamental right of the human person is one such expression.[92]

It is doubtful whether in India religious liberty is granted from this perspective. Religious liberty is mainly considered as a means of maintaining religious coexistence and harmony among different religious communities in India.

Within the Hindu tradition, religious liberty is understood primarily in an individual sense, i.e., freedom of the individual to realize God. This is equivalent to freedom of conscience. This is something that no state can interfere with. Since Hinduism views man's religious quest as essentially an individual matter, the social aspect of religious freedom is not given much importance. One Hindu writer observes:

> Real freedom therefore is not harnessed to social freedoms, however worthy. It is the freedom of the transcendental or the Deity. It is the primary duty of every individual to seek God for it is in his nature to attain Him. Man seeks a greater life and no social institution, however big and pretentious, can

---

91. Syed Vahiduddin, "Need for Religion in a Secular State," *The Aryan Path* 37, no. 2 (February 1966):83.
92. *The Christian Community within the Human Community*, pp. 21-22.

fulfil the need for freedom and existence that God grants.[93]

It is this individualistic approach to religion that has made Hinduism as a religious institution not highly organized. There is less concern about the social nature of religious freedom in traditional Hinduism than in Christianity.

But religion cannot remain for long a merely personal affair. It is shared with others, and the religious experience is sustained by the company of and communication with others. Then religion becomes social and institutional, and the state is confronted with the question of religious liberty.[94] Christianity and Islam are highly organized and institutionalized, and hence there is greater concern for religious liberty among these religions. The Christian community has a special responsibility to affirm the real basis of religious liberty in man's prior loyalty to God and the social nature of religious expression.

Religious liberty, though, "a freedom sui generis," is closely related to, and can exist only in the context of general human freedoms. As Carrillo de Albornoz points out,[95] religious liberty presupposes the exercise of other human rights. "Freedom of conscience" is related to "freedom of thought," and freedom of religious witness to the right of "free expression." So also, freedom of public worship is closely related to the fundamental right to freedom of assembly, and freedom of religious groups to the general "freedom of association." When the former right in each of these pairs is violated, the latter more general freedom is also in jeopardy. It is important that this fundamental connection between religious liberty and other fundamental rights be emphasized when Christians advocate religious freedom. Christians should also work for the strengthening of the clauses that guarantee the "fundamental rights" of the individual.

Mere constitutional provisions cannot guarantee that there will be religious freedom in a country. A favorable social environment is also necessary to strengthen it.[96] It is important that various sections of the population be educated as to the importance

---

93. K. C. Varadachari, "The Hindu Conception of Religious Freedom," in J. R. Chandran and M. M. Thomas, eds., *Religious Freedom* (Bangalore: Committee for Literature on Social Concerns, 1956), p. 29.

94. Vahiduddin, p. 83.

95. A. F. Carrillo de Albornoz, "Religious Liberty, Human Freedom and Responsible Government," in Matthews, ed., p. 234. See also *idem, The Basis of Religious Liberty*, pp. 33–41.

96. *The Christian Community within the Human Community*, p. 22.

of religious freedom and its relation to general human freedoms. In a democratic country like India, those who are elected to govern the country should be those who are committed to the principle of religious liberty.

There should be a continuing dialogue between the religious communities and the state on matters pertaining to religious freedom and nation-building. The state should make opportunities for this and the religious communities should respond. It is gratifying that the National Christian Council of India and the Christian Institute for the Study of Religion and Society have appointed secretaries to be stationed in New Delhi, who will keep in touch with the government not only in matters concerning the Christian community, but also in studying and advising government and churches regarding legislation.[97] These types of informal contact with government officials at various levels of government can facilitate dialogue, remove misunderstandings and offer helpful advice to government when occasions arise for the same.

In Indonesia representatives of the church, along with other religious leaders, sit in the advisory councils of the state. While this can promote cooperation between church and state, it can also create difficulties. There is no department for religious affairs in India. At present it would be a problem to decide how to give adequate representation to the various denominations in India if the government were to set up a consultative body for Christians. The hierarchy and the Christian leadership might not represent the opinions of the rank and file of the Christian community. Political motives might be involved in appointing members to a consultative body. Thus an officially appointed consultative body, either for each religious community or for all the religious communities as a whole, may not be feasible or desirable. In the absence of such officially constituted consultative bodies, the Christian community should have highly representative organizations, which reflect not merely the opinions of certain classes or groups of Christians, but all Christians as far as possible, which the state can consult for advice and suggestions in dealing with matters that particularly concern the Christian community. The National Christian Council of India, if further expanded, can become highly representative of the Protestant and Orthodox churches, especially at the official level. The NCCI, in conjunction with the Catholic Bishops' Conference of India,

---

97. *Guardian* 46, no. 39 (19 September 1968):299; *NCCR* 88, no. 8 (August 1968):325-26.

can be spokesman for the Christian community in India in advising the government of India. Along with this, organizations like the Christian Union of India and the Catholic Union of India may also become bodies that the government could consult. There should also always be openings for any individual Christian or other Christian organizations to make their voices heard. But it is advantageous to both the state and the Christian community that there be well-organized bodies that can speak with some authority in behalf of the community.

In discussing new patterns of church-state consultation and cooperation, it is evident that there is no one pattern or patterns that completely avoid the twin dangers of indifference by the state to religion and the indirect establishment of religion. Different methods have to be tried and evaluated, keeping what is best. But it is essential that channels of communication and cooperation exist between churches and the state.

Conclusions

We have examined some of the areas and patterns for service and witness for Christians in the Indian secular state. From this study emerge certain major conclusions:

1. It is an essential part of Christian responsibility to be active in politics. Christians should fulfill their appropriate role in politics as churches, as a community, and as individuals.

2. Christians should seek active cooperation with non-Christians for purposes of nation-building, for promoting national integration, and for providing a spiritual and philosophical basis for the Indian secular state. This cooperation and dialogue should be based on common humanity rather than on religion as such.

3. The Christian community as a minority has a special role to play in defending the principle of religious freedom and, consequently, human rights in general. Religious freedom and human rights are closely related to each other and when the former right is curtailed, the latter rights also will inevitably be compromised.

4. Service is an essential part of Christian witness. It is not to be thought of as primarily an instrument for evangelism. Christian service should be based on common humanity, and hence should not be limited to Christians only. While Christians should serve others because of Christ's command to love one another, its two important by-products are nation-building and creating good

will toward and acceptance of the Christian community by the majority community.

5. The Christian community and the Indian secular state should open and maintain channels of intercommunication for mutual understanding and benefit. Christian organizations of an ecumenical nature can most effectively promote these contacts with the state.

6
Summary and Conclusions

I have tried from three vantage points to explore the meaning of the secular state in India and to suggest the potential role of the Indian Christian community in a secular Indian state. These three vantage points are: 1) the self-understanding and practice of the Indian secular state; 2) the self-understanding and practice of the Indian Christian community in its relation to the state (in each case set in its historical context); and 3) the potential role of the Christian community in the Indian secular state. In defining the secular state, I have emphasized not only the separation between religion and state and religious freedom and the equality of citizens before the law, but also the idea of social justice and social reform as a positive responsibility of the secular state. The idea of a secular state without the last component would be detrimental to the welfare of a developing society like India, where much social reform is to be effected and where religion and society are closely integrated with each other. For this reason, the process of secularization is to be welcomed, whereas the acceptance of the ideology of *closed* or *integral* secularism would be against the spirit of the Indian secular state, which is not anti-religious. We have seen too that in India the terms *the idea of the secular state* and *secularism* are often interchangeably used.

Next we embarked on a survey of the historical and cultural roots of the secular state in the Indian tradition. Hindu religion and society were closely intermingled during the classical Hindu period. But the Hindu polity contained several features that favored the emergence of the secular state. The kingship was not considered primarily divine in origin, and the king's relationship with the people was contractual, at least in theory, if not always in practice. The separation of the functions of the Brahmins (priests) and the Kshatriyas (warriors and rulers), and the ideal of tolerance exemplified by Hindu monarchs (most eminently by Asoka the Buddhist emperor), also provide historical under-girding for the secular-state ideal. And we should not ignore the strong tradition of having had democratic republics in India during the fourth and fifth centuries A.D.

The Muslim ideology of the state generally militated against the concept of the secular state. In India, Muslim rule contained, on the one hand, examples of state patronage of Islam, forced conversions, and persecution of Hindus under the rule of a number of Muslim leaders. On the other hand, we also have the example of Akbar, who practiced complete tolerance of all religions and gave high positions to Hindus in his administration.

Muslim rule in India was followed by British colonial rule. The British administration, as in other Asian countries, followed, to a great extent, a policy of religious neutrality. This was good preparation for the emergence of the Indian secular state. Britain established the principle of equality before the law for all citizens, irrespective of caste and creed. The independent civil and judicial systems that the British left also provided a good framework for the secular government.

An equally important contribution of the British rule was the influence of Western liberal thought on India. This profoundly molded the thought of the Indian intelligentsia and particularly the leaders of the Indian national movement. The Westernizing influences of English education and the work of the Christian missionaries also contributed to the development of the secular-state ideal.

In reviewing the impact of ideas that favored the secular-state ideal, we found that there was a significant tradition in Hindu thought that emphasized the pursuit of *artha* (material wealth), and the Charvaka system in Hindu thought was both atheistic and materialistic. The Hindu renaissance during the nineteenth century was also rationalistic and progressive.

Indian nationalism had two aspects. One was the communal nationalism of both Hindus and Muslims, which finally led to the partition of India into India and Pakistan. The other was secular nationalism, which aimed at the establishment of an independent secular democracy. The declaration of independence by the people of East Pakistan and the emergence of the new Republic of Bangladesh may also be seen as a result of the affirmation of the ideology of secular nationalism. Even though both ideologies were represented in the Indian National Congress party (which pri-

CHRISTIANS IN SECULAR INDIA

marily gave leadership to India to attain freedom), the latter
ideology was dominant, especially under the leadership of Gandhi
and Nehru. The disturbances immediately preceding and following independence only reinforced the will of the founding fathers
of the nation to keep the Indian state secular.

We also noted many forces that were against the spirit of the
secular state. The close relation between religion and state in the
Hindu tradition; the idea of the theocratic state and religious
discrimination during much of Muslim rule; the "divide and
rule" policies of the British government, which encouraged communal policies in India and the communal aspects of the Congress
party, all these were factors that did not favor the emergence of
the secular state. Even though the forces that favored its establishment were stronger, and prevailed over the others, we see that
some of the latter are still operative in the Indian secular state
and, moreover, pose potential dangers to its secular character.

Having reviewed the historical antecedents of the Indian secular state, we next analyzed the self-understanding of India as a
secular state. We examined the ideology of the Indian National
Congress party (which led India to freedom and has been in
power in the central government and most of the state governments since independence) with regard to the secular state.
Jawaharlal Nehru, the leader of the Congress party and Prime
Minister of independent India until his death in 1964 was the
most ardent supporter of the secular-state ideal and his ideas are
important in understanding its meaning in India. The members
of the Constituent Assembly debated at length about the nature
of the Indian secular state before they completed the Indian Constitution, and their debates provide a rich mine of information on
the various ideas of the founding fathers regarding the meaning
of the secular state.

We noted these ideas and also the provisions of the Indian Constitution with regard to the religion-state relationship. Another
profitable way for exploring the self-understanding of India as a
secular state lay in interviews with eminent leaders of the various
political parties of India, in which their views regarding the
principles and practice of the secular state in India were sought.

The Indian National Congress had two major concerns in relation to the secular state ideology. They were: 1) insuring communal harmony, and 2) guaranteeing fundamental rights for all
citizens, especially the minorities. Communal harmony and the
confidence of minority communities in the majority community

were to a great extent preconditions for attainment of Indian freedom through peaceful means. The Congress party worked incessantly for communal harmony (even though its actions did not always have the desired effect), and it redeemed its pledges regarding fundamental rights by incorporating necessary clauses in the Indian constitution. Nehru's secularism was based on practical needs as well as on his philosophic convictions as a scientific humanist. He was against archaic forms of religion and communalism but was not anti-religious. His philosophy of secularism, which may be called *open secularism,* provides much of the ideological content for the Indian secular state.

From the debates of the Constituent Assembly, we noted six major points as to the interpretation given the secular state by the framers of the Indian Constitution. They are the following: 1) the secular state is an arrangement by which different religions and cultural communities may live together peacefully and harmoniously. This has to be understood in the context of pre-independent and the immediate post-independent period of communal conflict and tension; 2) the neutrality or nondiscrimination of the state with regard to different religions does not imply any anti-religious bias on the part of the state; 3) social reform is an essential part of the secular state and the state reserves the right to interfere in the secular aspects of religion in order to promote social reform; 4) while religious education is excluded from public schools, the need for some kind of moral education is affirmed; 5) the secular-state idea as enshrined in the Indian Constitution represented compromises at different levels for those who represented different points of view, such as Hindu communalism and minority rights; and 6) to men like Nehru, a secular state involved thinking beyond membership in religious or social communities alone to membership in economic, political, and other different groupings.

Then we examined the interpretations given the secular state by different political leaders and parties. While there is general agreement regarding the desirability of a secular state, various leaders gave different interpretations. For example, while everyone agrees that the secular state is not anti-religious, the Communist leader emphasized that the state should not encourage religion. The Jana Sangh (Hindu communal party) leader saw Hindu culture as the basis of the secular state, and not any composite culture as suggested by Lohia and Nehru. As far as the right to propagate religion is concerned, non-Christian leaders would like to limit it to Indian citizens only, while the Communist leader would have it only to individuals and not to organizations. There was general agreement on the need to separate church and state, as well as restrict religion from interfering in affairs of state. While some leaders took a very positive attitude toward religion, including organized religion, and said that it was legitimate for the secular state to help all religions, others advocated a neutral or even negative attitude toward religion, also in the name of the secular state.

Thus we see that while there are agreements on the broad outline, there are fundamental disagreements regarding what the attitude of the state should be to religion. This polarity we also noticed in the debates of the Constituent Assembly. There are many areas, such as the dividing line between religious freedom and state interference, that are not well defined. The Constitution does not define the state's attitude toward religion, and here again various shades of interpretation are given by different leaders and parties. In some instances (e.g., freedom to propagate religion) even when certain rights are well defined, leaders do not agree to it or interpret it differently. The different ideologies and interests of different groups in the nation are reflected in the various interpretations given the secular state.

In examining the role that the Christian community played in the evolution of the secular state, and its understanding of its meaning, we explored the relationship between the Christian community and the state before Indian independence. The Syrian Christians of Kerala had an honorable position in the former "native states" in which they lived but they were not identified with it. Under the Portuguese rule the Roman Catholics of Goa and other Portuguese territories in India were closely linked with the state. During the British rule, the Christian community did not get much direct help from the government even though it benefited greatly in many indirect ways. But Christians on the whole suffered from over-Westernization and identification by others with the imperial rule.

Many Indian Christians, especially from the educated class, took part in the national freedom movement, but large sections of the Christian community supported the British rule. The All-India Conference of Indian Christians and the local Indian Christian associations in the various cities on the whole were in favor of the idea of Indian independence but did not support the civil-disobedience and noncooperation movement of Gandhi and the

Congress. These associations opposed the principle of communal electorates even though they often pleaded with the governments for Christian representation in the government at various levels. There were also some groups who favored the principle of communal representation. When the Indian Constitution was being framed, the Christian leaders in the Constituent Assembly set the example for other minority communities by renouncing not only separate electorates but also reservation of seats for Christians. By this they made a worthy contribution to strengthening the secular character of the Constitution.

Since independence, major Christian organizations (mainly Protestant) like the National Christian Council of India (NCCI) and the Christian Institute for the Study of Religion and Society (CISRS) have made significant contributions to the discussion on the secular state. The NCCI has emphasized the following points in its pronouncements regarding the secular state: 1) the secular state is the only practical ideal in a multi-religious country like India; 2) the state should recognize the authority of a higher moral law and should not assume absolute sovereignty. It should serve the moral ends of man; 3) in the secular state, Christians should not demand any special privileges but should actively participate in national life. The church and Christian organizations should educate Christians in moral issues in political and public life and offer responsible criticism to the state; 4) the church has the responsibility of representing the interests of the Christian community within the framework of the government. The NCCI acts as a liaison between the churches and the government; 5) Christians, including foreign missionaries, have a right to propagate their religion; 6) along with other voluntary organizations, Christian educational and social agencies have an important role in strengthening the democratic spirit of society.

While the NCCI has been more concerned with the practical issues of church-state relationship, the CISRS has emphasized the philosophical and theological aspects. It defines the secular state in terms of *open* secularism, which is open to the influences of "social ethics inspired by religious beliefs." The secular state presupposes secularization, which should be welcomed for practical and Christian reasons. But there is the danger that this may lead to a *closed* secularism. Religion should inspire the secular culture from within rather than attempt to dominate it. A secular state, not being based on traditional religious integration of society, may lead to loss of national integration. A new philosophy

of open secularism is necessary to fill this vacuum. Here the
CISRS thinking is very similar to that of Nehru and Lohia. Paul
Varghese of the Orthodox church has warned that the "theology
of the secular" should not become "the philosophy of the secular."
He sees the need for greater awareness of the transcendent realm
in the theology of the secular.

On balance we may say that the Christian contribution to the
evolution of the secular state in India was positive. This is particularly true of the period immediately preceding independence
and during the framing of the Constitution.

The independent secular state presented the Christian community with a new situation. It was able to shed much of the stigma
of having been associated with colonial rulers and Western customs. Christianity was more and more recognized as an Indian
and not a foreign religion in India. In the context of mobilization
of society for nation-building, the Christian community was presented with new opportunities for service in traditional as well as
in new areas. In the working out of the provision of the Constitution regarding religious freedom and other fundamental rights,
as well as in the attitudes of extreme communal groups in the
majority community, Christians faced new challenges also. How
has the Christian community responded to these opportunities and
challenges during the last two decades and more of independence,
since 1947?

We have examined some representative examples of how the
churches have responded to challenges and opportunities presented
by the secular state. Since I am most familiar with Kerala, and
since it has a very high percentage of Christians, I have given
special importance to the study of examples from that state. We
have found that some of these responses have been positive and
others negative, from the point of view of the larger interests of
the Christian community and the nation as a whole.

We find that, in some instances, the churches have acted in line
with those aspirations and goals of the secular state which are
also in accord with Christian principles. The Industrial Team
Service of Bangalore provides a good example of this. The rapid
pace of industrialization and urbanization that is going on in
India has presented the need for work in this area, and the
church in Bangalore (as well as in a few other cities in India)
has responded to this. Here Christians try to cooperate with government agencies as well as with non-Christians in rendering service to the industrial community.

Another area where the goals of the secular state and those of the Christian community parallel each other is that of moral and religious education in Christian colleges. Here the record has not been very good. While religious education has been offered mainly to Christian students in most Christian colleges for a long time (but rather unsatisfactorily), only recently have the Christian educationalists begun to think seriously about the expressed desire of the secular state to provide some kind of moral education to all Indian students. So far, the response of Christian leaders to government proposals regarding introducing moral education in all schools and colleges has been primarily negative, without offering positive alternatives. Fortunately, there are a few exceptions to this picture.

We have also noted that the churches have made a small beginning in some areas in organizing Christian professional groups so that they will be better equipped to serve the interests of the Christian community as well as the nation.

In the 1965 general election in Kerala, the hierarchy of the churches in Kerala took an active interest in bringing about a reconciliation between the Congress party and its splinter group, the Kerala Congress, with a view to averting the success of the Communist-led coalition in the elections. The churches were not successful in either objective. We have noted that they tend to take active interest in politics only during crisis situations, when their institutional security seems to be at stake, and that they have failed in the task of giving their members political education so as to inspire them to be active in politics through democratic parties. The negative response of Kerala church leaders to the Dowry Prohibition Act is another example of the preoccupation of church leaders with the economic security of the institutional church rather than with the welfare of the people in general, and of their unwillingness to cooperate with the secular state in achieving needed social reform.

We have also examined two situations in which the freedom to propagate religion and to conduct schools without undue interference from the government, rights which are guaranteed by the Constitution, was attempted to be curtailed. The Christian community in India as a whole reacted strongly, but with restraint and dignity, against the patently false allegations of the Niyogi Commission Report against foreign missionaries and the Christian community in general. By restrained but strong action to vindicate truth regarding the situation that called for the Report, and to assert their legitimate rights, the Christian community contributed to the strengthening of the secular ideal of the state.

The second situation refers to Kerala. The Education Bill of 1957 that the Communist government in power introduced would have resulted in considerable loss of freedom for the Christian minority in conducting schools of their choice and in maintaining their Christian character. The Christian churches firmly opposed it. In addition to this, the general dissatisfaction with Communist rule resulted in the "liberation struggle," in which the vast majority of the people in the state took part. Christians on the whole vigorously supported this move, which persuaded the central government to remove the Communist ministry from office. Here, too, we have given credit to the Kerala Christian community for decisive action at a time of crisis, but the record is marred by long inaction in the matter of integrating "backward Christians" into the general community, and by much criticism of corruption, which many of the Christian schools are open to.

A survey of some instances of Christian response to involvement in the secular state shows that the Christian community has been both creative as well as narrow and communal. On the basis of empirical observations and biblical and theological principles that should guide Christian actions, and of the needs and nature of the Indian secular state, I have suggested some principles, modes, and areas of Christian involvement in the secular state. The formulation of the new role that the Christian community should play in the Indian secular state has been the prime focus of this study.

In trying to understand the meaning of the secular state in India, the history of the church-state relationship in India, and the Christian community's understanding of and involvement in the Indian secular state, I have attempted to form some guidelines for the future role of the Christian community in the Indian secular state. They are as follows:

1) India is a secular state. The historical and cultural roots of the idea of the secular state in India are not limited to the British rule or Western political and philosophical thought and ideas. There are genuine indigenous historical and philosophical influences that have also contributed to the growth of the secular-state ideal. However, the former forms the major basis of the Indian secular state.

2) The Indian secular state is not anti-religious, but the state has broad powers to interfere in the affairs of religious organiza-

tions. The state may not show special favor to one religion, but may show favor or disfavor to all religions. The state may even discriminate against a religion when discrimination is based on other than religious reasons. While the ruling Congress party has so far followed a policy of religious neutrality, it is possible that other parties in power might violate the secular spirit of the Constitution even when not violating its letter.

3) The Indian secular state is as much the product of historical circumstances as it is the result of deliberate choice. Consequently, it encompasses within itself many contradictions and compromises. These contradictions have their origin in the differences of opinion as to what ideology should be the basis of the Indian state. If the secular-state experiment is to succeed, it should be reinforced with the propagation and acceptance of secularization and the ideology of open secularism as advocated by leaders like Nehru and progressive Christian thinkers in India.

4) While Christianity has an ancient history in India, its more recent history is closely linked to the colonial rule; with some justification, the Christian community was identified with British rule and Western culture. However, the educated sections of the community and its progressive leadership supported the national freedom movement and the evolution of the secular state. The Christian leadership did make a significant contribution to the framing of the secular constitution of India.

5) The progressive leadership of the Indian Christian community is aware of the possibilities and potential dangers of the secular state and the important role that the community should play in it.

6) The Christian community's response to the secular state has been both positive and negative on different occasions and in different sections of the community. This situation calls for rethinking as to the new role the churches should play in the Indian secular state in the future.

These conclusions lead to more specific conclusions regarding the new role of the Christian community in the future of the Indian secular state:

7) Christians should participate in politics more actively than in the past. This Christian participation is demanded by biblical teachings as well as the theological understanding of the nature of the state and the church.

8) Christians may participate in politics as churches, as individuals, and as a community. The main responsibilities of the

churches should be to speak out on moral and ethical aspects of political issues, and to educate their members on the responsibility of Christian participation in politics.

Christian individuals should work through the various democratic political parties that are committed to the welfare of the people. Through this political involvement informed by Christian understanding, Christian principles should be brought to bear upon the life of the Indian nation.

The Christian community as a whole may organize itself not as a political party but as a civic organization for sociopolitical action and education. In this way specific Christian insights may be better heard and accepted by the national and regional political parties and leaders. Recent attempts to form such national organizations should be judged on the basis of how much noncommunal political education and participation they are able to inspire and achieve among Christians. In cooperation with other groups, both secular and religious, these organizations may work for the material and spiritual progress of India.

9) Christians should give up separatist (*qaum*) mentality and seek to identify more with the communities around them in social, economic, and political matters. The Christian community should not be a closed community. It should seek active cooperation with non-Christian religious and secular bodies in India for purposes of: a) nation-building, b) promoting national integration by developing a composite culture, c) providing a spiritual basis for the Indian secular state, and d) for the de-alienation of the Christian community itself. Christian cooperation and dialogue with men of other faiths and no faith should be based on common humanity rather than on religion as such. The reasons for this cooperation and dialogue are both practical and theological.

10) The Christian community as a minority community in India has a special role to play to insure that religious freedom guaranteed in the Constitution is practiced by state and society both in letter and in spirit. This is a historic role that minorities in many countries have fulfilled. In defending their legitimate fundamental rights forcefully and effectively, the Christian minority will be rendering great service not only to themselves but to the nation as a whole. To be effective in doing this, Christians, in addition to working through existing political parties, may have to act through organizations like the National Christian Council, the Christian Union of India, and the Catholic Union of India. The more ecumenical and representative these organizations are,

the greater will be their effectiveness in putting pressure on the government and other political parties to conform to the secular-state ideal when they deviate from it. Christians as individuals and groups may, where necessary, form and work with organizations like the Civil Liberties Union in the United States, in which men of all communities and groups work together to promote civil liberty, of which religious liberty is the keystone.

11) Christian service, whatever its motive, has always been an important part of the work of the Christian church in India. In spite of some criticism that Indian Christians have rendered service to the nation with the ulterior motive of winning converts to Christianity, the predominant non-Christian opinion in the past and at present has highly commended both the spirit and nature of Christian service in India. It may be surmised that the general good will and friendship that were shown to Christians and to their demands regarding religious freedom (especially, freedom to propagate religion) at the time of the framing of the Constitution, were mainly due to the reservoir of good will that the Christian community had built up in the country through its philanthropic work in the educational, medical, and other fields. If the Christian community is to merit the continued good will and appreciation of the state and of other communities in India, this work has to be continued. However, Christian *diakonia* is not to be understood in utilitarian terms, either for the purpose mentioned above or to attract converts. It is part and parcel of the Christian gospel. Christian *diakonia* has to be expressed in new ways so as to meet the changing needs and conditions of Indian society and the state. Whenever possible, it has to be exercised in cooperation with the state, and non-Christians and its beneficiaries should be members of all communities.

12) Since religion and society are still closely interrelated in India, and since they can never be completely divorced, the state in India often has to deal with religious communities as such. In proposing changes in the personal laws of minority communities, the state consults the communities concerned. The state may also want to enlist the support of all groups, including religious groups in their programs for nation-building. As for the Christian community, it has to communicate with the state on several issues that might particularly affect them both. They might also wish to contribute their opinions and insights to the state regarding national plans, programs, and legislative measures. It would be advantageous both to the state and to the Christian community to

improve and increase channels of communication between them. The National Christian Council of India and the Catholic Bishops' Conference are already serving as agencies of the churches for contact with the state at different levels. Both formal and informal channels of communication should be increased and new forms for achieving this purpose should be explored. The state also should be more open to such a dialogue with the Christian community and other religious groups (as significant social groups in the country) and, without establishing any religion or giving undue advantage to any religious body, should experiment with opening up new channels of communication.

In following these principles, the Christian community can play a most significant role in helping to continue and strengthen the secular-state ideal in India.

Bibliography

Books

Appasamy, A. J. *The Christian Task in Independent India*. London: S.P.C.K., 1951.

Asirvatham, Eddy. *Christianity in the Indian Crucible*. 2d rev. ed. Calcutta: Y.M.C.A. Publishing House, 1957.

———. *The Future Constitution of India*. Madras: Rochouse and Sons, Ltd., 1945.

Bannerjee, A. C. *The Constituent Assembly of India*. Calcutta: A. Mukherjee and Co., 1947.

———. *Indian Constitutional Documents*, Vol. III: *1917–1939*. Calcutta: A. Mukherjee and Co., 1949.

Basham, A. L. *The Wonder That was India*. New York: Grove Press, Inc., 1959.

Basu, Das Durga. *Cases on the Constitution of India (1950–51)*. Calcutta: S. C. Sarkar and Sons, Ltd., 1952.

———. 3d ed. *Commentary on the Constitution of India*. Vol. I (Articles 1–151). Calcutta: S. C. Sarkar and Sons, Ltd., 1955.

Bates, Searle M. *Religious Liberty: An Inquiry*. New York: International Missionary Council, 1945.

Bearce, George D. *British Attitudes towards India, 1784–1858*. London: Oxford University Press, 1961.

Bellah, Robert N. *Tokugawa Religion*. Glencoe, Ill.: The Free Press, 1957.

Bennett, John C., ed. *Christian Social Ethics in a Changing World: An Ecumenical Theological Inquiry*. New York: Association Press, 1966.

———. *Christians and the State*. New York: Charles Scribner's Sons, 1958.

———. *When Christians Make Political Decisions*. New York: Association Press, 1964.

Beth, Loren P. *The American Theory of Church and State*. Gainesville: University of Florida Press, 1958.

Bidney, David. *Theoretical Anthropology*. New York: Columbia University Press, 1954.

Binder, Leonard. *Religion and Politics in Pakistan*. Berkeley: University of California Press, 1961.

Bowles, Chester. *Ambassador's Report*. New York: Harper and Brothers, 1954.

Brecher, Michael. *Nehru: A Political Biography*. London: Oxford University Press, 1959.

Brown, L. W. *The Indian Christians of St. Thomas: An Account of the Ancient Syrian Church of Malabar*. Cambridge: University Press, 1956.

Brown, D. Mackenzie. *The Nationalist Movement: Indian Political Thought from Ranade to Bhave*. Berkeley and Los Angeles: University of California Press, 1965.

Butler, J. F., and Samuel S. *The Right of Conversion*. Madras: The Christian Literature Society for India, 1946.

Carillo de Albornoz, A. F. *The Basis of Religious Liberty*. London: SCM Press, Ltd., 1963.

———. *Religious Liberty*. New York: Sheed and Ward, 1967.

Chandran, J. R., and Thomas, M. M., ed. *Political Outlook in India Today: A Pre-election Study*. Bangalore: Committee for Literature on Social Concerns, 1956.

———. *Religious Freedom*. Bangalore: Committee for Literature on Social Concerns, 1956.

The Christian Community within the Human Community. (Containing Statements from the Bangkok Assembly of the E.A.C.C., February–March, 1964, Minutes, Part 2.) Bangkok: East Asia Christian Conference, 1964.

Christian Service in the Revolution: Report of the Consultation held November 14–18, 1962 in Sukavumi, Indonesia. The Committees on Inter-Church Aid and on Church and Society of the East Asia Christian Conference, 1963.

Church, Society and State in Kerala—A Christian Evaluation. Alwaye Consultation 1959. Bangalore: Christian Institute for the Study of Religion and Society, 1960.

Constituent Assembly Debates. Vols. I–XI. New Delhi: Government of India.

Constituent Assembly of India. *Draft Constitution of India*. New Delhi: Manager, Government of India Press, 1948.

The Constitution of India. New Delhi: Ministry of Law, Government of India, 1966.

Coupland, R. *The Indian Problem. Report on the Constitutional Problem of India*. London: Oxford University Press, 1944.

Daniel, I. *The Malabar Church and Other Orthodox Churches*. Haripad, Travancore: Suvarna Bharthi Press, 1950.

———. *The Syrian Church of Malabar*. Madras: The Diocesan Press, 1945.

Das, M. N. *The Political Philosophy of Jawaharlal Nehru*. New York: The John Day Company, 1961.

Datta, Bhupendra Nath. *Studies in Indian Social Polity*. Calcutta: Purabi Publishers, 1944.

Datta, K. K. *Renaissance, Nationalism and Social Changes in Modern India*. Calcutta: Bookland Private Ltd., 1965.

Deats, Richard L. *Nationalism and Christianity in the Philippines*. Dallas: Southern Methodist University Press, 1967.

de Bary, William Theodore. *Sources of Indian Tradition*. New York: Columbia University Press, 1958.

Devanandan, Paul David. *Christian Concern in Hinduism*. Bangalore: The Christian Institute for the Study of Religion and Society, 1961.

————. *The Gospel and Renascent Hinduism*. London: S.C.M. Press, Ltd., 1959.

————. *I Will Lift Up Mine Eyes unto the Hills*. Bangalore: The Christian Institute for the Study of Religion and Society, 1963.

————. *Preparation for Dialogue*. Bangalore: The Christian Institute for the Study of Religion and Society, 1964.

————, and· Thomas, M. M., eds. *Christian Participation in Nation-Building*. Bangalore: The National Christian Council of India and the C.I.S.R.S., 1960.

————, and Thomas, M. M., eds. *Cultural Foundations of Indian Democracy*. Bangalore: Committee for Literature on Social Concerns, 1955.

————, and Thomas, M. M., eds. *Human Person, Society and State*. Bangalore: Committee for Literature on Social Concerns, 1957.

————, and Thomas, M. M., eds. *Indian Quest for Democracy*. Calcutta: Y.M.C.A. Publishing House, 1955.

————, and Thomas, M. M., eds. *Problems of Indian Democracy*. Bangalore: Christian Institute for the Study of Religion and Society, 1962.

De Vries, Egbert. *Man in Community: Christian Concern for the Human in Changing Society*. New York: Association Press, 1966.

Dilemmas and Opportunities: Christian Action in Rapid Social Change. Report of an International Ecumenical Study Conference, Thessalonica, Greece July 25–August 2, 1959. Geneva: World Council of Churches, 1959.

Documents of the Three-Self Movement: Source Materials for the Study of the Protestant Church in Communist China. New York: National Council of the Churches of Christ in the U.S.A., 1963.

Douglas, William O. *We the Judges: Studies in American and Indian Constitutional Law from Marshall to Mukherjee*. Garden City, N.Y.: Doubleday and Co., Inc., 1956.

D'Souza, Jerome, S.J. *The Church and Civilization*. Garden City, N.Y.: Doubleday and Co., Inc., 1967.

East Asia Christian Conference, Inaugural Assembly, Kuala Lumpur, Malaya, 1959. *The Witness of the Churches in the Midst of Social Change. A Survey of Ecumenical Thought* (Papers for Preparatory Reading for the Assembly). Kottayam: C.M.S. Press, 1959.

Ebright, Donald Fossett. *The National Missionary Society of India, 1905–1942. An Expression of the Movement toward Indigenization within the Indian Christian Community*. Chicago: University of Chicago, 1944.

Eddy, Sherwood. *India Awakening*. New York: Missionary Education Movement of the United States and Canada, 1912.

Facts about India. New Delhi: Ministry of Information and Broadcasting, Government of India, 1957.

Forman, Charles W. *Christianity in the Non-Western World*. Englewood Cliffs, N.J.: Prentice-Hall, Inc., 1967.

Gandhi, M. K. *Communal Unity*. Ahmedabad: Navajivan Publishing House, 1949.

————. *The Mahatma and the Missionary*. Selected writings by Mohandas K. Gandhi. Edited by Clifford Manshardt. Chicago, Ill.: Henry Regnery Co., 1949.

Gandhi, Mahatma. *Swaraj in One Year*. Madras: Ganesh and Co., 1921.

Gopal, Ram. *How India Struggled for Freedom (A Political History)*. Bombay: The Book Centre Private Ltd., 1967.

Griffiths, Percival. *The British Impact on India*. London: Macdonald & Co., 1952.

————. *Modern India*. New York: Frederick A. Praeger, 1957.

Gwyer, Sir Maurice, and Appadorai, A. *Speeches and Documents on the Indian Constitution 1921–47*. Vols. I and II. Bombay: Oxford University Press, 1957.

Haas, Harry. *Christianity in the Asian Revolution*. Baltimore: Helicon, 1966.

Hall, D. G. E. *A History of South-East Asia*. London: Macmillan and Co., Ltd., 1960.

Harrison, Selig S. *India: The Most Dangerous Decades*. Princeton, N.J.: Princeton University Press, 1960.

Hayward, Victor E. W., ed. *The Church as a Christian Community: Three Studies of North Indian Churches*. London: Lutterworth Press, 1966.

Heimsath, Charles H. *Indian Nationalism and Hindu Social Reform*. Princeton, N.J.: Princeton University Press, 1964.

Hodge, J. Z. *Salute to India*. New York: Friendship Press, 1944.

Hoffman, Bengt R. *Christian Social Thought in India: 1947–1962. An Evaluation*. Bangalore: Christian Institute for the Study of Religion and Society, 1967.

Hogg, A. G. *The Christian Message to the Hindu*. London: S.C.M. Press, 1947.

Holland, William L., ed. *Asian Nationalism and the West*. A Symposium Based on Documents and Reports of the Eleventh Conference, Institute of Pacific Relations. New York: The Macmillan Company, 1953.

Husain, S. Abid. *The Way of Gandhi and Nehru*. London: Asia Publishing House, 1961.

Ikram, S. M. *Muslim Civilization in India*. New York: Columbia University Press, 1964.

Ingham, Kenneth. *Reformers in India 1793–1833:* An Account of the Work of Christian Missionaries on Behalf of Social Reform. Cambridge: University Press, 1956.

Jai Singh, Herbert. *Inter-Religious Dialogue.* Bangalore: Christian Institute for the Study of Religion and Society, 1967.

————, and Rao, Mark Sunder, ed. *Indian Politics After Nehru.* Bangalore: The Christian Institute for the Study of Religion and Society, 1967.

Joseph, S. C. *Kerala the "Communist" State.* Madras: The Madras Premier Co., 1959.

Joshi, G. N. *The Constitution of India.* London: The Macmillan Co., 1952.

Kahin, George McTurnan. *Nationalism and Revolution in Indonesia.* Ithaca, N.Y.: Cornell University Press, 1959.

Kaushik, P. D. *The Congress Ideology and Programme 1920–1947. Ideological Foundations of Indian Nationalism during the Gandhian Era.* Bombay: Allied Publishers Private Ltd., 1964.

Keay, F. E. *A History of the Syrian Church in India.* London: S.P.C.K., 1938.

Kulandran, S. *Resurgent Religions.* London: Lutterworth Press, 1957.

Kurian, George. *The Indian Family in Transition.* The Hague: Mouton and Co., 1961.

Kuruvilla, K. K. *A History of the Mar Thoma Church and Its Doctrines.* Madras: The Christian Literature Society for India, 1951.

Lacy, Creighton. *The Conscience of India: Moral Traditions in the Modern World.* New York: Holt, Rinehart and Winston, 1965.

Latourette, Kenneth Scott. *A Short History of the Far East.* New York: The Macmillan Company, 1957.

Levai, Blaise, ed. *Revolution in Missions.* Vellore, India: The Popular Press, 1957.

Lewis, Martin D. *The British in India—Imperialism or Trusteeship?* Boston: D. C. Heath and Company, 1965.

Luthera, Ved Parkash. *The Concept of the Secular State and India.* London: Oxford University Press, 1964.

Lyall, Alfred C. *The Rise and Expansion of the British Dominion in India.* London: John Murray & Co., 1920.

MacIntyre, Alasdair C. *Secularization and Moral Change.* London: Oxford University Press, 1967.

Madhok, Balraj. *What Bharatiya Jana-Sangh Stands For.* Ahmedabad: Ahmedabad Junior Chamber, 1966.

Majumdar, R. C., gen. ed. *The History and Culture of the Indian People,* Vol. IX: *British Parmontey and Indian Renaissance,* Part I. Bombay: Bharatiya Vidya Bhavan, 1965.

————. *The History and Culture of the Indian People,* Vol. X: *British Paramountcy and Indian Renaissance,* Part II. Bombay: Bharatiya Vidya Bhavan, 1965.

Malaviya, H. D. *Kerala: A Report to the Nation.* New Delhi: People's Publishing House Ltd., 1958.

Manikam, Rajah B., ed. *Christianity and the Asian Revolution.* The Joint East Asia Secretariat of the International Missionary Council and the World Council of Churches, 1954.

Manorama Year Book, 1966. Kottayam (India): Manorama Publishing House, 1966.

Mar Thoma, Juhanon. *Christianity in India and the Mar Thoma Syrian Church.* Madras: Diocesan Press, 1952.

Mathew, C. P. and Thomas, M. M. *The Indian Churches of Saint Thomas.* Delhi: I.S.P.C.K., 1967.

Mathew, E. V. *Role of Law in a Revolutionary Age.* Bangalore: The Christian Institute for the Study of Religion and Society, 1965.

Mathews, Basil. *The Church Takes Root in India.* New York: Friendship Press, 1938.

Matthews, Z. K., ed. *Responsible Government in a Revolutionary Age.* New York: Association Press, 1966.

Mayhew, Arthur J. *Christianity and the Government of India.* London: Faber and Gwyer Ltd., 1929.

Moraes, Frank. *India Today.* New York: The Macmillan Company, 1960.

Moraes, George Mark. *A History of Christianity in India: From Early Times to St. Francis Xavier A.D. 52–1542.* Bombay: Manaktalas, 1964.

Muelder, Walter S. *Foundations of the Responsible Society.* New York: Abingdon Press, 1959.

Munby, D. L. *The Idea of a Secular Society and its Significance for Christians.* London: Oxford University Press, 1963.

Murray, A. Victor. *The State and the Church in Free Society.* Cambridge: The University Press, 1958.

Nanda, B. R. *Mahatma Gandhi: A Biography.* Woodbury, N.Y.: Barron's Educational Series, Inc., 1958.

Natarajan, S. *A Century of Social Reform in India.* Bombay: Asia Publishing House (1959), 1962.

———. *Main Currents in Indian Culture.* Hyderabad: The Institute of Indo-Middle East Cultural Studies, 1960.

Nehru, Jawaharlal. *The Discovery of India.* New York: The John Day Company, 1946.

———. *India's Freedom.* London: George Allen and Unwin Ltd. (1936), 1962.

———. *Jawaharlal Nehru's Speeches,* Vol. I: *Sept., 1946–May, 1949.* New Delhi: The Publications Division, Government of India, 1958.

———. *Nehru on Gandhi:* A Selection Arranged in the Order of Events, from the Writings and Speeches of Jawaharlal Nehru. New York: The John Day Company, 1948.

———. *Talks with Nehru: A Discussion Between Jawaharlal Nehru and Norman Cousins.* London: Victor Gollancz Ltd., 1951.

———. *Toward Freedom: The Autobiography of Jawaharlal Nehru.*

New York: The John Day Company, 1941.

Neill, Stephen. *Colonialism and Christian Missions.* New York: McGraw Hill Book Company, 1966.

————. *Under Three Flags.* New York: Friendship Press, 1954.

Neksatkhan, Sam M. *Some Political Achievements of the Congress.* Bombay: Hamara Hindustan Publications, 1946.

Newbigin, James Edward Leslie. *Honest Religion for Secular Man.* Philadelphia: The Westminster Press, 1966.

Northcott, Cecil. *Religious Liberty.* New York: The Macmillan Company, 1949.

Panikkar, K. M. *Asia and Western Dominance.* London: George Allen and Unwin Ltd., 1953.

————. *The Foundations of New India.* London: George Allen and Unwin Ltd., 1963.

————. *Hinduism and the Modern World.* Allahabad: Kitabistan, 1938.

————. *The Ideas of Sovereignty and State in Indian Political Thought.* Bombay: Bharatiya Vidya Bhavan, 1963.

————. *A Survey of Indian History.* Bombay: The National Information and Publications Ltd., 1947.

Park, Richard L. and Tinker, Irene, ed. *Leadership and Political Institutions in India.* Princeton, N.J.: Princeton University Press, 1959.

Patel, Sardar. *On Indian Problems.* Delhi: Publications Division, Ministry of Information and Broadcasting, Government of India, 1949.

Paul, Rajaiah D. *The Cross Over India.* London: SCM Press Ltd., 1952.

Philips, C. H. *India.* London: Hutchinson's University Library, 1948.

————, ed. *Politics and Society in India.* London: George Allen and Unwin Ltd., 1963.

Pillai, Kainikara Padmanabha. *The Red Interlude in Kerala.* Trivandrum: Kerala Pradesh Congress Committee, 1959.

Plattner, F. A., S.J. *The Catholic Church in India—Yesterday and Today.* Allahabad, U.P.: St. Paul Publications, 1964.

————. *Christian India.* New York: The Vanguard Press, 1957.

Popley, H. A. *K. T. Paul: Christian Leader* (Builders of Modern India Series). Calcutta: Y.M.C.A. Publishing House, 1938.

Pothacamury, Thomas. *The Church in Independent India.* Maryknoll, N.Y.: Maryknoll Publications, n.d.

Radhakrishnan, S., ed. *Mahatma Gandhi 100 Years.* New Delhi: Gandhi Peace Foundation, 1968.

Rai, Lajpat. *Young India: The Nationalist Movement.* New York: B. W. Huebsch, 1916.

Raichur, Sunder Raj Sathianathan. *Religion in Public Education in India.* Mysore: The Wesley Press and Publishing House, n.d.

Rajagopalachari, C. *Reconciliation, Why and How. A Plea for Immediate Action.* Bombay: Hind Kitabs, 1945.

Ramsey, Arthur Michael. *Sacred and Secular:* A Study in the other worldly and this-worldly aspects of Christianity (The Holland Lectures for 1964). New York: Harper and Row, Publishers, 1965.

Ramaswamy, M. *The United States of America: A Secular State—How It was Built and How It Works*. Bangalore: Gokhale Institute of Public Affairs, 1949.

Report of the Committee on Religious and Moral Instruction. Ministⅼy of Education, Government of India, 1964.

Report of the University Education Commission (Dec., 1948–Aug., 1949) (Radhakrishnan Commission). Delhi: Manager of Publications, Government of India, 1950.

Robinson, John A. T. *On Being the Church in the World*. London: S.C.M. Press Ltd., 1960.

Romein, Jan. *The Asian Century: A History of Modern Nationalism in Asia*. London: George Allen and Unwin Ltd., 1962.

Rycroft, Stanley W. *A Factual Study of Asia*. New York: The United Presbyterian Church in the U.S.A., 1963.

Saletore, Bhasker Anand. *Ancient Indian Political Thought and Institutions*. Bombay: Asia Publishing House, 1963.

Sanders, Thomas G. *Protestant Concepts of Church and State*. New York: Doubleday and Co., Inc., 1965.

Sarma, V. P. *Studies in Hindu Political Thought*. Delhi: Motilal Banarsidas, 1959.

Scopes, Wilfred. *Indian Opportunity*. London: Edinburgh House Press, 1961.

The Secular State in India: A Christian Point of View. Calcutta: Y.M.C.A. Publishing House, 1954.

Segal, Ronald. *The Anguish of India*. New York: Stein and Day, 1965.

Sharma, G. S., ed. *Secularism: Its Implications for Law and Life in India*. Bombay: N. M. Tripathy Private Ltd., 1966.

Sherring, M. A. *The Indian Church during the Great Rebellion*. An Authentic Narrative of the Disasters That Befell It, Its Sufferings and Faithfulness unto Death of Many of Its European and Native Members. 2d ed. London: James Nisbet and Co., 1859.

Shukla, Chandrashankar. *Gandhi's View of Life*. Bombay: Bharatiya Vidya Bhavan, 1960.

Singh, Jitendra. *Communist Rule in Kerala*. New Delhi: Diwan Chand Indian Information Centre, 1959.

Sinha, H. N. *The Development of Indian Polity*. Bombay: Asia Publishing House, 1963.

Sitaramayya, B. Pattabhi. *The History of the Congress*. Allahabad: Congress Working Committee, 1935.

Smith, Donald Eugene. *India as a Secular State*. Princeton, N.J.: Princeton University Press, 1963.

————, ed. *South Asian Politics and Religion*. Princeton, N.J.: Princeton University Press, 1966.

Smith, Elwyn A. *Church and State in Your Community*. Philadelphia: The Westminster Press, 1968.

————, ed. *Church-State Relations in Ecumenical Perspective*. Louvain: Duquesne Press, 1966.

Soares, A., *et al. Truth Shall Prevail: Reply to Niyogi Committee*. Bombay: Catholic Association of Bombay, 1957.

A Socialistic Pattern of Society. Report of an Ecumenical Christian Conference, Bombay, January, 1956. Bangalore: C.I.S.R.S., 1956.

Spear, Percival. *India: A Modern History*. Ann Arbor: The University of Michigan Press, 1961.

————. *India, Pakistan and the West*. London: Oxford University Press, 1958.

Stokes, Anson Phelps, and Pfeffer, Leo. *Church and State in the United States*. 1-vol. rev. ed. New York: Harper and Row, Publishers, 1964.

Stotts, Herbert E., and Deats, Paul, Jr. *Methodism and Society: Guidelines for Strategy*. New York: Abingdon Press, 1962.

Sundkler, Bengt. *Church of South India: The Movement Towards Union 1900–1947*. London: Lutterworth Press, 1954.

Temple, William. *Christianity and the Social Order*. London: S.C.M. Press, 1950.

Thomas, M. M. *The Christian Response to the Asian Revolution*. London: S.C.M. Press Ltd., 1966.

————, and Daniel, H. F. J., ed. *Human Problems of Industry in Bangalore*. Bangalore: C.I.S.R.S. and St. Mark's Cathedral Industrial Team Service, 1964.

Thomas, P. *Christians and Christianity in India and Pakistan*. London: George Allen and Unwin Ltd., 1954.

Thomsen, Harry. *The New Religions of Japan*. Rutland, Vt.: Charles E. Tuttle Company, 1963.

Varma, V. P. *Studies in Hindu Political Thought*. Delhi: Motilal Banarsidas, 1954.

Wallbank, T. Walter. *India: A Study of the Heritage and Growth of Indian Nationalism*. New York: Henry Holt and Company, 1948.

Watson, Vincent C. *Communal Politics in India and the United States: A Comparative Analysis*. Atlanta, Ga.: School of Arts and Science Research Papers, Georgia State College, 1965.

Weiner, Myron. *Party Politics in India: The Development of a Multi-Party System*. Princeton, N.J.: Princeton University Press, 1957.

————. *The Politics of Scarcity: Public Pressure and Political Response in India*. Chicago: The University of Chicago Press, 1962.

Wilson, Bryan R. *Religion in Secular Society: A Sociological Comment*. London: C. A. Watts and Co., Ltd., 1966.

World Conference on Church and Society: Official Report. Geneva: World Council of Churches, 1967.

Wriggins, Howard W. *Ceylon: Dilemmas of a New Nation*. Princeton, N.J.: Princeton University Press, 1960.

Zinkin, Maurice. *Asia and the West*. London: Chatto and Windus, 1951.

Zinkin, Taya. *India Change!* New York: Oxford University Press, 1958.

Articles

Abraham, C. E. "The Rise and Growth of Christianity in India." *The Cultural Heritage of India*. Edited by Haridas Bhattacharya. Vol. IV, 2d ed. Calcutta: The Ramakrishna Mission Institute of Culture, 1956.

Abrecht, Paul. "Rapid Social Change and Human Need." *National Christian Council Review* 80, no. 12 (1960).

Asirvatham, Eddy. "Letter to the Editor." *Guardian* Madras 46, no. 22 (30 May 1968).

Baxi, Upendra. "The Little Done, The Vast Undone—Some Reflections on Reading Granville Austin's *The Indian Constitution*." *Journal of the Indian Law Institute* 9, no. 3 (July–September 1968).

Bhatty, C. E. "The Church's Contribution to Social Development in India." *National Christian Council Review* 81, no. 4 (1961).

————. "The Indian Christian Community and the Nationalist Movement." *National Christian Council Review* 62, no. 11 (November 1942).

"Christian Missionary Role Found in Non-Christian Religions." *Christian Science Monitor*, 16 December 1968.

"Christian Union of India—Policy and Programme." *Guardian* Madras 46, no. 1 (4 January 1968).

Clemis, Metropolitan Abraham Mar. "Pastoral Letter." *Edessa Magazine* (Kerala, India) (15 September 1968). In Malayalam.

Carman, John B. "The Place of the Study of World Religions in a College's Religious and Moral Education Programme." *Journal of Christian Colleges in India* 1, no. 2 (1968).

Deccan Herald (Bangalore). "Editorial: The Secular Ideal," 6 February 1966.

Devadutt, V. E. "A Christian Apologetic in Relation to Secularism." *National Christian Council Review* 63, no. 3 (March 1943).

Devanandan, P. D. "Contemporary Hindu Secularism." *Religion and Society* 9 (March 1962).

Dickinson, Richard D. N. "Indian Christian Colleges: Do They Have a Future?" *National Christian Council Review* 88, no. 4 (1968).

"Eighteen Years of Secular Democracy." *Malayala Manorama*. 26 January 1968. In Malayalam.

"Findings of the Nagpur Theological Study Conference, 1957." *Religion and Society* 4, no. 3 (1957).

Glover, Willis B. "Christian Origins of Modern Secular Culture." *Religion in Life*. Summer 1963.

Horsey, Mother Anita. "The Xavier Board Draft Syllabus for Moral Instruction in Colleges." *Journal of Christian Colleges in India* 1, no 2 (1968).

"The Idea of a Secular State—Editorial." *Religion and Society* 9, no. 1 (1962).

Kelly, William A. "Religious and Moral Instruction in Christian Colleges: An Appraisal." *Journal of Christian Colleges in India* 1, no. 2 (1968).

Langdon, John. "The Sri Prakasa Report: A Christian Appraisal of the Committee's Recommendations." *National Christian Council Review* 81, no. 1 (1961).

"The M.P. Questionnaire—Editorial." *National Christian Council Review* 75, no. 1 (1955).

Madgavakar, Kusum. "The Concept of the Secular State and India: A Review." *Seminar* (New Delhi, India), 67 (March 1965).

Mathew, C. P. "Churches in Kerala and the New Education Act." *National Christian Council Review* 79 (August 1959).

Mathew, E. V. "Towards a Uniform Law of Christian Succession." *Guardian* (Madras) (22 February 1968).

Mathew, K. A.."Kerala Seminar for Christian Writers and Journalists." *Guardian* (Madras) 46, no. 23 (6 June 1968).

————. "Lawyers' Seminar held by the Kerala Christian Council at Ernakulam." *Religion and Society* 15, no. 2 (1968).

Muelder, Walter G. "Communism, Secularism and Christianity." *Zions Herald* (19 April 1950).

Munshi, K. M. "Our Secularism: Precept and Practice." *Bhavan's Journal* 13, no. 14 (29 January 1967).

Narasimhayya, P. "The Rational Quest for Philosophy and Discipline: The Materialism of Charvaka." *Bhavan's Journal* 13, no. 6 (1966).

"New Patterns of Christian Social Witness in India—Nasrapur Findings—111." *Religion and Society* 7, no. 1 (1960).

"The Niyogi Recommendations—Editorial." *National Christian Council Review* 76, no. 10 (1956).

"The Niyogi Report—Editorial." *National Christian Council Review* 76, no. 9 (1956).

Panikkar, R. "Common Grounds for Christian–non-Christian Collaboration." *Religion and Society* 5, no. 1 (1958).

Rao, P. Kodanda. "Cow Slaughter—Letter to the Editor." *Deccan Herald* (Bangalore) (6 September 1966).

Rasmussen, Albert Terril. "Review of *Man in Community,* ed. by Egbert de Vries." *Social Action and Social Progress* (January–February, 1966).

"The Secular Ideal—Editorial." *Deccan Herald* (Bangalore) (6 February 1966).

Shastri, Shiv. "The Secular State in Inter-State Relations." *Indian Express* (Madras) (16 February 1966).

Shiner, Larry. "The Concept of Secularization in Empirical Research." *Journal for the Scientific Study of Religion* 6, no. 2 (Fall 1967).

Smith, W. Cantwell. "The Problem." *Seminar* (New Delhi) 67 (March 1965).

Thangasamy, D. A. "The Church's Diakonia in the Present Political and Economic Situation in India." *National Christian Council Review* 88, no. 1 (1968).

Thomas, M. M. "Christian Citizens and Minority Consciousness." *National Christian Council Review* 79, no. 11 (1959).

————. "The Ecumenical Movement and Christian Social Thought in India." *The Indian Journal of Theology* 10, no. 2 (April–June 1961).

————. "Nehru's Secularism—An Interpretation." *Religion and Society* 9, no. 1 (1962).

————. "State and Other Spheres of Life." *National Christian Council Review* 76, no. 10 (1956).

"The Theological Basis of Christian–non-Christian Cooperation in Social Thought and Action." Nagpur Theological Study Conference, October 1957. *Religion and Society* 4, no. 3 (1957).

Tyabji, Badr-ud-Din. "A Means to an End." *Seminar* (New Delhi) 67 (March 1965).

Vahiduddin, Syed. "Need for Religion in a Secular State." *Aryan Path* 37, no. 2 (1966).

Varghese, Paul. "Why We Serve." *Frontier* (London) 7 (Spring 1964).

Warren, Max. "Church and State in Asia and Africa." *Frontier* (Autumn 1965).

West, C. C. "Towards an Understanding of Secularism." *Religion and Society* 9, no. 1 (1962).

Others

Abraham, V. O. "The Dowry Prohibition Act and the Payment of Streedhanam." (Typewritten).

The Christian Medical Association of India: Constitution, By-Laws and Memorandum of Association. As revised, January 1963.

Daniel, H. F. J. Talk given at the United Theological College, Bangalore, June 1966.

Deepika. Malayalam Daily Newspaper, Kottayam, Kerala, India. January–March 1965.

Guardian. "A Christian Weekly Journal of Public Affairs," Madras, India. Present Chief Editor: M. M. Thomas, Director, Christian Institute for the Study of Religion and Society. 1923–1968.

Indian Christian Association, Delhi. Golden Jubilee 1911–1961, Souvenir.

Industrial Service News. Bangalore: Industrial Team Service, St. Mark's Cathedral 4 (May 1966).

Malankara Association Managing Committee, *Planning Committee Reports on Education, Theological Seminary, and Organizations,* n.d.

Malayala Manorama. Malayalam Daily Newspaper, Kottayam, Kerala, India. January–March 1965.

National Christian Council Review. Published monthly by The National Christian Council of India, Nagpur. 1924–1968.

Religion and Society (quarterly journal of the Christian Institute for the Study of Religion and Society, Bangalore) 9, no. 1 (1962). Theme: "Secularism in India Today."

Religion and Society (quarterly journal of the Christian Institute for the Study of Religion and Society, Bangalore) 11, no. 2 (1964). Theme: "Secularism."

Religious Formation of Our Students. JEA Seminar, Bombay, 12–17 May 1966. Delhi: Jesuit Educational Association of India, 1967.

Seminar (New Delhi) 67 (March 1965). Special issue on Secularism.

Thomas, M. M., ed. *Religion, State and Ideologies in East Asia.* Bangalore: Church and Society Committee of the East Asia Christian Council, 1965. (Mimeographed.)

Vetticad, Baben. *Kottayam Seminar Souvenir and Kerala Christian Writer's and Journalist's Directory* (Malayalam). Changanancherry: The Kerala Digest (India) Press, 1966.

Index